The Great
Hill Stations
of Asia

THE GREAT HILL STATIONS OF ASIA

Barbara Crossette

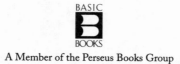

A Member of the Perseus Books Group

Library of Congress Cataloging-in-Publication Data
Crossette, Barbara.
    The great hill stations of Asia / Barbara Crossette.
        p. cm.
    Includes bibliographical references and index.
    ISBN 0-8133-3326-1 (cloth)
    ISBN 0-465-01488-7 (pbk.)
    1. Asia—Description and travel. 2. Mountain resorts—Asia.
I. Title
DS10.C7   1998
950'.0943—dc21   97-51950
                                                                                  CIP

Design by Heather Hutchison

99 00 01 02 ❖/RRD 10 9 8 7 6 5 4 3 2 1

. . . the heights of God

Ah! Yes, 'tis good to be up here
In this thrice blessed clime,
Where Jacks and Gills may climb the hills
And have a jolly time.
'Tis good to watch the babes we love
Who to our heart chords cling,
To see them grow in beauty's glow,
Like flowers in the spring.
'Tis good to see the virgin snows
No man has ever trod
The saints alone around His throne
May walk the heights of God.

—Anonymous
Darjeeling Advertiser, 1917

Contents

1

How It All Began

A misty afternoon in the Cameron Highlands of Malaysia

*P*ITY JOHN OUCHTERLONY. By the time they brought him to the healing hills, it was too late. On April 29, 1863, Lieutenant Colonel Ouchterlony of the Royal Madras Engineers died of "jungle fever brought on by exposure while in the execution of his duty," says a memorial plaque at St. Stephen's Church in Ootacamund, a British colonial town in the Nilgiri Hills of southern India. Others were luckier. They got to Ooty in time and survived the perilous East, at least for another season, by rising above its pestilential lower reaches. On litters, in chairs, on ponies, by foot if they were able, Europeans in Asia nearly two centuries ago began climbing into the hills in search of health, relaxation, and sometimes their sanity.

They called the refuges they created "hill stations." These little towns carved from rocky mountainsides or nestled in the meadows of high plateaus began mostly as sanitariums or convalescent centers, but they soon became Europeanized highland resorts and, ultimately, escapist retreats far from the tumultuous cities and hot, parched lowlands below. Colonialism came and went, but the hill stations are still there, from Pakistan on the old Northwest Frontier of imperial Asia, across India, Sri Lanka, Burma, Malaysia, Indonesia, and Vietnam to the mountains of Luzon in the Philippines, where Americans built one too. The hill stations are overgrown, often overpopulated, and no longer European now, but most have not lost their unique appeal. Air-conditioning notwithstanding, the plains still fry in the sun, and the cities of Asia have only grown larger, noisier, and more polluted.

For the European or American colonial soldier, the civil administrator and his clerk, the merchant, the missionary, and the families who followed them east of Suez, daily life was less a matter of advancing the glory of God or empire than a battle for survival against sunstroke, dysentery, cholera, malaria, and a host of other unnamed deadly fevers as well as little-examined, vague indispositions that in hindsight would probably be diagnosed as clinical symptoms of depression. Later medical scholars coined a phrase for it: "tropical fatigue." Even a contemporary traveler in Asia, armed with the newest medications, knows the fear of falling sick in a very strange place. Within a few hours, a once-exotic environment can suddenly become an alarming, perhaps threatening one, as panic and disorientation compound the illness. Imagine the terror that gripped the afflicted when there were no reliable diagnoses, let alone cures.

A British army doctor in Ceylon in the early nineteenth century calculated that a soldier between the ages of twenty and forty was five times as likely to die in the island's tropical climate, war or no war, than if he had been based in the British Isles. Ruskin Bond, the great essayist of India's Garhwal Himalayas, said that the average life span for a Briton in India in the first half of the nineteenth century was thirty-one for a man and twenty-eight for a woman, figures that reflect the deaths of many children. Bond wrote of a common grave in a town below his hills where ten members of an English family were buried together after dying of cholera in a period of only three days. In the 1830s, a group of American missionaries who arrived to open a new beachhead for the Lord's work in Madurai, in southern India, lost six of their number to diseases within a decade, only to be struck again, this time by a "fearful" cholera epidemic, when they thought the worst was over. The survivors, casting about for an escape, first considered buying a ship to sail away from infested India. On second thought, they took the advice of the British and joined the new trend. They, too, built a hill station.

Among Europeans in the colonies, culture shock was also certainly felt, if not identified or understood, by insensitive, blustering bureaucrats. Breakdowns sometimes followed long periods of stress punctuated by useless explosions of frustration. And all of it in the blistering, suffocating heat. "It rains hot water here," the nineteenth-century traveler Florence Caddy, who was good at one-liners, noted in Singapore. These were obviously not salubrious climes for the hot-tempered or inflexibly self-righteous. People almost literally burned out. Rudyard Kipling's oft-quoted bit of doggerel, injected into the odd little story he wrote with Walcott Balestier called "The Naulahka," struck a chord in the memories of many, to judge from the popularity it enjoyed in England:

> Now it is not good for the Christian's health to hustle the Aryan
>   brown,
> For the Christian riles, and the Aryan smiles, and he weareth the
>   Christian down;
> At the end of the fight is a tombstone white, with the name of the
>   late deceased,
> And the epitaph drear: "A fool lies here who tried to hustle the
>   East."

A flight to the hills gave many a nineteenth- or early-twentieth-century European beaten down by the debilitating tropics the strength to go back into the ring for another bout of administering, ministering, or running a colonial household. Although these men and women are long gone, their hill stations are being rediscovered by Asians, Europeans, and travelers from other continents and regions. Remote and rustic, hill stations are novelties to postcolonial Asians born and raised in increasingly affluent but traffic-choked cities. Furthermore, a century after Europeans first sought refuge in the highlands of Asia, the worst epidemic diseases may be under control, if not entirely gone, but new scourges have created new needs. Asian cities are among the world's most polluted because emission standards, where they exist, are often not enforced and unregulated industries, with the help of corrupt politicians, have made the air dangerous to breathe in New Delhi, Bangkok, and Manila, among other places. Great rivers have died, turned into stinking sewers. Coastal waters and shore resorts do not escape the poisonous by-products of rapid industrial growth and the press of population explosions.

Traveling around Asia now, one sees advertisements for hill stations pitched to local tourists in terms similar to those that publicized them first among colonial elites. Governments still use hill stations as rest and recreation areas for officials; large companies maintain substantial homes for executives and family resorts with lodges or cottages for employees. For foreigners who have done the palaces, temples, and beaches, hill stations are a quirky alternative, with eccentric inns nestling a lot closer to the land and the people than walled-off international tourists resorts with mass-produced hotels.

The universal resurgence of interest in hill stations is evident in the steady stream of old European books about this genre and its historical period now being reprinted in toto or extracted in anthologies. There is a rich deposit to mine. Colonials, whether government servants or private citizens, were often meticulous cataloguers and diarists. The joy and astonishment of discovery, tempered with the extreme hardship of the effort, leap from the writings of early travelers, both men and women, who were seeing wonderful things that none of their compatriots—or for that matter, many local people—had seen before. When Etienne Tardif, a young military doctor in Vietnam at the end of the nineteenth century, was searching for the right spot to build a French sanitarium, he encountered hill-tribe people in the highlands of Annam who were as strange to the Vietnamese in his party as they were to him. So was the sudden change in climate, since the towns of both the French and the Vietnamese tended to hug the torrid coast of the South China Sea and a few river valleys and deltas. "How well one sleeps when it is cold!" Tardif wrote of his first night in the hills, as it occurred to him that this was the first refreshing rest he had enjoyed in four months. "A light mist blurs the landscape. Am I in the colonies or in France, wrapped in the clouds of the Rhone?"

Whether or not these European intruders had the right to be wandering around Asia building towns and cities—apparently intending to stay forever, as they did in the Americas—is another matter. A crop of recent historians has sought to reduce their accomplishments to mere acts of cultural suppression. But to take a longer view of history than is now apparently fashionable, European explorers and settlers were certainly not the first people to migrate into Asia and change it. Arab traders in dhows and Chinese merchants in junks had transformed coastal populations in numerous places before the Europeans came. Before them, larger ethnic migrations had taken place almost everywhere, often pushing indigenous peoples into the hills and hinterlands or boxing them in there on subsistence land. Empires—Hellenistic, Muslim, Hindu, and Buddhist—were on the move, conquering and converting, from the Indus Valley to the islands of what is now the Indonesian archipelago. Europeans were neither the first nor the only intruders to cajole, trick, or intimidate native populations while looting the land, which the great Western mercantile companies certainly did at some times and in some places. Now and then Europeans also fought one another, blowing up rivals' fortifications and sinking their ships, to the astonishment and bewilderment of the local audience.

Yet individual adventurers—among them Victorian tourists who chose, courageously or recklessly, to venture beyond the European Grand Tour, along with scholars, writers, and the first Western administrators assigned to Asian posts by the trading companies—made tremendous contributions to the world's understanding of various Asian cultures. Of necessity, the pioneers learned languages, often without dictionaries or formal teachers. They ate and drank with native rulers and sometimes ordinary villagers, trading lore and absorbing local customs. Even the drunken misfit or the brawler who broke the cultural china everywhere he went often had an encyclopedic knowledge and a shrewd understanding of the neighborhood. Short stories and novels about colonial life draw vividly on such characters.

The first Europeans slogged through suffocating rain forests thick with ravenous leeches and mosquitoes and slashed their way into jungles alive with tigers and other predators. Alone and on foot, they approached indigenous settlements, not knowing if they would be welcomed, ignored, or summarily hacked to death; all had proved possible. They took measurements of everything: the longitude and latitude, the height of mountains, the depth of rivers, the temperature by day and night. They collected specimens and samples that enriched the museums and research organizations of Europe. They analyzed the composition of the soil and ground water. They observed and noted the existing wild and cultivated fruits, grains, or vegetables and calculated the potential for new species. They catalogued insects, animals, and trees. Those with the requisite talents made drawings and watercolors of the birds, the flowers, the untouched landscapes that unfolded before them. Some tried their hands at rudimentary photography when that became possible. All across colonized South Asia and Southeast Asia, European experts and their local colleagues established scientific, medical, archaeological, geographical, cartographic, and artistic institutions, museums, and libraries that sustain modern scholarship to this day.

Hill stations began to appear, albeit at different times in different places, when the era of initial exploration and conquest was waning, wives and families were arriving in substantial numbers, and life had become a bit more routine. By then, colonial societies could take stock of their longer-term needs and, regrettably, look for ways to build walls around themselves to shut out native populations. Though the age of European mercantile empire building and colonialism began with the turn of the sixteenth century, hill stations were largely a nineteenth-century phenomenon. Most were established between 1820 and about 1885, though the French came late with Dalat, in Vietnam, and the Americans with Baguio, in the Philippines, at the beginning of the twentieth century. The British themselves created a second generation of hill stations in peninsular Malaya even later, after World War I. All had the example of British India's older hill stations to emulate—or not.

The age of the hill station mirrored the period when seaside resorts, spas, and great mountains lodges were built in Europe and the United States. In some cases, the style and atmosphere of these European or American mountain retreats were consciously copied in the colonies. A planner of Baguio, in the Philippines, was influenced by the Adirondacks, for example. But in colonial Asia, the relatively high altitude hill station, usually at 5,000 to 8,000 feet above sea level, always had to be more than just a resort. It had to be a medical center of sorts to justify an officer's taking recuperative leave, however flimsy the excuse or ineffectual the cure. The site had to be beyond the reach of mosquitoes, though it was not known until the end of the nineteenth century that the malaria parasite was carried by these insects. The hill station was also a genteel fanta-syland, a retreat from reality where the homesick colonial could be cos-seted by the atmosphere of a European hometown, down to its familiar architecture and its cozy institutions: the club, the library, the village church. The hill station at its homiest is a phenomenon most often associ-ated with the British in India, but the French, the Americans, and to some extent the Dutch also endowed them with similar properties.

The hill station was not confined to Asia. In Africa, the British found highlands that served similar needs in Kenya, Uganda, and elsewhere. But it was in Asia, in countries so far from home and so radically different in culture, where strong old civilizations stood their ground against the in-cursions of Westerners, that the hill stations thrived. Their place in his-tory was strengthened when the British in India began the practice of moving the entire apparatus of regional and national government to the hills during the hottest, beastliest months of the year, turning hill towns into summer capitals. The greatest of these part-time capitals was Simla, in the Himalayan foothills of North India, where the viceroy's lodge ri-valed a maharajah's palace. But there were others. British officers on the Northwest Frontier had a hot-weather headquarters at Murree. Maha-baleshwar served the sahibs and memsahibs based in the East India Com-pany's Bombay region, and Ootacamund was the summer capital of the Madras presidency, Britain's first foothold on the Subcontinent. The British governor of Burma went to Maymyo for part of the year, and in the Vietnamese town of Dalat, the French planned to create a regional capital for an Indo-Chinese federation of Vietnam, Laos, and Cambodia. The American ambassador to the Philippines and the Philippine presi-dent continue to have formal residences at their disposal in Baguio, and the president of Indonesia has a palace at Bogor.

Although the most important hill stations served as seasonal centers of government, administrative buildings were not always the defining or en-during landmarks. Hill stations often had and still have—in addition to their offices, hospitals, country homes, churches, clubs, and libraries—at least one grand hotel or rustic lodge, boarding schools, a brewery, a lake (usually created by damming a stream), a botanical garden, wildlife sanctu-aries, a golf course, hiking trails, a race course or gymkhana ground for competitive games, and plenty of horses or ponies for mountain rides. A lot of hill stations have ghosts, "European" flowers, strawberries, and, alas, armies of uninvited monkeys. The monkeys are especially numerous in In-dia, where Hanuman, the monkey god, is an important mythological figure and an object of worship. Hanuman's descendants are marvelously adept at finding tourist attractions and picnic spots. I noticed a gang of them panhandling beside a speed bump on the road up to Ooty, where they knew they couldn't be missed when the tourist buses slowed to negotiate the bump. In Darjeeling, they hang out at the temples on Observatory Hill trying to look very hungry and forlorn. In Simla, half a dozen of them were entertaining themselves by removing and tossing around a traveler's laundry that had been hung outside a guest house window to dry.

Rehan Khan, who describes himself as a "lifer" at one of the most famous of boarding schools in the Indian hills, Woodstock, in Mussoorie, spent all his secondary-school years there in the 1980s and remembers a lush campus with a lot of "red-butted monkeys" among the prolific wildlife. "In my first year at school," he recalled, "I was walking down the path to the dormitories eating a sandwich when a group of monkeys started to chase me. Needless to say, they were after my sandwich. I remembered the oft-repeated chant of my peers: Do not ever run away from a monkey. If you happen to visit Mussoorie and a monkey chases you, muster up your best growl and run *toward* the animal. In my five years at Woodstock I always kept my food—and also perfected a pretty mean growl." A decade earlier, Gil Halstead, another student hiking in the hills, was pelted with pine cones tossed by silver langurs, who also enjoyed sitting on a cliff overlooking the Woodstock campus and taunting boys and girls as they walked to classes.

The presence and ultimately the proliferation of boarding schools in the hills stemmed from a distressing dilemma faced by many parents during the colonial era. Sending children back to the West for schooling split families for long periods. But keeping sons and daughters at home in the colonies reduced their educational opportunities and risked their health. Life in the Asian colonies could be hard on children. Their small graves are scattered everywhere, painful even to an uninvolved traveler, who cannot help but feel the parents' intolerable sorrow. In southern India, I happened upon a nineteenth-century stone decorated with watchful angels hovering over the grave of a little English girl "swept away by an unknown fever." In Vietnam, an overgrown French cemetery had, among other small tombs, one where six-year-old Alain Rouget was buried beside his thirteen-month-old sister, Odile. The two children had died within a year of each other, as late as the 1940s. In the Pakistani hill town of Murree, Jonathan Addleton, who was born there in 1957 of American Baptist missionary parents and educated at the Murree Christian School in the 1960s and 1970s, was haunted by dead children. Addleton, now an American diplomat who has written a sensitive, thoughtful book about his Pakistani childhood, *Some Far and Distant Place*, remembers a brass plaque at Murree's Holy Trinity Church memorializing Hyacinth Swinhoe, who died in 1913, two weeks before her third birthday. On it, her family had engraved a verse:

> *I wonder, oh, I wonder where*
> *The little faces go*
> *That come and smile and stay awhile*
> *Then pass like flakes of snow*

Many children were sent back to England or another home country, sometimes as babies. But separation from their young sons and daughters was trying for parents, particularly mothers, as stories and diaries from the period reflect poignantly. "A Mother in India," a Victorian-era short story by Sara Jeanette Duncan, is one of the more painful to read. I found a copy of the story, part of a collection now out of print, in an old anthology tucked among the romantic novels in the library of the Kodaikanal Club. Duncan, who apparently knew India well, wrote of a baby dispatched to England soon after birth to be raised by an aunt, and of the mother's aching inability to relate to the little girl, still a toddler, when they met again on the family's next home leave. Brought to the crib of her sleeping daughter, the mother shrank back, mumbling something about not wanting to invade the child's privacy by picking her up and holding her.

Boarding schools in the hills were the solution for many parents, especially for families without the means or the connections to obtain a good education for their children in Europe or the United States, or the money to be able to arrange regular visits if sons and daughters were sent abroad. In the hill stations, parents could join their children for vacations, or make regular trips to see them during the school term. The best of the schools did not die with colonialism. The Murree Christian School, where Addleton recalls "living a Victorian childhood," was not even established until 1956, nearly a decade after Pakistani independence. During the colonial era, American Protestant missionaries in India had established two notable boarding schools, at Kodaikanal in the Palni Hills of the South and Mussoorie in the northern Himalayan foothills, which developed into internationally known and respected institutions that still draw students from around the world as well as from many parts of India. Roman Catholic orders also opened schools in the hills, as they had in the cities, giving the label of "convent school" such cachet in India that educational institutions all over the country adopted the description, though they may have had little or no connection with churches or religious orders. Secular private schools and colleges also appeared. Dehra Dun, at the gateway to the Himalayas, is the home of the Doon School, one of India's most exclusive private boarding schools. In Vietnam, the French built their rigorous and distinguished Lycée Yersin in the hill town of Dalat. Military academies were established in hill stations in the Philippines, Vietnam, and Burma. India's military academy is also at Dehra Dun, not far from Mussoorie, the hill station where the country's high-ranking civil servants study at the Lal Bahadur Shastri Academy, a national school for government administrators.

Social life was taken very seriously in colonial hill stations, especially in the "official" resorts of India. Newcomers left cards in all the appropriate places until communities grew too large and diverse. Dinners were formal affairs, and there were numerous full-dress balls and costume-party evenings. The best imported wines and spirits were hauled up from distant ports across the plains. From accounts of some of the menus of the time, it appears that the food and drink available to those privileged enclaves would no longer be procurable in most hill stations today, certainly not in much of the Indian subcontinent, despite more modern means of transportation and rising incomes. The sheer audacity of colonial society assuming that households could eat as if in Europe, with fine food on fine linens and an abundance of silver and crystal, is truly extraordinary. "Isn't it strange to dine in silk stockings in such a place, to drink a bottle of French wine and another of champagne every evening, to have delicious Mocha coffee and receive the Calcutta papers every morning?" a French naturalist, Victor Jacquemont, wrote of a visit as early as 1830. Others recalled smoked salmon from Scotland, pâtés from France, and Mediterranean sardines. Jacquemont eventually concluded that rich food and excessive drink were undermining the health of Europeans who thought they could carry on eating in India, in the steaming cities as well as the hills, the way they would at home. Some colonial doctors supported that contention; they were usually ignored.

Between social events at clubs and summer residences, there were horse races and horse shows—the ability to ride well was a necessity in most places where roads were few or nonexistent—as well as team games at the gymkhana clubs and amateur theatricals for amusement. Some reasonably good libraries served to expand the mind, titillate the imagination, or just pass time. Shelves of popular novels and romances were escape hatches when life got boring. One viceroy's wife was thankful there was a Shakespeare collection at her disposal to recharge her mind now and then during a season of incessant entertaining. There were also assignations to enliven long afternoons and dark mountain nights.

The hills, where all cares and cautions seemed to be left behind, became famous for dalliances of every kind. Simla, the summer headquarters of the British Raj in India, had perhaps the worst reputation, though Ruskin Bond thought Mussoorie gave it competition. Rudyard Kipling suggested a cause for this propensity for mischief in "Bitters Neat," a story in *Plain Tales from the Hills:* "In India, where life goes quicker than at Home, things are more obviously tangled and therefore more pitiful to look at," he wrote. A mid-nineteenth-century cartoon from the "Delhi Sketch Book" in the Indian version of *Punch* warned horseback riders pictorially to slow down at Jakhu Hill, a well-known assignation point, lest they intrude too suddenly on a stolen kiss in passionate progress around the next bend. Adultery apart, hill stations were considered fine hunting grounds for lonely bachelors from the cantonments or collectors' bungalows, who sometimes in their rush to marry fell in love instantly and unwisely, as well as for single women shipped out from England under pressure by families to find a good match. In colonial parlance, these women were the "fishing fleet." If they went back unsuccessful, they were unkindly labeled "returned empties."

Decolonization began in the 1940s in Asia, earlier than in Africa. By the middle of the twentieth century, India, Pakistan, Ceylon, the Philippines, and Indonesia had become independent, with Vietnam and Malaya soon to follow. By then, the hill stations had lost much of their practical importance. Antimalarial drugs, insecticides, and antibiotics dealt with some of the worst diseases and their carriers; "air-cooled" and eventually air-conditioned offices and homes made life more tolerable at lower altitudes. Trips home to Europe during long breaks had for decades been easier and more affordable. Although many local people traveled or moved to hill stations for work or pleasure and often formed a significant majority of the population, the towns remained socially very much redolent of colonialism to the end, and thus a little irrelevant to the majority of local populations. Of course in some hill towns, the Japanese army occupation during World War II had cracked or shattered, if only temporarily, what was left of the effectively segregated colonial ambiance. The apparent ease with which the Japanese overran large areas of Asia, incidentally, suggested to many Asians that European invincibility had limits, a tremendous psychological catalyst to burgeoning independence movements.

But Japan's treatment of conquered populations during the occupation also demonstrated, paradoxically, that fellow Asians could be as brutal, if not much more brutal, than European colonizers. In a number of hill stations, the elderly relate that as children they were put to work at hard labor by the Japanese. In Indonesia, indignation at Japanese wartime atrocities was passed on to younger generations, contributing to widespread unease over Japan's economic power and its new reach over regions that Tokyo once called its "co-prosperity sphere." The brutality of Asian against Asian is part of history in other settings, too. Malays told the British in the nineteenth century about Siamese troops who ripped open the bellies of pregnant women to settle bets on the gender of unborn babies. Everywhere there are variants of stories about captive people tied down over fast-growing shoots of one or another jungle plant, usually bamboo or rattan, that pierce the body, causing insufferable pain.

Though the Westerners came rushing back after the defeat of Japan in 1945—except for the British in India proper, who never left, since the country escaped invasion—most hill stations had barely resumed functioning before the age of European empires was over. Hill stations went into a decline, and some observers at the time thought that they would never recover. For the people of the newly independent nations that inherited these orphaned towns, there were rankling memories of humiliating discrimination suffered at the hands of colonial masters, who in those artificially created settlements could make all the rules and often used their power to draw racial boundaries around their retreats. Freed of colonial domination, countries like India, Ceylon (now Sri Lanka), Burma, the Philippines, Indonesia, and, later, Vietnam and Malaya (now Malaysia and Singapore) were in any case eager to get on with building new economies, political systems, and institutions. There were other preoccupations. Armed leftists in several countries, boosted in some cases by the Japanese during the war, carried on fighting after independence to "complete the revolution" by co-opting and harnessing anticolonial fervor to the service of Communist movements. The hills became both hideouts and battlegrounds. In India, there was horrific bloodshed over the division of the old British Raj into predominantly Muslim and Hindu countries. In Burma the hero of independence, General Aung San—the father of Aung San Suu Kyi—was assassinated, along with his cabinet. In India, Mohandas Gandhi, the Mahatma, met the same fate.

The hill stations may have languished somewhat in the postcolonial years, but they were never completely forgotten. By the 1960s, local elites had taken over the exclusive clubs, the solidly built bungalows, and the tea and coffee plantations. Numerous maharajas and sultans never gave up their retreats in the hills; middle-class professional families had also bought property during colonial times and were well established. In a number of places, Europeans who felt more at home in Asia than in the countries of their birth—along with a substantial group of men and women born in Asia of Western parents or mixed marriages—retired or stayed on around hill stations to work, learning to live with new masters and often dwindling resources. Anglo-Indians—in the original meaning of the phrase, Britons who were born or had settled in India—were frequently more Indian than they realized, although they spoke of England as "home." They capitalized it: Home. In her book, *Ooty Preserved: A Victorian Hill Station*, Molly Panter-Downes told the story of a woman in her eighties who, when finally forced to return to Britain because she could no longer manage alone, packed a stone mortar and pestle so that she would always have freshly ground chilies and spices for her curry.

Recently, it has become apparent that the old hill stations of Asia are not just going to survive, but are indeed reviving so quickly that they may be victims of their own successes. In the last decade or two of the twentieth century, when the hill stations began to experience a significant rebirth, in fact a boom, it dawned on those who love them that these little towns perched on their cliffsides and mountain meadows were going to be altered forever unless local planners curtailed or zoned development. Rising affluence and greater mobility all over Asia have made the hill stations accessible to millions, surely a democratic trend to be applauded. But the majority of those in the crowds now arriving almost year-round no longer are satisfied with bracing walks in the woods or a snooze in the garden under the fragrant evergreens. They want theme parks, fast food, discos, karaoke, casinos, lavish buffet tables and well-stocked bars, video players in every hotel room, and high-decibel popular bands in the gazebo, where the string quartet once played. "Indians love noise," said Nilam Macdonald, the Bombay-born wife and innkeeper partner of Tim Macdonald, who inherited the quietly elegant Himalayan Hotel in Kalimpong. Southeast Asians love golf more than forests.

In many hill towns, trash piles up, choking drains and fouling footpaths no longer pleasant to walk along. Bookstores have all but vanished, except in India and Sri Lanka—significantly, both established democracies—and library collections have dwindled. Many classic old hotels are struggling, managers say, as newer ones with extravagant names and flashy images carve out places for themselves on already denuded hillsides, gashing the landscape, transforming the skyline with concrete blocks, and smudging the black night sky with neon. Condominiums and time-share holiday flats have also begun to migrate toward the hills. How the people who inherited the fragile hill resorts cope with the challenges they now face will determine which towns will survive the longest. Environmentally, all hill stations are probably as endangered as the tigers that once stalked the encircling forests. The woods themselves are disappearing, with forest cover dropping by 20 to 50 percent or more in only a few decades in most countries.

It is perhaps not surprising that a number of leading environmentalists in Asia have their bases in the hills and see the fate of hill towns as part of the larger problem of conserving valuable ecological systems. Saving forested watersheds that nurture the plains below is a high priority for activists across Asia, whose efforts all too often earn the scorn of politicians. "The Government believes that we should enjoy what nature provides," Mahathir Mohamad, Malaysia's prime minister, said, as he defended his decision to resurrect plans for a new federal highway that would slice through some of the most beautiful hill country in Southeast Asia in order to link three Malaysian hill towns now reached by separate roads from the lowlands. Repudiating environmentalists' charges that it was needlessly destructive to crack open whole hillsides and bulldoze away thousands of acres of rain forest for the greater convenience of motorists, the prime minister retorted that activists didn't seem to mind clearing land to build their own homes. "In order to preserve the forests, are we supposed to live in trees?" he asked rhetorically, as he cut the ribbon on a new tramway to another resort complex. Southeast Asians are infatuated with funicular railways and cable cars. In Vietnam, I read about government plans to build cable connections to the peaceful hilltop Linh Phong Pagoda and other attractions scattered around the pine forests of Dalat. Terminals would be buttressed with restaurants, shopping arcades, electronic games centers, and karaoke bars to draw and satiate the crowds.

All over Asia, this kind of development has already produced significant ecological and climatological effects, beginning with rising temperatures and the disappearance of plant and animal species. A resident of the southern Indian hill station of Kodaikanal, the environmentalist M. S. Viraraghavan, explained that deforestation in the highlands significantly raises the temperature of the earth itself and makes the reintroduction of important old species, accustomed to lower soil temperatures, much harder. Many of these older species were useful regulators of water, retaining moisture and releasing it slowly to flow to the plains, helping farmers many miles away. Upland meadows and grasslands also played a part in this process. Without these natural regulators, rainwater cascades down the mountainsides, taking the shallow topsoil with it and causing choked waterways and floods thousands of feet below.

The men and women who created hill stations almost two centuries ago were not guiltless of environmental destruction. By 1904 in Simla, the wildflowers that had covered the surrounding hills and meadows in the 1830s were all gone, Edward J. Buck wrote in *Simla Past and Present,* the standard reference work on the town for nearly a century until the publication of Pamela Kanwar's *Imperial Simla* in 1990, which added to accounts of early ecological devastation. Buck thought most of the flowers had been sacrificed to dining room tables. Women noted in their diaries that they sent servants into the meadows to pull up whole plants by the roots. Around other hill stations, tea plantations razed thousands of rolling acres of jungle or consumed all available pasture land. Roads (followed by railroads) began cutting into virgin hillsides more than 150 years ago, facilitating erosion and landslides—and, of course, opening the hills to crowds. Subsequent deforestation has only made the instability of the land more pronounced. Some new trees introduced for landscaping or mercantile gain, with eucalyptus and wattle the most common, proved to be destructive to the soil and to other species.

But there is a more positive side to the environmental record of colonialism. The heyday of hill stations coincided with a great age of gardening and of horticulture and agricultural experimentation, symbolized and often inspired by the Royal Botanical Gardens at Kew, in London, which were established in 1759 and opened to the public about a century later. From Kew, botanists armed with seeds and seedlings roamed the world, changing whole colonial economies. They took South American rubber trees to Southeast Asia by way of Ceylon, and cinchona, the source of quinine, to a number of countries, planting it in the new botanical gardens often created with the help of colleagues on loan from the Royal Botanical Gardens. In the hill stations, a great deal of effort went into the planting of trees, grass, and flowers around private homes. Across Asia, hill stations continue to support nursery industries and hold wonderful flower shows. The cultivation of fresh vegetables was encouraged, and orchards with both tropical and temperate fruits appeared on many slopes. Cows were herded up to high-altitude pastures, and dairies opened, adding to the general sense of wholesomeness by providing safe fresh milk (when not watered down by rogues) and cheeses.

For the Western sojourner in Asia, the hill stations still offer some keys to understanding a long-gone, geographically distant past. And although they were creations of the ancestors of Westerners, a point of interest in itself for many, hill stations are also still-living remnants of an earlier age for Asians themselves. They are returning to these towns to become reacquainted with a part of their own history, to learn why the misty mountains had such attraction. From the beginning, it must not be forgotten, Asians—Indians, Ceylonese, Burmese, Malays, and others—were part of life despite the social prohibitions. They sometimes went to schools and churches and often traded with the foreigners or created lucrative service industries, renting ponies or sedan chairs from the earliest days and supplying provisions. Later, local people were recruited by hotels, restaurants, and shops. Some eventually built their own substantial homes, temples, and businesses. India's Oberoi hotel chain got its start in Simla, when Mohan Singh Oberoi sold some of his wife's jewelry to buy Clarkes on the Mall, where he had been a manager.

With the passing of years, the hill stations become more a part of Asian than of Western history and are increasingly recognized as such. "In British times," an Indian will say by way of preface to a historical account, in much the same matter-of-fact way an American would talk about the days before the Revolution. "When the French were here . . . ," echoes a Vietnamese, with the emphasis on "here"—that is, in *our* place. In more than one hill station, Europeans are in fact back on the scene, advising local governments on tourism and sometimes restoring old hotels and villas for the leisure use of international corporations. Tourists from the old colonial powers come back to learn their own history, too: Witness the Dutch package tours to Indonesia.

Although natural settings may be under threat, there is still almost always enough wild terrain left in the hills, or along the way to them, to give the visitor at least a taste of the glorious Asian landscapes the first adventurers encountered. This was the environment in which earlier generations of Asians lived before the rush to the urban centers began in the latter part of the twentieth century. In very recent times, Asian cities, even more than Western ones, have simply bulldozed nature out of the way, making wild places more and more distant. Experienced tourists learn that beach resorts may seem largely interchangeable and Asian cities all begin to look alike. But hill stations, with their individual histories and vistas of arresting landscapes and other natural wonders, cannot be mass-produced or even reproduced anywhere but where they are.

As hill stations change, they also reveal something of the countries that inherited them and demonstrate how different these nations are from one another. Murree, now in Pakistan, could never be mistaken at the end of the twentieth century for the Cameron Highlands of Malaysia, though both countries were once British colonies and both now call themselves Islamic. The old tea planters' Hill Club in Sri Lanka's Nuwara Eliya has an entirely different atmosphere than similar establishments in northern India. The metamorphoses of the hill stations are yet another reminder that there is no such thing as a monolithic "Asia," an invention of the Oc-cidental mind, into which everything from the Levantine through the In-dus civilizations to the courts of Imperial China and Japan was filed.

I first encountered hill stations years ago while teaching at an Indian university in Chandigarh, not too far from where the Sivalak Hills, the first step to the Himalayas, descend to meet the Punjabi plain. Chandigarh is an entirely planned city, the creation of Le Corbusier and a team of archi-tects called in by India after independence to build the Punjab a city to compensate for the loss of its historical capital, Lahore, to Pakistan. One evening, walking near the city's artificial lake, I noticed under the vast Pun-jabi sky a cluster of twinkling lights high above the horizon. It was Kasauli, at more than 6,000 feet the first of a series of hill stations leading higher and higher into the mountains. Not long after that introduction, I made my first trip to the hills, to Simla, and was astounded at what had been cre-ated there despite the formidable natural obstacles. In subsequent years, as a correspondent in Asia, I stumbled from time to time into other hill sta-tions, often because there was trouble of one kind or another: guerrilla warfare, rebellion at a military academy, or an environmental confrontation over a proposed dam or other development project.

Eventually the hill station as an idea, a point of historical reference, and a kind of social litmus test in fast-changing Asian nations began to take hold of my imagination. In early 1997, I set off on a journey of several months: to see Asia anew just through its great hill stations, moving from mountain to mountain from Pakistan, across India, to Sri Lanka, Burma, Malaysia, Vietnam, and the Philippines. A year earlier I had made a trip to the highlands of Indonesian Sumatra, and it was there, at Bukittinggi, in the land of the Minangkabau people, that the idea of this kind of jour-ney came together. In the unlikely Sumatran interior, comfortable new hotels were rising to serve new generations of Southeast Asians with the time and money to take one vacation there and perhaps the next in the Malaysian highlands, Burma, India, or Vietnam. Hill stations were back on the tourist map everywhere.

I knew that it would never be possible to see them all in a matter of months—there are literally dozens of hill towns in India alone; the geographer Nora Mitchell plotted ninety-six of them. What could be accomplished was a tour of the classic Asian hill stations, including at least one built by each of the colonial powers. Not all the European imperialists established such towns. The Portuguese appear to have left no hill stations, and the Spanish never quite got around to building true sanitarium resorts in their 375-odd years in the Philippines, though they had taken a look at Baguio before the Americans came. The Dutch barely qualified. Although Bogor was their invention, it was greatly enhanced by Sir Thomas Stamford Raffles during the short period when the British ruled Java. In choosing which hill stations to visit, I gravitated first to those I had seen and might have enough familiarity with to discern the changes taking place. I limited the choice to the former colonies of South Asia and Southeast Asia, regions where I had lived for the better part of a decade. Thailand, Nepal, and China were eliminated because they were never formally colonized, though Europeans did have varying degrees of influence. In China, for example, American missionaries built a hill station near Moganshan, about 150 miles from Shanghai, which became a popular resort for Europeans.

The journey to any hill station is a major part of the experience. With very few exceptions, hill stations do not have airports. Getting to them involves heading away from today's manic Asian cities and rambling through farmland and back-country villages or towns, past rice fields and orchards, and under canopies of tamarind and banyan trees, to the narrow, winding colonial-era roads that snake upward thousands of feet into the mountains. Most hill stations are reachable only by car or bus, though a few have narrow-gauge rail lines, also built in the age of empire. Getting to the destination can foster a new respect for the grit and perseverance of colonial planners and their impressive engineering achievements. With explosives but no large earth-moving equipment, the builders of mountain roads depended on local labor—not always voluntary—to dig and level the roadbed. They called the workers "coolies," derived from *kuli*, an Indian word whose origins and meaning are still disputed between colonizers and the colonized.

The gang-labor system continues in India and Burma, where poor men, women, and children swarm construction sites, carrying bricks, earth, and concrete in shallow pans on their heads to build overpasses and air-conditioned office towers. Just out of Bagdogra on my way to Darjeeling, I saw a common sight made especially ironic by its historical context. Dozens of ragged, dust-covered people sat among piles of large rocks on the highway shoulders. They were breaking stones slowly by hand, with hammers or by banging one rock against another, preparing to lay the foundation needed to widen a colonial-era road to the hills. The scene might have been the same 150 years earlier.

In renewing my acquaintance with the great hill stations of Asia, I traveled around the world from New York through Europe to the mountainous frontiers of the Indian subcontinent in Pakistan. Then I progressed eastward through India, Sri Lanka, and Burma to the lusher, sweeter lands of Southeast Asia, where Americans experienced their most intimate relations with the Asian world, for better or worse, in the Philippines and Vietnam. As the plane bringing me home across the Pacific slid into Los Angeles at dusk, there was a dusting of snow on the Sierra Nevadas, as there had been on Pakistan's Margala Hills, my first stop. I saw houses built along the razorback ridges of the hills behind Los Angeles, cool retreats for a new elite escaping the ills of lower elevations. With their lights twinkling in the dusk, they seemed not very different as night fell from those colonial outposts on their Asian heights.

2

THE HILLS
OF PAKISTAN

Murree and the Galis

A Murree hillside blanketed in snow

$\mathcal{I}$ FIRST WENT TO MURREE for the almonds. Abdul Toheed, our cook in Delhi, often gave me a shopping list when I set off for Islamic Pakistan. Usually he wanted poetry books in Urdu. But if the season was right, he suggested almonds. Toheed's father had been a chef for Field Marshal Claude Auchinleck, the commander in chief of Britain's Indian army in the waning days of empire. It was General Auchinleck who in the years leading to Indian independence in 1947 negotiated with Jawaharlal Nehru, later to be India's first prime minister, over how to make the difficult and delicate transfer of military power to a new Indian government. General Auchinleck, and thus Toheed's family, had done stints on British India's Northwest Frontier, now Pakistan, and in the Himalayan hills of India. Like so many Indians, especially Muslim Indians, whose world was torn apart by Partition in 1947, Toheed, a poet himself, cherished memories of places he would never visit because his Islamic family had cast its lot with India, not Pakistan, and travel across the border has been very difficult. "You have seen Lahore!" he once said with appreciation when I returned from the airport in Delhi. Lahore, a worn but wonderful city, was (and in a spiritually truncated way still is) the heartland of North Indian culture, a place of glory to Sikhs, Muslims, and those Hindus sorrowful over the butchery of this civilization that took place half a century ago along sectarian lines.

Because of his unusual childhood, Toheed carried in his head a library of lore about subcontinental crops and regional specialties. Thus the almonds. The Murree Hills are famous for their walnuts and their orchards of temperate-climate fruits, but good almonds also reach the Murree bazaar from other parts of Pakistan and from Afghanistan, only hours away by truck or bus—an easy trip for vendors eager to tap Murree's affluent shoppers. I went eagerly to Murree, too, because I had been to Simla, the hill station of all hill stations and the one most travelers know most about. Murree was the only hill station in Pakistan that I had ever heard or read much about—Murree and its smaller neighbors, the Galis. I made the trip several times over the years, in several seasons: in winter, in the spring-summer "season," and again in early autumn, to walk Murree's Mall, the shopping and dining promenade where colonial and, later, Pakistani high society took its leisurely exercise in more formal olden times. The almonds were in abundance among the other nuts and fruits, overflowing the rude woven baskets, basins, and buckets arranged around competing hawkers.

The shopping done, I went off to explore the Murree Hills, with their panoramic views of Kashmiri peaks, more remote and challenging than many others in the Himalayas. I got no farther that day than Bhurban. Rounding a bend on a muddy mountainside work-in-progress that would one day be a road, I saw ahead a most magnificent sight. On a promontory overlooking a mountain chasm an eternity wide, a great lodge was rising—the first such grand hotel to be built in any Himalayan hill station for possibly a century—certainly since the end of the British Empire in India in 1947. The taxi driver and I explored the vast construction site. But I left the Subcontinent before the lodge at Bhurban, an ambitious project of Pakistan's Pearl Continental hotel group, was finished, and I never saw how it all turned out. I hoped to come back. That the unpredictable mountain weather later intervened to deprive me of this pleasure barely five miles from my goal is another story.

Murree was founded in the 1850s as the summer capital of the British Indian army's Northern Command, and some top officials of the counterpart civilian government, also based in Rawalpindi, had seasonal residences there. Among the well-known hill stations of British India, Murree alone went to Islamic Pakistan at Partition, taking with it all the trappings of any mountain resort: dancing, café life, movies, concerts, and theater, along with an easy intermingling of the sexes. Although Muslims, Hindus, and Sikhs hacked and bludgeoned one another by the thousands as they raced in panic to exchange places over a new border baptized in blood—Hindus and Sikhs from Pakistan fleeing to India, and Muslims from India hellbent for Pakistan—the two countries they created from Britain's Indian empire were not initially very different, at least not in the lives of the ruling elite. The social engineering of conservative Islamicists and nationalist Hindus would come later. At independence in 1947, the decision to split India along sectarian lines was as much political as religious.

"There was, mercifully, no rule that we couldn't eat a certain meat or whatever; it was up to us," said Begum Nargis Jan, a strong-willed woman now in her eighties who has lived part of every year in Murree since she was a little girl in the 1920s. That is when her wealthy parents, who owned a home there, enrolled her in a convent school. "Whether we had ham or bacon, that was up to us. Whether we drank, that was up to us. And we were better people, I can assure you. Simpson and Company—an English company—sold everything from ham to imported wines and whiskeys and things like that. But the best thing was the beer made by the Murree Brewery."

Of all the hill station breweries, and they were a regular feature because there were both clear water for the brewing and thirsty people with leisure time in the mountains, the Murree brewery was one of the most famous. Now just a ruin near the hamlet of Ghora Gali, the original Murree Brewery Company opened in 1861, less than a decade after the hill station's birth. "Consequent to the British ascendancy of the Punjab in 1849 and the stationing of British troops in northern India, the need for some quenchable solace, locally available, became imperative," says the company's official history. "Ghora Gali, a dreamy, pine-thicketed village near the hill station of Murree, famous since time immemorial for its sweet and bracing water, was selected as the venue." The Murree brewers pioneered the cultivation of hops in the Subcontinent, using the blessedly receptive cropland of Kashmir. By the end of the century, the brewery was so successful that it became an investor in breweries in Quetta, now the capital of Pakistan's Baluchistan Province, and in the hill stations of Ootacamund, in South India, and Nuwara Eliya, in Sri Lanka, then Ceylon. A stroke of luck led the brewery's owners to build a big plant in Rawalpindi also. This brewery, producing beer and malt whisky, would be the sole survivor of the Murree company's operations after the breakup of British India. It remains the country's only (legal) brewery, owned by Parsis, an influential minority in Muslim Pakistan.

Begum Nargis, whose late husband, Mohammed Jan, was a Muslim and a judge in the Lahore High Court, grew up in a liberal Parsi family that intermingled with Murree's British society. Her father, Jamsedji Planji Kaikobad, was a successful businessman and property owner who had an eclectic group of friends and acquaintances. Begum Nargis was reminiscing recently at her winter home in Lahore with her friend Hamid Alvi, a political analyst. Begum Nargis remembers more than seven decades of life in Murree; Hamid, a Muslim, came of age after the British had gone. But their recollections of the past and opinions on what is happening today to the Murree they knew are not dissimilar.

"You have a date in history—Independence, Partition in 1947—but a lot of things don't disappear right away; things don't automatically change 100 percent," Alvi had told me earlier during an evening at his home in Islamabad. He was sixteen at the time India and Pakistan split, an age just on the verge of adult pleasures. In his circle, weekends in Murree were among these. Alvi grew up in Lahore and was educated at Government College, where native sons who competed fiercely to wear the maroon blazer and gray slacks of this Subcontinental Eton-cum-Oxford prepared for the professions or the high ranks of the civil service. He learned his social graces carefully, in an environment of a genteel café and tea-room society. "As college students in Lahore, we had four or five places on the Mall Road to go to where there were drinks, a band, and cabaret. There was also Faletti's. You had to dress up to go to Faletti's. You couldn't just walk in there. You were first taken and introduced by someone who knew what to do. And that's how we learned how to behave."

Faletti's was Lahore's grand hotel, part of a chain that also included Flashman's in Rawalpindi, Dean's in Peshawar, and the Cecil in Murree. The hotels, all but the Cecil, are sprawling one-story affairs fronted by sunny gardens shielded from the avenues outside by a wall or hedge and trees. Built by the Faletti family but taken over by the Pakistan government after independence, the properties have been slowly but steadily sinking into decrepitude, kept alive mostly by romantics untroubled by discomfort and budget travelers lucky to find such inexpensive lodgings with so much history. Only the Cecil appears to have made some efforts to renovate, a testimony to the bright future of the hill station.

In Murree, Begum Nargis said, there was never the segregation that marked life under the British in Simla, where in the shadow of a viceregal court, a lot of English sahibs and memsahibs looked down with distaste even on maharajas. Few real lords and ladies inhabited the colonies, but there were plenty of untitled middle-class Britons happy to inflate themselves into a quasi aristocracy through colonial service. Surrounded by servants and far from the correctives of British town life, they took on unaccustomed airs. Malcolm Muggeridge, making his first trip to India in the waning days of the Raj, wrote in *The Green Stick*, the first volume of his autobiography, how the propensity to become more "la-di-da" increased in direct proportion to the sailing distance from England, and how by the time the ship reached the Suez Canal former Home Counties suburbanites were throwing around words like "tiffin" and "chota peg" and summoning the stewards with a brisk "Boy!"

Though often no less formal in its entertainment than Simla, Murree had no viceroy or other colonial bigwigs, but rather more junior officers and their families and therefore a small-town feel about it. Most houses were not so grand, and not too far from one another. The "Europeans," as the British and the few other Westerners, including Americans, were known collectively, mixed easily. Close enough to the British regional military headquarters at Rawalpindi for weekend commuting and with a climate considered healthy for children, Murree became a year-round home for some British families. Francis Younghusband, the British explorer, and Maud Marshall Diver, a writer of novels and short stories popular in Britain earlier in the twentieth century, were among those born there.

"The men used to come for a long weekend," Begum Nargis recalled.

> They used to come on Friday evenings round about four o'clock, go straight to the club. The club was a nucleus of all that the Europeans had. They had their parties there. They had their christenings there. They had their marriages there. They had their dances there. They had a lot of things going on in that club. If you know Murree you'll know that the club is not anywhere in town; it is a little off from town, on the Kuldanna Road. There was good fellowship, very good fellowship, with the British. They really liked it here very much. They encouraged us to come up to Murree, to buy property and to be one of them. They didn't stop us from going to the club. We were part and parcel of it.

An old-fashioned preference for snobby but spartan clubs survived independence in both Pakistan and India, at least for a while. Even after independence, throwing money around was not considered an acceptable way to apply for membership, and more than one gymkhana or other crusty, British-inspired establishment in the liberated Subcontinent stoically and sniffily chose mended tablecloths, thinner soup, or even slow death rather than lower standards. In India this attitude eventually drove large numbers of the new rich into the arms of the splashy hotels, which were only too eager to host the extravagant, even garishly vulgar, wedding parties and to provide the pseudo-elegant venues for business entertainment and political deal making. In both Pakistan and India (and elsewhere in Asia) politicians occasionally get more or less locked up in luxury hotels by their party leaders to prevent their bolting on important votes, lured by the many, many rupees that can change hands in a critical moment of decision. Room service helps.

"Clubs used to evaluate potential members on the old members' terms," Hamid Alvi recalled of the early years of independent Pakistan.

> They looked into the pedigree of the man. His financial resources counted, of course, but also his status in society. His family, his intellectual or professional achievements and other distinctions were weighed with his resources. That's the way it was in the hill stations, too. They also had their clubs and resorts that attracted a certain kind of guest. Murree had very formal customs. There were morning tea parties and afternoon tea parties. We used to dress up in the evening to go to the Mall—put on a necktie and suit just to

go walking from the Post Office to Pindi Point. Exercise was part of being there. You could meet almost the whole crowd in this mile and a half. People behaved very nicely. The restaurants were clean. In the summer in the evening, there were bands and dancing. There was no purdah; women were free. But we were an elite group.

Curiously, Pakistanis on the whole talk far less of slights, of racism or ostracism suffered at British hands, than Indians do, and the British often wrote in far more respectful terms of frontier Muslims they encountered than they did of their hapless Hindu servants. It was easier to loathe and ridicule a low-caste or outcaste Hindu; upper-caste Indians did and do it all the time. Pakistani society is on the whole more egalitarian, with ethnic or regional enmities rather than caste at the forefront of disdain and even violence. Begum Nargis did not have too much good to say about Afghans and Pathans, for example, frontier people who have moved into Murree since the British left. But the proud Pathans, whose lands were not far from Murree, would not know the meaning of the word *grovel*. Britain did not take over the governing of the Pathans' frontier city of Peshawar and the neighborhood around it until the mid–nineteenth century. In some areas beyond Jamrud, toward the Khyber Pass into Afghanistan, clan rulers were the government; the British could only station agents there. This arrangement continued into the time of independent Pakistan.

Begum Nargis said that after Partition, with the British gone and a large percentage of the houses in Murree damaged or destroyed by warring mobs, life began its irrevocable change, leaving her Parsi community and a few old Pakistani Muslim families the last remnants of the old order.

All kinds of people came. All kinds of property was sold. All that was left was sold, not to Hindus and Sikhs of course, but to us and to the Pathans. The Pathans made a great deal of money in Murree, a great deal. Quite a lot of Afghans came up to Murree, too. They're very nice people, I suppose, but there is no fraternization between anybody. If I went for a walk in the old days, somebody would say, "Hello, how are you?" and so on. We'd come back and we'd sit down at my house or their house and have dinner together. That sort of thing. Now we are isolated, and they don't like us. They don't fraternize with us. We don't fraternize with everybody, either. There is very little between them and us. If there is a wedding, they will certainly call us. If we go, they'd be very happy that we had been. If we don't go, they couldn't care less. That is the type of life that there is now in Murree.

Hearing her talk, I thought of the summer day when I encountered an ugly Afghan confrontation in the tiny parking lot of the Cecil Hotel. The

Afghan rebel leader, Gulbadin Hekmatyar, a truly dangerous misogynist of long reputation, had for some reason decided to say his afternoon prayers on the front lawn of the hotel, or so an advance party laying out the rugs told me. I knew him as one of the mujahideen who tried to bar foreign women from press conferences and who would later take his pre-Taliban brand of orthodoxy to Kabul after the Russians left. His henchmen, encumbered with automatic weapons, paid little attention to me in a corner gazebo. But even that was too close for me, and I moved off to take a walk. A muffled scream and the sounds of scuffle in the parking lot stopped me as I approached the hotel driveway. Several burly mujahideen were forcing a young woman into the back of a van. I caught her tear-stained face at the window, her fists raised to hammer on the glass. In South Asia, women are abused publicly in many ways, but this scene haunts me more than most because I hesitated for a long minute, knowing that only another woman might be able to help her but deciding that it might be too dangerous to intervene. I never knew what was happening—or what followed, because the van was gone when I came back up the hill—but I can still see her terrified face and feel a great remorse.

Begum Nargis had one good word for the Pathans and Afghans of the desolate border regions. "One thing is that these people haven't cut down any trees. The trees are still there, and it is March and they are sprouting, and like always everything will be beautifully green. Murree is a very beautiful place, very beautiful. And after the first shower of rain, it's washed clean, as it were." Perhaps these frontier people, a generation or less away from tribal life in terrain where water and trees may be more valuable than gold and gemstones, will be more protective of the environment than the Subcontinent's urbanites, with their preference for asphalt, neon, and concrete. Odd that an otherwise vicious Afghan warlord should be laying out his prayer rug in an English-style garden within view of a majestic forested mountain range that conveniently came between him and Mecca. The Afghanization of Murree must surely be one of the more bizarre turns in the story of Britain's legacy.

"I have been in Murree since a young girl of five, and lived there until I am eighty, so I have seen what Murree was and what Murree is now," Begum Nargis said.

The British were a majority and we were a minority. Overnight they built a beautiful road that still exists. All the roads in Murree that are still in use were made by the British. About 80 percent of the houses that were made there were made by British people. We have got our Dingley Dell. We have got Constancia Cottage. We've got the Rockledge Cottage. We've got Mall View, the house where I am staying. All these were made by the British. Their lives were very useful, very fruitful lives.

The convent schools came with them. There was the Presentation Convent, there was the Convent of Jesus and Mary, which is my school also. People from as far away as Delhi wished to send their children here simply because of the climate. We had both the Irish nuns and the English nuns teach us, and I am the product of those people. I have never forgotten either my mother or my teachers. Those teachers have played a very great part in my life. Every Sunday all the women, very beautifully dressed with hats and everything complete, and their little prayer books, too, in their hands, used to come and pray with us in the school chapel, right in the heart of Murree. I used to go to chapel too; I had to, because I was in the convent. My father didn't refuse. He was like that. It was a beautiful chapel. The bells that used to ring there have stopped, unfortunately. But they were a very beautiful clarion of bells. Now that those bells are silent, a bit of Murree is dead.

Much more of Murree died in Partition, Begum Nargis remembers.

There was a holocaust of Hindus and Muslims. It was terrible. We saw Murree burning. It so happened a gang came up to the cinema, which belonged to my father. The *chowkidar* said: "What are you doing? This belongs to the man who built the mosque for you!" They had come to torch the cinema, but they went back. But 80 percent of the properties in Murree were burnt. All those beautiful properties. The English never really came back after that.

"The lifestyle of the British women in colonial days?" She thought about it.

The Europeans lived very well. They came with their cooks and their staff and brought their horses with them. There was a lady called Flora MacDonald, who used to ride sidesaddle. A very beautiful woman. We never got tired of looking at her and wondering how on earth she could sit like this with both her legs over here. We'd never seen anything like it. The women would look after the house, where they would have good meals. Our *khansama*s could not cook in the manner in which they used to cook, so they taught them a great many things. They taught me, too. You must know this: You must know that I didn't know how to wash my clothes. I didn't know how to make a cake. They taught me a great deal. That is how they were, the British.

Begum Nargis remembers the riotous social life for which young British men developed outrageous reputations all over India, drinking too

much and indulging in fraternity party–style stunts around Pindi or Lahore after the New Year's Ball. But she said that in Murree, society was a
little more decorous.

On Saturday nights there used to be a big dance, where all the ladies used to
be dressed in their ball gowns. That ball used to go on to two or three in the
morning. Then there used to be a day of rest on Sunday. But by about eleven
o'clock on Sunday morning the ladies and the gentlemen and the officers
used to come out and give their children a treat of ice cream in what was
known in those days as Lintotts' Café. There was another café, Sam's, run by
a Jew called Sammy Hoof, whom I met later in Half Moon Street in London after many years. He had a place where you could get a very good cup of
coffee and a tea dance. From Scott's Garden, we used to get beautiful flowers
and walnuts, apples, and pears. Wonderful pears. Fantastic. I haven't seen
pears like that lately. Murree was very famous for that.

Before Partition, Hindus were also part of social life. "At Rowbury's—it
used to be a very big hotel—the Maharani of Cooch Behar used to come
every year, and every year on her husband's birthday, she would call the
whole of the people at the hotel to come and have a dinner and dance.
She would meet everybody. That sort of idea, that life, has gone. Completely." In its place are tourism and tourists with no stake in the place, she
said. "They are making a five-star hotel right in the heart of Murree. I
don't know that it's going to do Murree any good. There will be all sorts of
people that can afford 3,000 rupees a night just to be able to sleep on
those beds, and not even a cup of tea in the morning. No culture. Culture
is made by people. Now who is going to come to this hotel? You can just
imagine! They are rich but they've got no values."

All over Murree, new hotels are rising. They are striving hard to look
"modern." Neon, marble, flashy accouterments like the revolving dining
room at the Grand Heights Hotel, where I stayed. It was ineptly named
the Gaggan Restaurant. Mostly these buildings are austere, chilly places
in every sense. Colonial buildings in most hill stations may have been
drafty, but the new hotels in the hills are missing the psychological, if not
real, warmth of wood-paneled rooms with thick tapestries and fireplaces,
a luxury lost to deforestation and contemporary tastes. Glass walls and
deep, wide windows are the fashion of the times—and who can object
when the views are as grand as these. But such wide-open structures, fine
at beach resorts, lend a permanent chill to life on exposed hills and in the
wind-blown gullies that nestle below them—not only in winter.

South Asians seem to me to be inexplicably hard on public buildings. They scar walls, stain carpets, and slash upholstery with remarkable casualness. They allow grimy fingerprints to accumulate on doors, windows, light switches, and any number of other completely washable surfaces. Their uncontrolled children draw on walls and run up and down corridors shrieking and slamming doors well into the night. When it's time or past time to redecorate, workers are about as careful. Blobs and dribbles of paint are scattered everywhere. As more and more characterless concrete-box hotels are erected in Murree, the sense of sprawling, built-in degradation grows. My room at the Grand Heights, barely five years old, was already a museum of abuse. A potentially elegant space, with its magnificent view of rolling hills and snow-capped mountains, had walls looking as if someone in hiking boots had tried to walk on them or kick them down. Half a dozen brown triangles in the shape of a pressing-iron had been scorched into the haphazardly cut rose-colored carpet, which was also pockmarked with cigarette burns. A charming, carved-wood settee had a nasty gash and an even nastier stain on its almost-new upholstery. A hotel accountant who had recently returned from years of service in hotels in Europe and the Middle East blamed lax management as much as the guests. He was preparing to preside over a complete revamping of the place, hoping to upgrade it to multistar status. But he had a look of resignation about him.

Begum Nargis's friend Hamid Alvi still goes to Murree, too. Until recently he was a regular of the Golf Hotel, a members-only establishment for many years, though now open to the public. Nowadays he and his wife, Qaiserah, a professor of Urdu literature, stay at the Pearl Continental's new lodge at Bhurban because it strikes them as the salvation of a area otherwise going to seed. Murree is still very much alive and growing, sustained in large part by newly affluent Pakistanis who have made their money in commerce, industry, and sometimes government, where corruption flourished. Old-timers have no sympathy for the newcomers' fascination with neon-lit caverns that pass for discos, cheap souvenir shops, and traffic jams.

"Bhurban," Alvi said, "reminds me of the old days." More than five miles from the Murree Mall, Bhurban's Pearl Continental Hotel is cut off from the majority of day-trippers and short-stay visitors in the hills. It is prohibitively expensive for most Pakistanis. "I'm not a snob," said Alvi, "but I love beautiful things, and some comfort. The grounds are nicely laid out, with an open-air theater. Every evening, they invite a musician."

The silence and the entertainment offered do not hold out much attraction for "women in shiny dresses," he said, searching for an image to characterize the Pakistani nouveau riche. Begum Nargis added that this is the sort of person who says, "Hi, Pop! and stuff like that."

The approach to Murree, about 7,500 feet in altitude, is both similar to and different from trips to other hill stations. Mostly it is an easy practice run, a warm-up exercise for the stomach-turning, terrorizing ascents to other hill resorts of the Subcontinent. Murree is barely an hour and a half's drive from the flat Pokahara plateau cities of Rawalpindi and Islamabad, Pakistan's capital planned and built for that purpose. Murree had the good fortune after independence to stay in Punjab Province, where in recent years Nawaz Sharif, as provincial chief minister and later prime minister of Pakistan, took a special interest in road building, not something most South Asian politicians are noted for. The road to Murree is genuinely two-lane all the way, with widened bends and a continuous barrier of alternating guard rails and low concrete or stone walls built to minimize, if not prevent, the harrowing fatal plunges into ravines that regularly take place along many other mountain roads in this part of the world.

At night, Murree can be seen for miles as the road snakes toward its pool of lights spilling down and around several hills. A hill station always tantalizes an approaching traveler, sometimes for a hour or more, because it seems so near—and yet is still valleys and hilltops away. As the road rises and falls, twists and turns, it is there, then gone, then there again. For those in earlier times who hiked to Murree on foot or made the journey in a tonga or a horse-drawn landau, the cruelty of this teasing hussy must have been all the greater. However, like other people I met in the Asian hills whose long lives have spanned great changes, Begum Nargis rather enjoyed the old forms of transportation.

A Parsi with the help of two Hindus put up what was known as the Imperial Carrying Company. We rode a two-horse tonga, very broad, very comfortable. We used to change horses every six miles and go on up to Murree. It used to take us four hours to get there. There were no cars, mercifully, and none of those motor lorries. When we got up to Murree, there was what is known as the tonga stand, and we got down there, and we walked up the hill to the Mall. Rickshaws used to be plying in those days, and women like my mother and others of her age who could not walk very well used to be put into rickshaws. The European women had their own rickshaws and their own rickshaw coolies in their own uniforms, if you please. There were two coolies at the front and two at the back.

About the same time that Murree got electricity—much later than Simla—Begum Nargis's family got motorized. "Somehow or another grandfather got a car. The first car that came to Pindi belonged to him. It was called a Dedion, and of course it came with the chauffeur. We used to say our prayers and then get into that car. After that, the Hindus and the Sikhs got cars, too." No mention of the Muslims.

Murree was for years a special way station on the long Jhelum Road between Rawalpindi and Srinagar, the capital of the former kingdom of Kashmir. At Srinagar, the Moghul emperors had built, centuries earlier, one of two fabulous Shalimar Gardens (the other is in Lahore) and established the reputation of the Vale of Kashmir as a haven of near-unearthly pleasures. Kashmiris, living on fertile land and endowed with uncommon artistic talents, were influenced by the mystical, more pacific Sufi strain of Islam. Together, the qualities of the place and people later endeared Kashmir to the British, who, not permitted to own property there, turned instead to the magnificent rococo houseboats that made Srinagar's lakes floating fairylands. All this turned to tragedy in the 1990s, when a clumsy and violent Indian army occupation aiming to crush, not understand, a growing ethnic separatist movement by Kashmiris, transformed Srinagar into a heavily fortified and sandbagged camp. Subsequent elections have not done much to mitigate the sense of oppression.

Since 1947, India and Pakistan have fought two and a half wars over Kashmir, which at independence had a Hindu maharaja and a Muslim majority. Kashmir's status remains officially unresolved, its territory divided. The Jhelum Road has long been closed at the free-fire range along the cease-fire line separating India and Pakistan. But when this route flourished, largely because it was the only road open year-round, Murree was the last stop to relax and have fun. Beyond Murree, some tough travel begins, along narrow stony tracks that cling to cliff faces along a profoundly steep gorge and a deep jade-green river that I once saw swallow a tanker truck that took a bend too fast, rolled, and dropped in surreal silence into the chasm.

Begum Nargis was close to tears talking about Kashmir, where her family spent a few months every year. "Kashmir was given to us by God Almighty," she said. "I have been to some very fine hill resorts in Europe. I've been through the whole of Switzerland. It's never the same thing as Kashmir. The war has made things very difficult for everybody. Every year we used to go from Murree to Kashmir during the monsoons. My grandfather had a houseboat. My father bought me a houseboat, the *Topaz*. We used to go to the Dal Lake, with flowers on either side of our shikara."

But after the world turned upside down in 1947, the rabble came, the Begum said. "Do you know what they do now there? Shall I tell you what they do? They pinch your bottom! They actually pinch your bottom! These are the type of people. Now what am I to say?"

After the buildup to Murree from the plains, the arrival is anticlimactic: one last hairpin turn and some sort of kiosk or guest-house sign provides evidence that you are there, though you can't see the hill station for the hills. Like most mountain towns, Murree is a tangle of switchback lanes and alleys and outdoor stairways, climbing ever higher to one of two landmark elevations: Pindi Point, with a view south to Rawalpindi and Islamabad, forty miles away; and Kashmir Point, looking east across the Jhelum, one of five rivers that gave the Punjab its name. Most of Murree proper, with its jumble of shops and restaurants along the Mall, occupies a ridge running southwest to northeast between these points.

Murree, cool and green in the warmer months, is famous also for its crisp wintry landscape. Families bring their children to give them the rare experience of snow and of bundling up in unfamiliar clothes. If there were Christmas here, it would almost always be white. When I arrived the last time in mid-January, thankful that the roads were not snow-covered, Mumtaz Ahmed, chief executive of the Grand Heights Hotel, was apologetic about the dull brown scenery mitigated only by towering green fir trees. "I don't know why this is," he said. "In other years, there was always snow this time." Down on the dusty plateau to the south, the president of Pakistan had joined religious leaders that day in praying for rain to relieve a long drought. The message must have gone straight to heaven. Next morning, I barely had time to hike around the town to reacquaint myself and catch a glimpse of the distant peaks of the Pir Panjal range, when snow started to fall, first in flurries, then in a serious, howling blizzard.

It snowed all afternoon, tapering off after nightfall long enough to clear the air and reveal a Christmas-card scene in the valley beneath my window. The pinpoints of light from isolated homes, hamlets, and what looked like small military installations were magnified by fields of white. But then, shortly before midnight, a second blizzard struck with the force of a minor hurricane. Violent gusts of arctic wind blasted us, and my room's valiant little single-bar electric heater—an enduring artifact of modern British civilization—was cowed into pale submission but not yet beaten. Three times the power went out, only to be restored within half an hour. I began to think that this part of Pakistan had also overcome its energy problems as no equivalent place in India had. Then a few fatal, icy blasts cut the power again, and it could not be restarted. Murree sank slowly into a deep, dark, dangerous freeze. A third snow squall just before daybreak finished the job: Powerless Murree was now also cut off from the plains by snow-drifted roads and downed telephone lines. In only thirty hours, three and a half feet of snow had fallen, grounding birds and animals and people.

First to go were my plans to visit the Galis, smaller hill stations higher in the mountains north of Murree. Then I feared I would never get to Bhurban. As time passed, I was reduced to worrying if I would ever leave Murree. Or ever leave Murree alive. The storm never gave up. It snowed all the next day, too, while the power squad made several short-lived efforts to restart the electrical supply. Lines were cut, we were told, and would have to be reconnected in several places. At dusk, we were still without heat and light, and the hotel staff seemed astonishingly unconcerned that they might be on the point of losing a guest or two to hypothermia.

But then I must have been a nuisance to these otherwise helpful men, all men, who were not only freezing, but also fasting through the holy month of Ramadan. Many of the people of the Murree Hills are religious conservatives, many claiming descent from Abbas, an uncle of the Prophet. The name Abbasi is common here. Yet between the last predawn meal and the *iftar* feast that breaks the fast at nightfall (announced here by a fire siren), I was always able to get food, which was cheerfully cooked and served by a young man wrapped in layers of wool. I noticed a family of snow-struck Pakistani guests from the lowlands who had arrived with food and drink in jugs and thermoses, just in case. We were all at the Grand Heights Hotel, it seemed, because the Pearl Continental had closed its Bhurban lodge for Ramadan. Just as well, since drifts and landslides had just removed it from the map.

Lying in bed under rug-thick blankets made by people (Iranians, the label said) who know what to expect when winter hits the mountains, I tried to remember other seasons and the warm sun and soft breezes of the last time I saw Murree. In those days I could fritter away an hour in the garden of the Cecil Hotel, a colonial relic, drinking tea under the sun while an itinerant Kashmiri shawl seller laid out his wares on the fussed-over short grass of the lawn. The shops along the Mall were not so forlorn. Swarms of tourists, Pakistani and foreign, strolled along the promenade, exuding the day-tripper's cheerful determination to have a great time.

With Murree locked into winter, it seemed a much poorer, shabbier place. In a ditch outside the flashy Red Onion Restaurant, almost opposite the towering Holy Trinity Church, an emaciated man huddled in the ubiquitous Himalayan wrap of shawls and blankets was selling knitted woolen socks at 25 cents a pair, though he didn't have the energy to hawk them very effectively. No one tried to entice me with a souvenir or even a postcard. Coming out of what appeared to be the town's last bookshop, a disappointing place, I nearly collided with an anguished woman hastening along the road, cradling in her arms an unconscious child of nine or ten. Another woman ran ahead, searching frantically for someone or something.

When Murree is its off-season self, there are not many women to be seen anywhere in public. Their absence is felt in shops and hotels, where the atmosphere is harshly masculine, with no grace notes—all the more so on dismal winter days. This Pakistani masculinity does not manifest itself as a swaggering, threatening machismo, at least not to a foreign woman in a small town. Rather it is a unselfconscious maleness acquired from growing up, hanging out, eating, and going to work almost always in the company of only boys and men. This is reinforced by a religion where the place of worship is pretty much a male club and men have at their disposal certain convenient passages of the Koran, and the interpretations of it collectively known as Hadith, with which they can degrade women. Beyond the home, where rural girls and their mothers, aunties, and grannies are in any case often separated from the males, men just don't mingle and schmooze with them. When thrown into mixed company, they have no useful social skills. Of course in cities, especially among the rich and well educated, and on the staffs of international hotels, relationships are different. Women in public jobs seem to be on an at least superficially equal footing with male colleagues. Those famous prayers and Koranic texts recited before any Pakistani airliner takes off are often read by a woman from the cabin crew. Her mellifluous voice makes the familiar *bismi'llahi r-rehmani r-rahim*—"In the name of God, the compassionate, the merciful"—sound sweeter, more appealing, and more reassuring to the infidel than the male voice blasted periodically from a neighborhood mosque's loudspeakers.

Islamic life certainly pervades Pakistan, but it does not often intrude harshly in the world the tourist traverses. It is appreciated when women dress modestly, and it is plain good manners to do so, but foreign women are very, very rarely assaulted, otherwise threatened, or jeered at, as they might be in Iran or Saudi Arabia. There are women in all the secular professions, and they share much of the outlook of similar women anywhere. Their fashion designers have made the modest *shalwar-kamiz*—tunic and baggy trousers—into very attractive clothes with a universal appeal. Before she turned frumpy, Benazir Bhutto had some beautifully tailored sets.

Princess Diana acquired an ensemble on a visit to Pakistan a few years before her death. Entertainment pages of newspapers, most liberally in the English-language press, dwell on the lives of singers and film stars and routinely picture women with uncovered heads—though in the rural heartland or the Northwest Frontier other women may be completely covered by a burkha. Mostly, there is coexistence. In Murree, what would qualify as discreet nightclubs are beginning to appear, so far without negative consequences. The Grand Heights Hotel was swarming with workers trying to finish a Grand Music Hall in time for the final evening of Ramadan parties to break the fast. These *iftar* galas can get pretty raucous, much to the dismay of the more pious.

The skyline of Murree, where most of the people are Muslims, has both minarets and steeples. This ecumenicism, however uneasy and lopsided in Mecca's favor, is intrinsic to Murree's history. So are bugles of reveille, ricocheting from one military post to another before dawn, beating the muezzin's first call to prayer by at least an hour. Murree was well established as a cantonment before it became a hill station in the purely civilian sense. And then its moment of glory was short-lived. Between the British annexation of Punjab in 1849 and the decision to transfer the summer headquarters of the colonial administration for the province to Simla in 1876, Murree barely got started. It was newly independent Pakistan that made Murree the country's best known hill resort after 1947, when Punjab Province was split between India and Pakistan. Later, Murree was a major beneficiary of the creation of Islamabad—Pakistan's Brasilia or Canberra—in 1962. Foreign embassies and wealthy Pakistanis have weekend retreats in Murree and the Galis, enlarging towns that were once very small collections of simple summer homes built by prominent Pakistani families. One of those towns, Nathiagali, was the hot-weather headquarters of the Northwest Frontier government.

Mian Qadrud-din, a Pakistani diplomat, remembers his boyhood summer bucket baths and the only heat for cool nights provided by wood fires at the family's retreat in Dunga Gali, a smaller town that he says has not changed very much in the past half century.

I went there as a boy in the 1940s, and then in 1950 I went to boarding school in Abbotabad, not so far away. Dunga Gali is the water supply center for Murree. There's a pipeline of about five miles at 8,000 feet, all level, to Gora Dhaka, where there were British soldiers. Near Gora Dhaka it goes through a tunnel. Then it goes all the way down to Murree. It's level to a place called Garia, which is about five miles short of Murree, then it sort of goes down the slope to Murree. There's a track covering it, about five feet wide—no, six feet wide—and very good to walk on. The track was built in order to maintain the pipeline. When I was a boy we used to bike on it to Gora Dhaka. Now this whole area is called Ayubia. It has become a national park and the forest is virgin still. Untouched. It's a very, very pretty walk.

Dunga Gali was built on a ridge, more or less. All of the Galis were on ridges because they had to be high so that they were cool. Not hidden in a valley to keep them warm. Where there's a plateau, that's even better. Dunga Gali is 8,000 feet at the bazaar. Nathiagali is a little more. I would say it's about two, three, four hundred feet higher. Nathiagali is much bigger. The ridge is wider. At the top it even has a club, a sort of officers' club with a tennis court and so on. There's a very pretty church there. Still going—it's one of the Protestant denominations, maintained by the missions. In Dunga Gali the church is closed, but I think the building is still there. The last time I went there I saw it, a couple of years ago. It hasn't changed very much. We used to come to Dunga Gali for the summer for two months during school holidays and rent a house. I think there were at that time about ten to fifteen houses in Dunga Gali altogether. We used to drive over from Peshawar, where we lived. The rent in Dunga Gali was not high; the houses were not luxurious.

Gora Dhaka used to be a British R and R station. We had bicycles, or we used to rent little ponies and go riding there on the mountain tracks. We saw British soldiers. But in 1945—or if my memory fails me, it must have been 1944—an American battalion turned up. We started seeing American soldiers in the Dunga Gali bazaar. They would walk over. American Wrigley's chewing gum became available. It was wartime and you could not get a lot of chocolates and things; there were shortages everywhere. Of course when we started seeing chewing gum and these things, the prices of the ponies went up. I do remember talking to the odd American GI. I remember seeing for the first time these American nail clippers. Their uniforms had a different color than those of the British. These are things I remember. These Americans probably came in from Burma or somewhere. But for some strange reason we had a whole lot of them. Rawalpindi was far from the front in Burma, but maybe they had some supply function here, or they were on their way out, or all the other R and R places were filled up. Maybe Murree was filled up, too, and so they brought them here. I'm sure they were bored to tears, because there are only mountains and trees around.

Murree had the cinema, and it used to be a big treat to take the bus there. In the early years; that is, '43, '44, we had a narrow road—unpaved, of course, to Murree. At one time buses would travel from one side and at another time from the other side. You'd take the bus, twenty to twenty-two miles in those days, and they'd have difficulty negotiating the hills. They boiled over.

You'd stop at various places where there were springs. They would put cooler water in and then take off. This used to be quite thrilling. In Murree there was a cinema! And the Mall, where you could walk around and look at people. It was a great treat. They had a roller skating rink—one of the restaurants had a sort of wooden floor for skating. There were the restaurants. It was an interesting place. Murree was a much more lively place then than it is now. We as children didn't particularly like being in the mountains. It rained a lot in July and August. We had to take cold baths in a wooden tub. There were no movies. Nothing. It was just nature. Did us a lot of good in the long run, I think, but at that time we did not enjoy it.

Mian Qadrud-din, whose father was a well-traveled barrister from a prominent frontier family, said that Murree was a favorite haunt of Anglo-Indians—British or mixed-race people born in imperial India, which then included what is now Pakistan.

They came to the tea dances. The Muslims didn't dance, except the elite families. In Peshawar, we knew one family whose women would go dancing, but I think it was the only local family. The Parsis, yes. And of course the Anglo-Indians, the Eurasians, definitely. They were Christians, and they claimed to be closer to the Europeans. They were the ones who ran the bands, played the music, did all those things. They were the entertainment. In the restaurants and hotels, they were managers or assistant managers. The Muslims were more traditional landowning families or the professional class. Even though our women were educated, dancing was a little too advanced.

In colonial times, not every British officer, civilian or military, wanted an assignment in Murree, which could never be more than a pale imitation of Simla, where real power congregated. "I cannot say I am particularly anxious to go to a hill station," George Elsmie, an official in Punjab, confided to his diary on February 15, 1863. "Still, of course, I would very much rather go than grind on at Lahore as an Assistant Commissioner. I would not, however, give up the slightest chance of getting a better appointment in the plains for all the hills that ever reared themselves to Heaven." He was assigned to Murree the next month. After a 210-mile trip by "doolie," a one-seater chair carried by coolies or strapped to a wagon, Elsmie and his wife arrived in Murree, cold and wet, on April 11 and were shown a small, empty, cheerless house where they would live when the carts bearing their possessions finally arrived. This did not improve his spirits.

The new assistant commissioner of Murree had been told that one of his chief duties would be to subdue the European property owners who must have spent a lot of time fighting with authority and each other. His first major crisis was domestic violence. A European man was threatening his unfaithful wife with an unspecified vengeance, and she had fled to the plains. Elsmie, having business at a lower elevation himself, set off down the hill and encountered a sedan chair carried by four coolies that seemed to be in a hurry. Accosting the lady inside, he discovered that she was the wife of the archdeacon of Calcutta and not the errant spouse whose husband Elsmie had just put under restraint. It was not an auspicious start. People who lived in hill stations often complained of the petty quarreling that went on when folks did not have enough to do. Kipling immortalized those women of Simla who whiled away the hours undercutting each other for the attentions of men. Families were often thrown together in a shared house, which produced friction. By the time Elsmie left Murree, he had grown to dislike his European civilian charges intensely. The relative idleness of life in any hill station, not only Murree, seemed to encourage not only pettiness but also an odd dependence. He was once asked to find a canine wet nurse for someone's orphaned puppies.

One of the burdens Elsmie had to bear as assistant commissioner of Murree was Sir Robert Montgomery, then the lieutenant governor of Punjab and his boss. From the vantage point of Elsmie's diary of the period, parts of which he reproduced later in a book, *Thirty-Five Years in the Punjab*, Sir Robert was a maniac for detail and didn't find much time for enjoyment. The happiest Elsmie ever saw him was when a maharaja sent an army of footmen to hold big red umbrellas over the members of the lieutenant governor's traveling party, making the event look like a royal procession. Sir Robert dispatched a flurry of demands to his assistant commissioner: Stop the coolies' dumping dirt shoveled from drains on the roads; meet me at 7 A.M. to look at locust damage; lay out more paths for walking. The lieutenant governor disapproved of dancing and amateur theatricals. However, since the military outnumbered civilians in authority in Murree, a group of officers simply ignored these obstacles. The lieutenant governor would not be there forever. The officers built a stage in the barracks area, and there were suddenly actors galore to fill a range of roles, including Elsmie, whose specialty was playing middle-aged women.

Trapped in a blizzard without modern conveniences, I was able to venture out now and then into what could have been a nineteenth-century town untroubled by the vehicular traffic that has so drastically changed the atmosphere of this and other hill stations. The transformation was remarkable. Even when the electric power came back to stay in snowy Murree late one afternoon, only a few moments before the end of twilight, the glory that enveloped us was worth much more than the price of two bitter, cold-water days. I put away my books and blankets and sat by the window. The lights of the valley below again cast pools of gold on the snow. On the hill leading to the ridge along which Murree is centered, dozens of houses—odd-shaped boxes with caps of snow on their roofs of tin or galvanized iron—were piled atop one another in artistic relief, yellow lightbulbs visible through their windows.

The next morning life restarted. Birds I had not seen for days, mynahs and magpies, showed up to scramble for food, joining the aggressive crows. A huge rumbling machine with a rotating brush where a road-grader might be in summer chewed its way up the hill, lights flashing. More effective than a plow, it crunched into its maw both loose and packed snow, then shot the stuff out through a long chute that cleared the shoulder of the narrow road. Along the Mall, snow was piled high in front of shops and restaurants. But in most places, the roads were surprisingly clear and already clogged with traffic and trash. One more day, and I made my escape, in a minuscule yellow taxi that slipped and slid very little in the hands of a skillful driver.

Within half a hour, we had cleared the snow line and descended into fog. The road was still slippery, and we passed a family car that had skidded into a deep culvert along one side. The driver flagged us down, and the next car, and another coming in the opposite direction. No car failed to stop, and no motorist hesitated before joining the enlarging band of men in their rough *shalwar-kamize*s and wool Pathan caps who were trying with their bare hands to lift the car out of the ditch and back on the road, while an unbelievable number of women and children who were the little auto's passengers watched. After little more than a quarter of an hour, the pick-up rescue crew succeeded in righting the car. The passengers wedged themselves back in. We all drove away with friendly waves. A few miles later the air got warmer, grass grew, flowers bloomed, and contemporary Pakistan took over.

3

❧

An Indian Sextet

Simla

Mussoorie

Darjeeling and Kalimpong

Kodaikanal and Ootacamund

The Viceregal Lodge in Simla

SIMLA

No hill station in Asia has mesmerized more historians, politicians, journalists, and tourists of all kinds than Simla, a town studied to death not only for its astonishing creation but also for its symbolism. There is no mystery about this. For long periods of the year and for more than a century Simla was, unofficially and then officially, the summer capital of British India, and no place more succinctly displayed, not just in that season, the hard core of the British Raj, with all its political trappings and social and racial distinctions. For decades—right up to World War II—it was also the year-round headquarters of the British Indian army and, after 1876, the part-time capital of Punjab, arguably the most important Indian province. The absurdity of all this justifies the attention Simla gets. Here was a hill town at 7,000 feet and higher, devilishly hard to reach and 1,200 miles from the winter capital at Calcutta. Getting there and back every year, with the government of India largely loaded on wagons, was a logistical operation larger than many a military campaign. Below the top officials, nearly everyone ultimately felt the outrageous cost of this pilgrimage in one way or another, most harshly the thousands of Indian villagers recruited or dragooned as porters to carry the empire to and fro for little or no pay.

"I doubt if any government has ever existed so cut off from the governed as the Government of India nestling among the Himalayas in Simla," noted Malcolm Muggeridge, the British journalist doing a stint on the *Statesman* of Calcutta in the 1930s. In the second volume of his autobiography, *Chronicles of Wasted Time,* Muggeridge called the viceregal court "a honey-pot of authority" around which everyone and everything buzzed. Simla, the make-it-or-break-it town to a lot of colonial careers, seemed to Muggeridge to be more or less indifferent or blind to the vast nation of India below.

Victor Jacquemont, a French naturalist on an expedition in India a century earlier for the Museum of Natural History in Paris, watched as the personal and official baggage of Lord Bentinck, the governor-general of India (before there were viceroys), was loaded for the trip to Simla in late February of 1831. Jacquemont claimed to have counted roughly 300 elephants, 1,300 camels, and 8 oxcarts in the caravan, which was accompanied by two regiments of troops, one cavalry and the other infantry. Emily Eden, the sister of another governor-general, Lord Auckland, described in letters to their sister how equally cumbersome, lengthy, and disruptive the preparations for the return to the plains in autumn had become by the late 1830s. For many, including families with babies and small children, the trip to Simla in March or April and back again to Calcutta in October or November involved weeks of tramping or bumping away in a rough cart by day and camping at night, hoping to avoid disease, wild animals, and accidents along the route. Unwilling Bengali servants were dragged along from the Hooghly to the hills, shivering and protesting at the prospect of cold weather on the outward journey and stumbling back in weakened health on the return.

Not relishing another such expedition herself—and she went in style, to say the least—Emily Eden (who later became a novelist in England) enjoyed the irony of a punishing trek made in the name of well-being. She remarked sarcastically that "those camp preparations, I am happy to say, made everybody ill." But her letters, collected in the book *Up the Country*, hinted more than once that at least the outward journey might have been worth the trouble and that Simla, not Calcutta, was really considered home. Because she followed her governor-general brother on his rounds across India the rest of the year, Simla was stability. In one year she reckoned that she and Lord Auckland had spent five months on the road, sleeping in tents and being jostled along on all forms of pre-industrial-age transportation. Other British families of sufficient wealth and position bought land and built homes in Simla, which most Indians now spell and pronounce "Shimla." A substantial number of women and their children stayed in the hills all year, as they did in Murree. Most did not live in luxury, at least not at the start. Before galvanized iron and tin roofing was used widely, giving the hill towns vaguely similar skylines, there were leaky roofs of shingles or sod that sometimes collapsed under monsoon rains. Fleas and rats infested households. Pets got eaten by wild animals. A walk in any direction was a serious trek up and down steep inclines, and travelers on horseback were occasionally pitched into ravines or crushed by landslides.

Nonetheless, Simla soon created a surprisingly durable fantasy image for itself. It still lives on the romantic notion that it is somehow foreign: a tidy little corner of India that will be forever England. A 1996 *Guide to the Tourist Places of India with Hotels and Trains at a Glance,* published in New Delhi, talks of Simla as a moody foreign town whose atmosphere changes with the seasons. "The Mall is lined with stately English-looking houses bearing strangely displaced English names," it tells us. "Simla's English flavor is continued by buildings like Christ Church, which dates from 1857." But then the guide goes on to list the top sites to visit, and Europe fades. A few natural wonders, a Tibetan monastery, and more Hindu temples than British landmarks are recommended. Today's visitor can walk the Mall and the Ridge in vain looking for something other than derelict architectural details that recall the days of tea shops and the Gaiety Theatre, the hub of colonial culture before the cinema was born.

I have an enduring memory of Simla that will probably outlast most others. My husband and I were getting ready for dinner at the Oberoi Clarkes Hotel, a classic colonial throwback conveniently placed at one end of the Mall. There was plenty to do. After washing, we filled the bathtub as insurance against a break in the water supply, which did happen overnight. We tried to coax the fire into giving a little more heat to dress by. One searches old British hotels and lodges in India vainly for those huge hearths that warm English country inns; only the Windamere in Darjeeling seems to have mastered fireplace heating, and they do it with coal. But then British houses are more often noted for being damp, cold, and drafty, and India inherited the knack. At Clarkes, I telephoned for more wood, acutely aware (but with diminishing guilt) that deforestation was already a very serious problem. Then the electricity failed.

At just about the same time there came a knock on the door. Thinking the firewood had arrived, I flung the door open to confront in the dim light of the corridor the shrouded form and weather-beaten face of an old Tibetan monk. He was startled and stood motionless, wrapped in worn shawls and carrying a bundle and a prayer wheel. We stared at each other for a long moment without saying a word. Then, as if an apparition, he vanished into the dark. I never saw him again. At dinner in the spartan dining room, however, there were other Tibetans and exuberant men of Himachal in their distinctive caps, engrossed in some kind of official function. The few Indian tourists from the cities of the plains on that winter weekend were just about as alien as we. Simla was a Himalayan town populated by the people whose mountains the aliens had once invaded and briefly inhabited.

Colonial hill station life and travel in India probably contributed more contraptions to the world's collection of man-powered forms of transportation than any civilization since ancient times, as diaries and letters like Emily Eden's demonstrate. Only someone familiar with the annual trek to the hills before there were carriage roads or railways would have any idea what she meant when she wrote to her sister that "F. and I got into our *jonpauns*, which might just as well be called *tonjauns*, they are the same sort of conveyances, only they swing about more, and look like coffins." Nigel Hankin, in his absorbing and entertaining book, *Hanklyn-*

Janklin, tried in 1992 to catalogue the chairs and litters in which "men with power contrived to be carried by men without." But he cautions that names could change or designs vary from place to place, depending on local needs and ingenuities.

The *tonjaun,* or *tonjon,* to which Emily Eden referred, was an open sedan chair largely reserved for town and city use. The *jonpaun*—also spelled *jampan, jhampan,* or *jompon*—was at first a portable chair slung on poles, Hankin said. Some, however, were really enclosed boxes that contemporaries, like Emily Eden, described as upright coffins. Hankin asserted that the *jampan* evolved into the *jhampani* in Simla, Mussoorie, and Matheran in the hills above Bombay. The wheeled *jhampani* was powered by four men—two pulling, two pushing—making it a kind of mountain rickshaw. Memoirs from colonial Simla usually call this vehicle a rickshaw and the men who pushed and pulled it *jampanis.* The man-powered rickshaws served as family cars until modern times in part because no other vehicles, except for the viceroy's and occasionally those of other high-ranking people, were allowed on Simla's upper roads. Ladies liked to outfit *jampanis* in distinctive household livery. The brilliant, volatile Indian artist Amrita Sher-Gil, who lived in Simla in the 1930s with her Sikh father and Hungarian mother, had a bright yellow rickshaw, with *jampanis* dressed in uniforms to match. As wheeled vehicles went, the tonga was a better bet, when it could be maneuvered into the terrain in question. This horse-drawn cart with two wheels and a passenger seat facing backwards is still a common form of local transportation in Pakistan, where Begum Nargis Jan once enjoyed the efficient service they provided to Murree.

A *dhooli,* or *dooli,* was described by Hankin as "something equivalent to an upturned string cot" used at first to carry invalids. In Kodaikanal, a "doolie" looked more like a *jampan* and was not considered as comfortable as an open sedan chair, which cost twice as much to hire. Kodaikanal did not have the severe weather of the Himalayan foothills, and a covered box could have been a nuisance when there was so much wonderful scenery around. The open Kodaikanal sedan chair was slung on two poles and carried by four men. A "dandy," in contrast, was a sort of hammock slung on only one pole and borne by two coolies, said Hankin.

The palanquin, or *palki,* was the most elaborate kind of man-powered transporter, with its tiny cushioned carriage mounted on poles. Borne by four or six men, a palanquin was often low-slung, barely a foot or two off the ground. Being roomier and enclosed, it was good for long journeys, though a few passengers discovered that the swaying and bouncing produced motion sickness. A *palki* mounted on wheels became a *palki-ghari* of one sort or another, with varying degrees of comfort. Nina Mazuchelli, the wife of an army chaplain, Francis Mazuchelli, wrote in *The Indian Alps and How We Crossed Them* of hiring a *palki-ghari* on the way to Darjeeling that was no more than an oblong box in which they had to lie down; their luggage was piled on top. Almost any of the pole-mounted chairs or boxes could be attached to carts. George Elsmie, heading for his new job as assistant commissioner in Murree, started the trip in a doolie lashed to a mail wagon. In the mountains where there are no roads to this day, it is still possible to see a "kandy," a large, cone-shaped basket strapped to the back of a single porter that can carry a child or an elderly or sick person. In Nepal I encountered an old man being carried this way from the town of Lukla toward the Everest base camp of Namche Bazar.

Contemporary travel to Simla by car, bus, or train certainly makes the trip shorter, but for many, it is still an ordeal. The train journey may begin in a distant city in an overloaded carriage where there is no room to sleep or sit comfortably, the food is barely acceptable, and the toilets and washrooms are filthy beyond description. An Indian consumer group has busied itself in recent years measuring the level of fecal matter in the drinking water on the Calcutta run, not overlooking the luxury trains. Boxes and giant suitcases are stacked all around and overhead. Even in air-conditioned class, privacy is elusive. Trains that were state of the art in the nineteenth century are still just that: nineteenth century. Or pity the Indian middle-class families and poorer people without cars or the money to hire taxis who travel on stuffy, lurching buses up the twisting road to Simla—the culmination of a trip of ten hours or more from Delhi—clutching bottles of boiled water for relief and taking turns vomiting out of the windows. The experience must make not a few of them think nostalgically about the plodding oxcarts, slow-motion tongas, and quiet tent sites of yore. Long-gone early travelers could write in their meticulously kept journals of those fine moments, perhaps while changing horses, when a pause to take in the spectacular scenery and breathe pure air was tonic enough to carry one through another leg.

The story of Simla is woven into the history of the East India Company, which established the British Empire in India and ran it for more than two centuries. In fact, the British government did not directly administer India (including what is now Pakistan and Bangladesh and, for a time, Burma) until the mid–nineteenth century. The British East India Company—there were also Dutch and French versions—was chartered in 1600 by Queen Elizabeth I. The Company, as it was known, was intended to hold a monopoly in trade with Asia, though it was soon challenged not only by other European nations but also by private English entrepreneurs. A rival company was formed in the late seventeenth century, but the two were merged in 1708.

In the early years the Company, which exercised administrative and defense powers in its overseas bases, worked mostly through agreements with local rulers in India, leaving political power in their hands. There were three Company regions, called presidencies, in Madras, Bombay, and Calcutta—each with official hill stations of its own, in addition to the national summer capital at Simla. But in the eighteenth century, for a variety of reasons, including the decline in the effective power of some local sultans or maharajas and the growing influence of the French in India, the Company began to become involved in governing parts of India. After Robert Clive delivered a few decisive military blows to the French in the 1750s, blunting their commercial and territorial expansion, the Company began to rule Bengal, in eastern India. It was there in Calcutta that the first governor-general was installed, with the power to oversee all British possessions on the Subcontinent. By 1784, that power had been broadened and consolidated by an act of Parliament.

At the same time, the Company controlled the British army in India. It was known as the Indian army, but this usage has become confusing since Indian independence in 1947. The army consisted of a "European" (that is, mostly English, Irish, Scottish, or Welsh) officer corps and of troops whose majority became increasingly Indian. The ratio was a cause for alarm after the Indian Mutiny of 1857–1858, a watershed event in a number of ways for the British in India. The rebellion sent a chill through British colonial society. Women and children had been massacred on the plains, and rumors swept even the safe heights of Simla that Nepali Gurkha troops nearby were restive. By then thousands of Indians had settled in the hill stations, and they too suddenly became the objects of suspicion and fear.

The mutiny, which some Indians call the Uprising and others, the First War of Independence, led to the East India Company's losing both political and military power to the British crown and government. In his exhaustive *Oxford History of Modern India, 1740–1975,* Sir Percival Spear pointed out that by the time of the mutiny, the Company "had already become a husk of its former self," administering India on contract for the British government. The Government of India Act of 1858 finished the job by taking away whatever governing functions remained and establishing the post of secretary of state for India under the control of the British Cabinet. On the ground in India, however, the structure was not changed dramatically. Britons bearing titles that were a mixture of native Indian and colonial British nomenclature and function continued to carry on their political, judicial, and public service functions. The governor-general took on the additional title of viceroy as the direct representative of the British crown.

The British Indian army—in particular the Bengal army, one of three corresponding to the three presidencies—was reorganized. Spear noted that 120,000 of the 128,000 Indians in the Bengal army were involved in the mutiny, and most of them were dead or had fled when the uprising was finally put down. When the mutiny (almost entirely confined to North India) was over, there were only 16,000 European troops and a few Indian units that had not rebelled available to form the core of a new army. Care was taken to cut the proportion of Indian to European troops in the restructuring. Spear said that before the mutiny there were 238,000 Indian soldiers, called sepoys, and 45,000 Europeans in the three presidency armies combined, although the three were not actually merged until later in the nineteenth century. In 1863, there were 140,000 Indians and 65,000 native Europeans or soldiers of European descent. British officers were put in charge of all units, and it became military policy not to base Indian battalions alone without a complement of European troops.

William Howard Russell, who reported from India for the *Times* of London in the late 1850s—and would later cover the Crimean War and American Civil War for that newspaper—judged that the worst consequence of the mutiny "was that instantly the whole sepoy army was placed under the ban of suspicious distrust, and, there is reason to believe, in some instances the stigma of open and avowed insult. Every man, no matter how well inclined, was at once ranked among the intending mutineers."

While all of the postmutiny reorganizing was going on, Simla was growing in size and authority. A number of factors coincided to make Simla what it was, and is. In 1815, the Gurkha rulers of Nepal, who had harassed the British in the western Himalayan foothills, were defeated, and the way was open to exploration and settlement of a large region. The East India Company was always on the lookout for new routes into Tibet, the source of fine wools and salt, among other commodities. Approaches to Tibet were at the heart of Calcutta's relations with local rulers on the borders of West Bengal also, in Sikkim and Bhutan, from which the British wrested frontier territory later in the nineteenth century. Farther to the northwest and closer to Simla, the Tibet trade route passed through Kashmir and Ladakh, where it was subject to attack by a Sikh ruler, Ranjit Singh. After his death in 1839, his heirs would go down to defeat. But in the first decades of the nineteenth century, Ranjit Singh loomed large in the thinking of everyone along the upper reaches of British India.

Simla could be the focal point of a different Tibetan trade route through Rampur, the capital of a friendlier Indian state, Bushahr.

To these strategic and commercial interests was soon added the compelling issue of health. This was the dawn of the sanitarium age in India, and a number of British officers recommended the development of a hill station at Simla not only to enhance trade and trade and security but also because the military needed a convalescent resort. Until the creation of Simla and Mussoorie, soon after, troops had been sent by ship as far afield as Cape Town for a recuperative climate. Chance sojourners in the northern hills, among them soldiers who fought in the Gurkha wars, were struck by the invigorating air, fragrant with pine, and the lack of hostility among the local hill people.

In 1822, Captain Charles Kennedy, a garrison officer, built the first house on the forested ridge near a small village he understood to be named "Semla." His predecessor had erected a rustic cabin in the vicinity, but historians credit Kennedy, a resident until 1835, with establishing Simla and giving it its imperial style. Drawings of the period show his house in stately isolation on a rise, commanding a view over hills in every direction. Kennedy was a generous host, and numerous visitors who were entertained by him described his life and that of the town, bequeathing posterity good records of those early days. Among his guests was Victor Jacquemont, who was still in his twenties at the time. The French naturalist watched the captain with some admiration. In letters home to his father in France, Jacquemont praised the quality of food served at Kennedy's table and marveled at how little time his host seemed to spend on work, given the breadth of his political and judicial as well as military duties. In one letter, Jacquemont wrote that Kennedy seemed to enjoy "the independence of the Grand Turk as he acts as judge over his own subjects and, what is more, those of neighboring rajahs, Hindu, Tartar, and Tibetan, sending them to prison, fining them and even hanging them when he sees fit."

Jacquemont, visiting in 1830, thought Simla was "a resort of the very rich, the leisured, and the sick." Simla also attracted the fit and healthy who wanted to stay that way or who just wanted a break from the summer torpor of Calcutta or other lowland cities. Some found the promise of a salubrious climate overrated. The journalist Russell, for one, noted wryly in his diary that within days of his arrival his health was worse in Simla than at lower elevations. "A malady peculiar to Simla, which seizes on new-comers from the plains, has attacked me, and the doctors recommend me bed, starvation, and drastics—low diet, full physic." He took to his couch in pain, unable to move one leg and complaining generally of being "supine and sick."

Lord Amherst was the first governor-general to visit Simla, staying at Kennedy House for two months in the 1820s and setting a precedent. By 1830, the East India Company had formally acquired land from two local rulers, the maharaja of Patiala and the rana of Keonthal, to develop the town. Lord Bentinck, the governor-general whose moving caravan was observed by Jacquemont, was the first to construct a comfortable residence for himself, a house called Bentinck's Castle. Other governors and more houses followed. By midcentury, when Russell arrived, Simla had at least a hundred homes. Clubs, theaters, shops, and public offices were being built. Colonial administrators and military officers with their eyes on the important province of Punjab, the Northwest Frontier, and Afghanistan began to press for a larger role for Simla, complaining that Calcutta was no longer where the action was.

But Simla was still very difficult to reach, with only a dirt track a tortuous 40 miles long, passing through forests and along steep ravines from Kalka, the first town of importance at the edge of the plains. Kalka itself was little more than a way station. The main British presence, particularly for the military, was at Ambala, another 40 miles south. Had Delhi, an easy 120 miles farther south of Ambala, been the Indian capital then and not Calcutta, the selection of Simla as a summer headquarters might have made a little more sense. Criticism mounted at the extravagance of the biannual migration from Bengal. Nevertheless, the British, with their determination harnessed to their engineering skills, went to work on what they grandly titled the Hindustan-Tibet road from the foot of the hills to Simla, with plans to continue to the Tibetan border, a design that was never fully realized. Outposts were fortified between Simla and the plains. Soon after leaving Kalka, a side road from the main Hindustan-Tibet highway that follows the original horse track to Simla leads to Kasauli, the smaller hill station I saw from Chandigarh. The British made Kasauli a garrison town.

"There is Kussowlee!" Russell of *The Times* exclaimed to his diary, as he arrived after a "tiresome and sickening" *jampan* ride at his first stop in the hills en route to Simla.

It was 11 o'clock ere we reached this charming hill station, which is on a small plateau, and on the side of a long ridge of hill, covered with pines of great size. First we passed a dirty fakeer, sitting in a hole, burrowed out of the side of the road—then some poor native huts—then came in sight a handsome church, some large barracks; a few English children and soldiers playing and sauntering in the shade; then a few shops, and a long road, bounded by hedges, inside which were English bungalows, with names painted on the gateways, "Laburnam Lodge," "Prospect," "The Elms," and such like home reminiscences, and the clang of piano-fortes and streams of song rushed out through open windows.

These days, many Indians think Kasauli is a much prettier place than Simla because it has not been overbuilt, in part since the military still influences—and limits—development. Solan, about halfway between Kalka and Simla on the main road, was also turned into a military cantonment and rifle range but never became the pleasant town Kasauli was. At Solan, the famous Mohan Meakin brewery, established in colonial times, still produces some of India's most popular beer and, recently, bottled water.

Simla did not become the official summer capital of India until the mid-1860s, under the viceroy Sir John Lawrence, who nagged London endlessly on the subject. By then wheeled vehicles could make the trip from Kalka, and trains were not far behind. By 1891, the line connecting Ambala to Calcutta had been extended with a spur to Kalka. In 1903, the narrow-gauge Kalka-Simla Railway was completed to carry the little "toy train" and a swifter, smaller, more expensive one-coach, eighteen-seat rail car into the mountains through scores of tunnels, sharp bends, and switchbacks, with a stop for breakfast or tea at a rail-side rest house along the route.

At the turn of the twentieth century, the British were actively looking around for a new national capital to replace Calcutta, and fortunately for Simla, all the proposed locations were closer or more accessible to the hill station than the Bengali capital had been. In 1911, the British finally chose a site on the Jamuna River a few miles from Delhi, a centuries-old city that had been the seat of Muslim kings and emperors. Named New Delhi, the imperial city that arose there over the next two decades, designed by Sir Edwin Lutyens and Sir Herbert Baker, is still Asia's most magnificent capital. Although there were still many in India and in England who questioned the cost of two capitals, if there was to be an official hill station, the case for Simla was certainly stronger at that time than it had been earlier.

Once Simla had been formally designated the summer capital and military headquarters in the 1860s, more development followed, crowned by the completion in 1888 of the baronial Viceregal Lodge. The viceroy's retreat, built of stone and paneled inside with teak from Burma, now belongs to Himachal Pradesh University. At the time it was built, however, it quickly became symbolic of Simla's hierarchical professional and social system. A summons to a viceroy's reception or dinner was something to die for. Once in possession of the engraved invitation card and starchily outfitted in formal evening clothes—and medals if he could muster a few—an ambitious officer or colonial administrator of middling ranks would travel the three or four miles from Simla town to the viceroy's baronial hall in both hope and trepidation, aware that a casual remark or the wrong answer to a viceregal question from him or his wife could ruin a career. Commenting on the serious social climbing that went on at such formal events, the journalist William Howard Russell described the Simla scene as "ball after ball, each followed by a little backbiting."

At first glance, the imperial social system seems straightforward: The ranks descended through the white British line from the viceroy down to the lowest of imperial officials before crossing over into Indian or Eurasian society. In her *Up the Country* letters, Emily Eden wrote about the fuss caused by her suggestion that the wives of uncovenanted officers—usually locally hired clerks not under contract to the East India Company and often Eurasians or Anglo-Indians—be asked to contribute crafts to sell at the annual "fancy" fair, a charity extravaganza held at Annandale, the wide, pine-framed playing field where all manner of outdoor events from polo to picnics took place. Ladylike craft work, often embroidery or sketching, was encouraged in colonial society, and women in Simla had a lot of spare time to be as creative as their talents allowed. Eden rightly assumed that the fancy fair would benefit from a broadening of participation.

"This was rather a shock to the aristocracy of Simla, and they did suggest that some of the wives were very black," she recalled. She told them that "the black would not come off on their works" and won that round. She was, after all, the governor general's sister, and her drawings of local life were a centerpiece at the sale. She was not a social reformer, though; there were few of them to be found in colonial service. Indian servants were routinely derided in racial terms behind their backs and abused verbally to their faces by sahibs and memsahibs. Sometimes physical violence was used against them. As late as 1925, a coolie tangled in his blanket who did not stand up quickly enough to answer a summons was kicked to death in a Simla garden by a British army business manager. To be fair to colonial justice, the Briton was sent to jail, where he committed suicide.

In India, British notions of class and the Indian caste system often cross-pollinated to create some interesting anomalies. In her very valuable book, *Imperial Simla*, Pamela Kanwar took a look at the town and its social and political systems through Indian eyes as much as possible. Indian society was complex, mannered, and fraught with taboos. At the top were the brahmins and maharajas, who also bought property at Simla until the British began to fear they were amassing too much of it and tried to stall the process with red tape. Indian rulers paid formal calls on the viceroy or a lower official befitting the ruler's perceived place vis-à-vis the imperial hierarchy. Gifts were exchanged. Indian professionals and rich merchants from several higher Hindu castes bought homes and became influential in the affairs of the town as their numbers grew, although most local businesses were relegated to the Lower Bazar, which still tumbles down the cliff side below the Mall.

Unofficial Britons—known then as Anglo-Indians, though that term was later broadened to include mixed-race Eurasians—were able to start businesses and buy homes, whereas colonial officials were eventually prohibited from becoming property owners during their tours of duty. Not infrequently, the unofficial (especially commercial box-wala, or merchant) British and the middle-class Indians were equally shunned by imperial society and its clubs. Journalist Russell noted the rigidity of the British social system in Simla. "Wealth can do nothing for a man or woman in securing them honour or precedency in their march to dinner," he wrote. "A successful speculator, or a 'merchant prince' may force his way into good society in England; he may be presented at court, and flourish at court-balls, but in India he must remain forever outside the sacred barrier, which keeps the non-official world from the high society of the services." Moreover, the shunning of the merchant classes did not break down racial barriers by Indians and unofficial Britons' making common cause. Mixed marriages, though they occurred occasionally, were largely anathema to both Europeans and Indians.

Indians also discriminated against one another along caste lines, and these attitudes sometimes reinforced British distinctions and prejudices. At the bottom of everyone's social order were the outcastes who emptied latrines, and just above them, the coolies and rickshawalas, who carried goods and people. Even though imperial officials and military officers were always in need of porters, the law of supply and demand was not germane here. Instead of making the value of a professional porter's labor worth more and, therefore, his income grow, the shortfall led the British to impose and enforce a system called *begar* on the people of the hills. Pamela Kanwar explained how it worked: rulers of the hill areas, whose subjects were considered more docile than the people of the plains, were required to provide the human backs for transporting official baggage and often the paraphernalia of private hunting expeditions or other leisure excursions. Farmers were taken from their fields with no regard to the consequences for their crops. Indeed, rural lives were already beset by the gradual disappearance of farmland and forests, as a growing town fostered larger-scale agriculture and woodlands were set aside (and off limits) to meet Simla's need for timber. Some British residents of Simla opposed the *begar* system—one official called it serfdom—but even after its formal abolition, it went on well into the twentieth century, helping to fuel a minor hill revolt in 1921.

Much mythology is attached itself to the social history of Simla. On visits there, I was told that Indians were not allowed to walk on the Mall or the Ridge, where Christ Church towered over the town and made it look British long after the place had any English ambiance left at all. Though this story is retold again and again in articles and books, Kanwar said it was never strictly true. She set the myth to rest by including in her book the text of laws governing access to the Mall, where evening promenades took place and more exclusive shops were located. The rule in question said that from March 15 to October 15 "no job porter or coolie shall solicit employment, loiter or carry any load" on most of Simla's major roads from 4 to 8 P.M. Moreover, from 3 to 8 P.M., "no person shall lead or drive any animal used for slaughter or burden, or horned cattle, and no horse dealer, syce, grass cutter, native trainer, jockey or other native servant shall lead, drive or ride any horse, pony or mule or other animal." The prohibition was always a limited one. But, as Kanwar said, the letter of the law was often stretched on the Mall to facilitate the harassment of any Indians whom officials did not want around. Political demonstrations in particular and "ill-dressed Indians" in general—whatever that might mean—were removed in humiliating style. Naturally, when civil disobedience was planned in 1930, the Mall was the place to march. By that time, India was moving swiftly toward self-rule and then independence.

Simla is now a city in the hills, not a hill station any more. The state capital of Himachal Pradesh since 1966, Simla is a busy hub of politics and commerce. Viceregal Lodge belongs to the state, and British homes and businesses belong to Indians. But the old image refuses to fade, not only from tourist brochures. Pamela Kanwar made the fascinating observation that Simla had cast a spell on Indians. "That Simla was the facsimile of an original British town (which most had never seen) was never doubted," she wrote. "Thus a strange convoluted nostalgia shadows Indian memories." Everyone touched by it, from the wealthy professional to the lowly toilet cleaner, "all felt privileged to have lived in the Chota Vilayat—little England—of India."

Mussoorie: The grand old Savoy

MUSSOORIE

Ruskin Bond, whose evocative journals, stories, and poems have given life to a region known as the Garhwal Himalayas, was quick to discern what made Mussoorie different from Simla. There was nothing starchily official about Mussoorie's origins: It was created for pleasure, not work. There were no swarms of bureaucrats migrating from the plains, no army cantonment, not an excessive number of missionaries, not even much in the line of police. Mussoorie, born liberated, quickly embraced promiscuity. In an essay called "A Station for Scandal," part of the collection of his writings published as *Rain in the Mountains*, Bond wrote that "you could live there without feeling that the Viceroy or the Governor was looking over your shoulder." Mussoorie was where pukka British fellows built cottages for their mistresses and proper English ladies actually sold their kisses at fetes. Dancing and dallying along mountain trails led to this and that. In the lore that accumulated around Mussoorie was the story (also told of other hill stations) about how the Savoy Hotel, the Ritz of the mountains, rang a bell just before dawn to prepare the religious for prayer and chase the others back to their own beds before the sun came up.

Comparisons between official and unofficial hill stations were a reflection of rivalry and a measure of loyalty to competing towns, most of which laid claim to superiority for one reason or another. Of course, most hill stations have—or had—unique characters, even personalities. Two other Indian towns on the south flank of the Himalayas—Naini Tal and Almora in the Kumaon Hills—are good examples. Naini Tal was the official one, the summer capital of the colonial United Provinces of Agra and Oudh. Its setting was so beautiful that not many cosmetic changes were necessary. There was a natural lake, whereas other hill stations had to create one. At about 6,400 feet in altitude, Naini Tal was densely forested (and populated by tigers and wicked spirits), and so the population was sparse well into the nineteenth century. Like Kasauli, it clings today to a reputation for being quieter and more attractive than many other overdeveloped hills resorts.

In contrast, Almora, at only 5,000 feet but still considered healthy, was never a formal summer capital, and its unofficial status left room for alternate lifestyles. It was populated first by Himalayan traders and later attracted legions of people with causes, from environmentalists to spiritualists. Bill Aitken, a Scottish-born Indian, settled there for a spell more than three decades ago. "The Kumaon Hills for some reason seemed to attract eccentrics," he wrote later in *Seven Sacred Rivers*. "Almora, from the days of the exotic American disciples of Swami Vivekananda, has had a flourishing 'Cranks Ridge' which in its way had contributed to twentieth century mysticism." In Almora, Aitken found British Buddhists, Indian scientists given to alchemy and religious reform, Europeans of various origins dabbling in ashrams. Timothy Leary, a brother of Mick Jagger, and camp followers of D. H. Lawrence passed through. Among the mystics was Sunya Baba, "whose spiritual credentials were not quite top-drawer, since he had started out as Sorenson, the Danish gardener of the Nehrus," Aitken wrote. His favorite character was a blind former actor from Australia who ran an organic (he called it "biodynamic") orchard.

Mussoorie, which also liked to think of itself as independent minded, is not without its contemporary officialdom, however. The Lal Bahadur Shastri Academy for the Indian Administrative Service trains the cream of New Delhi's civil servants there. And in Dehra Dun, where the road from Mussoorie hits the plains, the Indian Military Academy has been functioning since colonial times. But the atmosphere of Mussoorie, although much changed over the years, is certainly different from that of contemporary Simla, where the Annandale picnic ground is now a heliport for the military and state government officials.

Like Simla, however, Mussoorie and about two dozen other hill settlements scattered along the northwestern Himalayan foothills were made possible by the British accession of Nepali Gurkha lands following the 1816 peace treaty that ended a two-year war. Despite the Gurkha defeat, Nepal managed to avoid becoming part of the British Empire in India, as did the two small kingdoms of Sikkim and Bhutan, but Gurkhas enlisted in the British forces stationed in the Garhwal and Kumaon hills and stayed on after independence to serve in India's army. Like many hill stations, Mussoorie was first widely known as a health resort for troops, a number of whom had fought in the Gurkha war. Their convalescent center was actually in Landour, a few miles above Mussoorie, but over time the two towns grew together into a single sprawling settlement. A British chronicler wrote in the nineteenth century that the rate of cure there was phenomenal for sick and wounded soldiers; the area was also reputed to be especially good for the health of children. By the 1840s, dozens of homes dotted the hills, along with farms for growing fresh produce and grains, a brewery, and, of course, a club, with at least 150 members in 1842.

Into this evolving social setting, the Savoy, like a debutante, made an entrance. The Savoy Hotel is now a dowager, crippled by assaults from upstart resorts new to Mussoorie, most recently a mammoth mountain lodge called the Residency, which advertises itself as "the first five-star deluxe hotel in the hills of North India." But it was the legendary Savoy— not the squash courts or pool of the Residency—that propelled me to Mussoorie in the dead of winter on my most recent trip. It was the second time I foolishly made the climb from Dehra Dun in cold weather. My son, Jonathan, and I had visited the Woodstock School in Landour more than a decade ago. He, hardened by short-pants British education, nonetheless remembers Woodstock as the coldest place he ever had to get out of bed in the morning. But at least our guest room had an efficient *bukhari*, a wood stove that can be started quickly with almost anything flammable and will produce warmth very quickly. In the 1950s, when Edith Theis-Nielsen was a student at Woodstock, she found the cold-water showers "trying" in winter. "For at least 15 years after my time at Woodstock, I was thankful every time I turned on the hot-water tap," she recalled. Theis-Nielsen, who is Danish, had brought along a Scandinavian eiderdown for her bed. "Once at room inspection the matron gave me a demerit because she didn't think my bed was properly made. I explained to her that an eiderdown has no way of being made flat as a pancake."

Rehan Khan, who was a student at Woodstock in the 1980s, said he never remembered it snowing, but "a few avalanches in the mountains every month provided badly needed excitement." The next time I arrived in Mussoorie the town was deep in snow, adding considerable adventure if not exactly excitement to the experience. Leaving a hired car and its dubious driver at the base of the hill crowned by the Savoy, I plodded up on foot, lugging my laptop and luggage along a frozen pathway with an angle of ascent approaching 45 degrees, if not more. It was dark, and there seemed no end to a slippery hike up a long curved driveway circling toward the Savoy's private hill. Then around the bend, there suddenly was a speck of light, a small cottage and a trellised doorway bearing a modest sign that read "Office." A naked yellow bulb illuminated it and the doorstep below. All else was lost in the black night, except the acres of snow. In the bitter cold, absolutely nothing moved; even the trees seemed frozen.

Decades vanished in the few moments that followed my opening the door, with some uncertainty about whether I had come to the right hotel. Inside was a small foyer with a chest-high barricade of bank-teller windows that would have made Dickens comfortable. One sign over an old metal grill said "Reception." Others said "Cashier," "Bills," and "Miscellaneous." On the wall, there were boards for pinning up one's calling card to inform other guests who was here and who was who. Old ledgers, coated with grime and dust, were piled about. A yellowing newspaper covered the small table this side of the barrier. I peered through the opening marked "Reception." There, huddled in a chair, back to the door and to me, an old man sat, wrapped in the ubiquitous shawl. He was motionless.

"Excuse me," I tried. He came to life slowly, turned and stood. I asked if this was indeed the Savoy. He said yes. I gave him my name, and he opened the top ledger on the pile nearest him and searched a penciled list with a bony finger for what seemed forever. Thoughts of what I could possibly do if turned away began to form in the panic zone. Then the old gentleman looked up, pleased. I existed. Collecting a key, he shuffled around through a back door and joined me, leading the way to a suite that had been set aside for me in an upper corner, "where there are good views," he said.

Crunching over ice and snow, we made our way through a kind of car-port, up numerous flights of frozen stairs (passing a sign pointing to a ball-room), and along a second-story veranda to Number 17. Now this was a suite to remember. When the double doors swung open, all I was conscious of was the temperature. Wearing, as I was, thermal underwear, a track suit, a heavy woolen tunic-style long-sleeved *pheran* from Kashmir, and a shawl, I would never have dared to sit down, fearing death from inaction. Sensing that I would not be capable of removing my gloves, the wizened reception-ist said that it would be all right if I signed the registration book required of foreigners in the morning. Could there be a morning? Out of the frigid black night, help soon arrived. Improbably, a waiter appeared, asking if I wanted the veg or non-veg dinner. Behind him was a housekeeper, an at-tractively casual man in a down jacket who looked more like a guest than the fellow in charge of hot water bottles, which he was. In a few minutes, he came back with one, and also a quilt. He was followed by a nineteenth-cen-tury figure bundled in Bob Cratchit scarves and carrying a lightbulb for the dark and cavernous bathroom—where no water ever ran from the taps dur-ing my stay. Mercifully, the toilet worked. And now I could see it.

The view was more of a problem. The vaunted windows were so coated with grime and laced with cobwebs that I thought it might be more useful to see what was out there by stepping onto the veranda, which at that time was bathed in moonlight. The moon, helped by a blanket of snow, also il-luminated other wings and outbuildings of the hotel. There seemed to be no other lights but mine. The canopied stairs leading to the elevated cen-tral entrance to the dining room and bar rose out of a snow drift, where there must have been a path. In the morning I could see that the potted plants that lined the covered staircase, among them a fern and a spider plant, seemed no worse for the cold. One of the pleasures of many Indian hills stations is the warmth of the daytime sun and the heat that unlikely plants can take from it to store against the nighttime chill, even against a substantial frost. European and American botanists and amateur British horticulturists alike were astounded in the nineteenth century by the sheer number and climatological variety of species they found growing naturally or could introduce successfully, particularly in the South Indian hills, only 11 degrees north of the Equator. Even this far north, species and seasons could be mixed in remarkable ways.

Suite 17 at the Savoy was huge and probably once magnificent. Regrettably but not unexpectedly, the front parlor had those ponderous, squarish, overstuffed British-inspired armchairs and settee upholstered in the red moquette that India has spent half a century trying to rid itself of. A cheap thin carpet, also red, more or less covered the floor. In one corner, a Gothic writing desk with a useless telephone stood by the door, through whose cracks arctic wind whistled. In one of the desk drawers, someone had secreted an empty Peter Scott whisky bottle, the room's only echo of a perhaps scandalous episode, albeit recent, since Peter Scott is an Indian imitation of scotch. They call it "Indian-made foreign liquor." A local newspaper used as a drawer liner featured this very Indian story: "Supervisor Beaten Up While Distributing Flood Relief."

But the room did have a fireplace. It was of the most basic sort, no more than a flueless hollow in the wall with a chimney above. Still, it was worth a try. "The fire will be 80 rupees extra," someone in the gathering crowd mentioned helpfully. At a little over $2.25, could I turn that down? Another ancient retainer arrived, carrying on his back a large tin bucket filled with chunks of solid, very dry hardwood. He also had the inevitable kerosene can, so beloved of fire starters all over the Himalayas. Dousing the wood he had arranged in the fireplace, he threw in a match and there was instant heat. But without a draft or flue, the fireplace was not likely to provide warmth for long, so I asked for another round of wood. "That will be 75 rupees more," was the answer. For each load I ordered, we had to complete the necessary paperwork in duplicate.

I pulled up one of the two armchairs to the fire to await the dinner. Ordered at 7 o'clock, it could not be served until 8:30 when the dining room opened, in a manner of speaking. With no discernible guests but me in this 121-room hotel, the dining room was closed for the season. But standards are standards. I unpacked my laptop computer to begin recording the trip up to Mussoorie from the plains. Not for long. A few paragraphs later, three short electronic shrieks said that the battery suddenly needed recharging, sooner than expected. The power seemed to be draining with uncommon haste, judging from the increasingly dire warnings on the screen. Unwrapping myself from my shawl, I searched for any electrical outlet that might be reasonably safe. In the bathroom there was a grounded socket for shavers, a kind of outlet I had used successfully many times in the third world. So I hitched up the machine to its cord and headed for the wash basin. No more than a second after the plug met the wall, smoke began pouring from the adapter and there was the unmistakable smell of burning electrical parts.

Though it would be hard to feel philosophical at such a moment, the meltdown of the adapter offered another example of India's mixed success at modernization and economic reform. The use of computers, Indian and foreign, is spreading rapidly, and with the resourceful help of the *New York Times* Indian office manager, P. J. Anthony, I was able to replace the IBM adapter within twenty-four hours in New Delhi. This would have been unthinkable a few years ago. But no adapter, even with a portable surge protector, can withstand an electrical system that was clearly sending a steady current in excess of 250 volts through the wiring of the Savoy. "It happens all the time," a computer expert told me a few weeks later in South India when I told him the story. The school where he teaches children to use these high technology tools plugs its state-of-the-art equipment into car batteries.

The trip to Mussoorie from Delhi by road is in itself a hard lesson in the reality of near-twenty-first-century India. The road crosses Uttar Pradesh, the country's most populous state, with more than 150 million people. The sheer magnitude of India is revealed in the claims on the billboards: Bagpiper Whisky, the world's sixth-best seller; Hero Bicycles, the world's Number One. Those honest claims can be made on Indian sales alone; there are no export markets, at least not for Indian whisky, sold all over the country (or rather in states without prohibition) at what are euphemistically referred to as "English wine shops," an old colonial designation transformed. A billion people, with a few hundred million of them in an internationally recognizable consumer society, are big business. It is the rest, those millions in material poverty, whose lifestyles are on display in Uttar Pradesh, however.

"U.P." is among the least developed, least humane places to be found in Asia and certainly difficult to accept or explain in a nation that calls itself a democracy and hopes to be the next Asian economic tiger. Horrifying police brutality and criminality are routine, literacy is low, women have scant status, and scrawny children with dull eyes and runny noses spend their days hanging around filthy market stalls instead of going to school. A Muslim writer once said that the state constabulary, laced with Hindu nationalists, is set loose on his people like a pack of hounds whenever there is a disturbance. Population growth is unsustainable and family planning programs are shams. The high-profile Thai family planning pioneer, Mechai Viravaidya, who was on a visit to India while I was last there, roundly rebuked Indians in places like this for their sloth in family planning. "You were the first to start a program forty years ago; we began only twenty years ago, but today our birthrate in Thailand has gone down from 7 percent to 2 percent. You, however, are still rolling around in the same place you were then. In sixty years at this rate, India will have 1.6 billion people." It will have by then overtaken China as the world's most populous country, and much of that growth will occur in places like Uttar Pradesh.

The road north to Dehra Dun and the hills, a major highway only two lanes wide, shared by bullock carts, bicycles, trucks, buses, and now imported high-powered cars, passes through town after town choked by people forced to live in the most degrading and debilitating of environments: open sewers, air thick with black soot and chemical pollutants that pour from vehicles and factories, mangled trees stripped of every reachable branch for firewood. Corruption lurks at every crossroads. My driver, Ebeneezer Massey—who felt he had to explain his unusual name by saying that his family were Punjabi Christians who had named all their children for biblical figures—began the trip by trying vainly to get a receipt for the road tax he had to pay at the Delhi-U.P. border. Naturally, up the road a few miles, a policeman stopped him and asked to see the nonexistent receipt. The indolent cop, roused from his chair by the sight of a new imported car with tourist plates, demanded a bribe to avoid a fine for not having the necessary piece of paper. Apparently intending to be both threatening and irritating, the overweight constable pored endlessly over all the car's documents. The driver offered 20 rupees (under $1). The cop said that wasn't enough: He needed at least 50 rupees. Massey told him that he would have to speak to the memsahib about that since 20 rupees was all the spare cash he had; he was only a driver. The cop relented, took the 20 rupees and went back to waiting for another victim. We headed for the next stretch of potholes that these "road taxes" will never repair.

The road to Dehra Dun and several holy cities of pilgrimage in the region is considered one of the most hazardous in India, a country where 60,000 people die and hundreds of thousands are injured every year in traffic accidents—and those are the reported cases. The Highway Users' Club in New Delhi, one of those nongovernmental organizations that is trying to change India from the grass roots up, says that the country has only 1 percent of the world's motor vehicles but accounts for 6 percent of its traffic accidents. A crash takes place every two minutes; every ten minutes somebody dies, often because there is no emergency medical service available. Another public-interest group calculated that more than half the truck drivers, the culprits in many fatal crashes, have fraudulently acquired driving licenses or no licenses at all.

What venal politicians and a law enforcement system beyond redemption have done to rob U.P.'s hardworking people of their due is evident from the natural wealth of the countryside. As we drove farther and farther from the industrial sprawl of the Delhi metropolitan area, fields of sugarcane and rice came closer and closer to the road. By Roorkhee, north of the sprawling, gridlocked city of Muzzafarnagar, shady groves of mango and papaya become more common, along with plantations of chilies and other crops. Some woodland has survived; there is more room to move and breathe. What many people of the hills fear, here and elsewhere in India, is that the sprawl and clutter and pollution of the plains is moving steadily toward them, bringing with it a sadly diminished quality of life and new hazards like lead poisoning, rejuvenated cholera, and clinical disorders caused by stress. Water resources are strained and already-meager sanitation efforts are overwhelmed. Temperatures rise as trees disappear.

Massey, the driver, fumed for miles over the ethical standards of the U.P. police, which clearly ran contrary to what he had been taught in a Christian school somewhere in neighboring Punjab. Another religious minority, the warlike but tolerant Sikhs, had made Punjab into one of India's most productive states in agriculture and industry. Massey had gone back to Punjab for a wife, a laboratory technician from the Christian Medical College in Ludhiana. They were to be married in a few months, now that he had saved enough to buy a car and a few other luxuries. Massey then segued for my benefit into an exposition of the differences between Protestants like him and Catholics. "Their God is Mary and our God is Jesus," he said. I hadn't thought of it quite that way before, but in the Indian context, this made sense. With a pantheon of gods in human and animal forms to chose from, most people in India's Hindu majority do not give much thought to divinity in the abstract but focus on the idols or symbolic representations of specific gods or goddesses. Even modern living gurus, so successful at luring Western seekers into their aura, are often treated as gods, with shrines erected in homes to honor them. Years ago, I had marveled at the splendid altar the mother of my Hindi tutor in Chandigarh had erected to Sai Baba. It taught me to recognize his image everywhere I went in India.

By the end of a daylong trip to Mussoorie, Massey had worked himself into such a righteous state that he decided to sleep in the car, a relatively new Toyota, rather than risk any harm coming to it. He had been offered a free room at the Savoy. In the morning, he admitted he had taken a look at the room and decided the car would be more comfortable. In my $30 Savoy suite, dinner—veg, which usually does one less harm in India than non-veg—had arrived on time. It was a wonderfully hot and tasty array of curried cauliflower, peas, spinach, and paneer, or local cheese, with a pile of fresh chapatis wrapped in a heavy linen napkin. My fire dwindling, an electric heater arrived, borne by a man who proceeded to connect it by adroitly inserting two bare wires into a wall socket in a wooden baseboard on a wood floor in the bedroom. If the whole thing followed my laptop adapter into a fiery oblivion, I reckoned, I could always escape through the sweeper's door to the bathroom, the only egress permitted those outcasts who traditionally clean toilets or, still today, carry away buckets of human waste.

Fully dressed for a hike in the hills (shoes excepted), I dug under several quilts and went to sleep, trying not to think about the computer. Fashion's layered look finds its definitive expression in the Himalayas and on the Tibetan plateau beyond. David Macdonald, who for twenty years in the first quarter of the twentieth century was the British trade agent in Tibet and later the empire's representative in Sikkim, explained in his book *The Land of the Lama* why "Tibetans are, generally speaking, not a cleanly race." Since there is not enough water for bathing, and if there were, it would be freezing, the Tibetan, he said, has little incentive to disrobe in such a climate, so he does the opposite. "Even when feeling chilled, the Tibetan does not make a fire for warmth, he simply puts on more clothing," Macdonald observed. To this day, the same tendency prevails in certain seasons in the hills of India, not only among the natives.

A long but peaceful night followed, punctuated only by occasional high-pitched screams that I imagined were coming from Ruskin Bond's brainfever bird. There are, of course, ghosts at the Savoy, but they are not known to be noisy. One of them is the restless spirit of Lady Ormsby-Gore, who succumbed here long years ago to a dose of strychnine in her medicine bottle. Her doctor died soon after, deepening the mystery. Agatha Christie drew on the story in 1920 in her first case for Hercule Poirot, *The Mysterious Affair at Styles*. Her tale, however, was set in Essex, not India, and mercifully it was summer. Landour also has a tradition of murders, Ruskin Bond asserted. Those occur at the extreme edge of erratic behavior that otherwise is limited to lifelong feuds and harmless offenses, he wrote in *Mussoorie and Landour: Days of Wine and Roses*. "Some residents of Landour past and present have been known to be slightly touched," he said with the tongue-in-cheek attitude of the observant native. "There is the theory that anyone who lives above 7,000 feet starts having delusions, illusions and hallucinations. People who, in the cities, are the models of respectability are know to fling more than stones and insults at each other when they come to live up here. Even those who have grown up and gone away still retain their cattiness."

A crystal morning dawned, and the golden Savoy, wrapped in drifts, glowed resplendent under the sun. Above its sloping rooftops, a panorama of high Himalayan peaks defined the skyline. Using the guide on my check-in brochure, I counted at least ten perennially snow-capped peaks over 20,000 feet. Three great Hindu shrines are perched in these mountains: Gangotri, Kedernath, and Badrinath, all more than 10,000 feet in altitude. Bill Aitken, whose richly descriptive *Seven Sacred Rivers* recounts his own efforts to reach some of Hinduism's most accessible holy places in these mountains, settled in Mussoorie for a spell in 1960 to learn Hindi at a missionary language school in Landour.

"One lived among the last weird vestiges of empire—elderly spinsters from Henley-in-Arden, posted to isolated mission compounds in the hinterland of Oudh, praying for guidance on the appropriateness of buying a kukri from an itinerant tradesman from church funds," he wrote. Within a few years, most of those missionaries would be gone from the Indian hills, withdrawn by their European and American churches, as a more assertive India began to turn against foreigners under Prime Minister Indira Gandhi, the daughter of Nehru but a personality as inward-looking as her father was outgoing in world affairs. Aitken found the air crackling with conversion in 1960, giving the atmosphere of Landour "a raw neurotic edge." When he revisited the town in 1990, he was pleased to see that his old pandit tutor had survived with his Hindu religion intact.

Landour's most famous institution, the Woodstock School, was founded in 1854 as a school for Protestant girls, many of them American or British children of missionaries. In 1874, the Board of Foreign Missions of the American Presbyterian church took over management, an arrangement that lasted until the early 1920s, when the school became interdenominational, though it never lost its earnest missionary atmosphere. At that point, boys were accepted as boarders; until then they were admitted only as day pupils. Like the Kodaikanal International School in South India, Woodstock has managed to keep alive strong links with American Protestant churches, despite India's unease about foreign Christians and their influence. Maureen Aung-Thwin, a Burmese-American who was educated at Kodai, where her mother also taught, told me that whole families became associated with these schools. The alumni are loyal friends who watch over Woodstock's fortunes just as Woodstock in turn watches over its natural environment. From the air, the school is enveloped in green. Rehan Khan remembers the lush, luxuriant foliage of the campus when he was there in the late 1980s—"a respite for sore eyes" after a walk through treeless Mussoorie town. The rainy, unspoiled forest presented its own problems, of course. "My most poignant memory of driving up to Mussoorie was the feeling of terrible gloom when the school reopens in July," he said. "The sky is overcast, it is raining heavily and it is a three-mile hike strewn with leeches from the town to the school." Gil Halsted learned about jungle wildlife in 1972 when he and his friends, exhausted from climbing Nag Tibba, decided to camp overnight at a deserted government rest house, only to be shocked out of their sleep by a water buffalo barging in through the front door.

Woodstock and the Kodaikanal school, which briefly considered a merger at one point, have had a powerful influence on many individuals, Americans and others, who support active alumni associations and retain their links to India and each other through these institutions. Edith Theis-Nielsen, who studied in a special class for Europeans and others at Woodstock who needed to take the British Cambridge secondary-school examinations, said the school had many activities that challenged students to think independently, though she and others bristled at the demonstrative Christianity of the missionary environment. But there was always also tolerance and an atmosphere of sharing. She later went to a boarding school in France and found it "run with military discipline separated from meaningful values." Students did not care for one another as they did at Woodstock, she said. "When I left Woodstock, I didn't think there was anything unusual about the school. But as the years passed, I realized how much Woodstock students and parents differed radically—in a positive way—from the people who surrounded me later in life in a purely secular context. I had given up being a believer. But in my search later for people who were like the ones at Woodstock, I also found faith rooted in the Bible."

Wilbur H. Lyon, a physician who lives in Idaho, was among those who feel, as he put it, "that exposure to international concerns at an early age helps one comprehend the complex world in which we live today." Lyon, who graduated from Woodstock in 1940, absorbed firsthand the tremors of approaching Indian independence. "India was then still British India," he wrote in an e-mail message to me. (Woodstock and Kodai schools have their own home pages on the World Wide Web.)

A classmate of mine was Chand Pandit. She was the daughter of Madame Jayalakshmi Pandit, the sister of Jawaharlal Nehru. He was to become the first Prime Minister of independent India and she would be India's Ambassador to the United Nations. Madame Pandit invited Chand's classmates to a party at her home after our baccalaureate service. At the party she stated that she expected to be imprisoned soon because of the stand she felt she needed to take, even though she knew it was against British laws. She wanted us, as Chand's classmates, to understand her views. She still stands out as one of the most intelligent and gracious people I have met in my nearly 73 years.

As a sixteen-year-old boy with nearly all my life experience in British India, I was concerned that India would be worse off if the British were forced out, since the British seemed to control the transportation, communications, financial structure, law enforcement and so on in such a large and diversified country. Her reply to my expression of this concern impressed me by making me realize the difficulty our very young country has in really understanding the thinking and philosophies of countries which are several thousand years old. She replied very calmly and graciously: "Yes, we will be worse off at first, and it may be 200 years until things are as good as they are today. Then things will get better, because that is the way it should be." At that time, my country was 166 years old. In the U.S.A. we are very impatient if our goals cannot be met in a four-year term or a fiscal year.

Young Wilbur also confronted other Indian realities at an early age, and came away sobered.

I remember as a thirteen-year-old student a feature speaker at one of our assemblies was one of India's top socioeconomists. He made one point that captured my youthful attention. He remarked that India had a serious problem because the previous year there had been an "unsuccessful famine." By that he meant that only about 20,000 people had died of starvation, rather than the predicted number ten times higher. This would result in many more people to feed and house in the years ahead than the country was prepared to support. This was entirely at odds with my thinking, even as a thirteen-year-old American boy.

The internationalism of Woodstock meant a lot to most of its students. "I remember the smells of breakfast and of the winter, the village and its northern influence on my experience of India and its culture," said Monica Flores, who entered Woodstock in 1988.

I was the was the only Mexican at the time, even the only Hispanic. The experience made me stronger in my own beliefs and more fully cultured. I learned a lot about uprooted children like myself; my father was in business and I never lived more than five years in one place. I have returned to Monterrey, Mexico, my birth town and work for a Dutch company now. I have a managerial position, a top staff job in a highly male culture. I know some of this is due to what the Woodstock experience taught me about being true to yourself—and how when you feel you represent only yourself you discover there is a lot of you in others.

Woodstock may have its lifelong friends and guardian angels, but other venerable institutions like the Savoy Hotel are in trouble in a new India. Anand Singh, the duty manager, told me the next morning how this came to be. As in Pakistan, many people in India with money to spend on vacations no longer want what an old hotel has to offer, a quiet formality tinged with eccentricity. Less-affluent tourists, coming to the hills in mushrooming numbers, would find it too expensive, even at the equivalent of about $35 a night, though it is doubtful it would hold any attraction for them either. Most visitors, including the busloads being disgorged that morning on a national holiday, the birthday of the Indian nationalist (and fascist sympathizer?) Subhas Chandra Bose, go to places with names like Sun 'n' Star, the Shilton, or the Honeymoon Inn. They ride a precarious cable car or hire the somnolent horses that are part of a hill station's repertoire. Like Murree, Mussoorie has a revolving restaurant and dozens of souvenir shops stocked by Kashmiris. Tibetans, perhaps even more successful merchants than Kashmiris, are also part of commercial life here, as they are now part of the scene in every hill station bazaar from the Himalayas to the blue Nilgiri Hills and the Palni highlands of the South.

The Savoy is willing to rent sections of the hotel to banks and corporations to use for staff recreation; "holiday homes" is the Indian expression.

That just about keeps things going. The seasonal summer crowd is still loyal, but shrinking. The hotel tried to add some amenities to attract a new generation, but old-timers are more outraged than pleased to find television sets added to their favorite rooms. "They tell me, 'Take it out!'" the manager said. For those who escape Mussoorie's noisy bazaars to find peace on the Savoy's hilltop, the traditional pastimes are the best: walking, reading, meeting in the bar with its upholstered armchairs, and lingering over dinner in a cathedral dining room complete with stained glass windows. In earlier times, the now-decrepit bandstand in the Library Bazaar just below the Savoy was the place where a regimental band performed most evenings during the season. A busy street barber has now set up shop—a chair and a mirror—to one side of the trash-strewn bandstand, alongside of which hooting buses and cars pass impatiently. Some yards away, a gaudy arch—an Indian described its decor as "the colors of Rajasthan"—has been erected over the entrance to Library Chowk by Hindu nationalist politicians. If the arch was intended to exorcise the ghost of British/Christian India from the chowk, there isn't much left to chase out.

When India was younger and less nationalistic, Mussoorie played its part in providing refuge for Tibetans fleeing a Chinese military attack on Lhasa in 1959. In Mussoorie, Rinchen Dolma Tsering, a well-educated woman from a prominent Tibetan family, and her husband, Jigme Taring, a Sikkimese prince and an aide to the fourteenth Dalai Lama, established a school for Tibetan refugee children even while they struggled to overcome a wrenching personal tragedy. When the Chinese shelling of Lhasa began in March of that year, both of them were about two miles out of the Tibetan capital at the temporary headquarters of the Dalai Lama, from which he soon fled to India. Rinchen Dolma's frantic efforts to return to Lhasa to rescue their two daughters, half a dozen grandchildren, two of them babies, and her elderly mother-in-law were thwarted by gunfire and menacing Chinese troops. She and a servant who had accompanied her out of the city were forced to flee. They made an impossible escape with the help of Tibetan rebels but without adequate clothing or supplies to sustain them across one of the highest, iciest Himalayan passes into the remote and landlocked Buddhist kingdom of Bhutan, and from there to India—and another hill station, Kalimpong.

Rinchen Dolma—who had picked up the Westernized name of Mary as a pupil in a Darjeeling boarding school many years earlier—had no idea whether her husband had survived until she reached India and learned that he was in Mussoorie, where the Dalai Lama stayed before he established his exile headquarters to the northwest at Dharamsala. All along the Himalayan foothills, thousands of Tibetans—monks, guerrilla fighters, and every kind of ordinary citizen—were flooding the hill stations, often their first safe stop in journeys of unimaginable horror and suffering.

For me, getting out of Mussoorie was harder than getting in, even though a warm sun was beginning to melt the snow and ice on the morning I returned to the plains. It was a beautiful day when Massey and I started back down the hill. But we didn't get much farther than the first bend out of the Library Chowk square when there was gridlock on the narrow road. Buses were snaking up the hill bumper to bumper, jammed with young people who wanted the rare chance to play in snow. At the slightest pause, passengers poured out to scramble into the drifts and make snowballs to throw at each other and other buses. Drivers honked and shouted; nobody could possibly move. Nobody was in charge. It took a shopkeeper to intervene, shooing a few wayward coaches out of the road and opening a lane for traffic going down. We left to the joyful sounds of laughter and singing and the screams of surprise as kids dressed for the heat below fell happily into snowbanks, slid crazily on ice, and seized a brief experience of an unusual winter they would remember for a long time.

The Windamere's garden gate: Darjeeling

Darjeeling and Kalimpong

The snow fell lazily outside. Inside, a fire glowed silently in Daisy's Music Room as Chandrika Kanade, teacup and saucer in hand, sat down at the piano and began to play. The tune was "Annie Laurie," rendered not sentimentally but in an accomplished pianist's clear, crisp notes that traveled into the bar next door and circled back over the finger sandwiches laid out for tea on a dark wooden table in the hallway. Then it was "Comin' Through the Rye" and "Loch Lomond" and so on and on. A small group began to gather in the music room, quietly, sitting properly on armchairs and on the settee by the bay window. Near the tempting, drag-up-a-chair fireplace, a discreet but prominent sign warned primly and peremptorily:

1. Visitors are respectfully requested *not* to move around furniture in this room in order that comfort may be shared in fair proportion by all.
2. Visitors are requested *not* to take off their footwear, or put up their feet on the furniture or lie supine on the hearth, or sleep behind the settees, lest unintended offence be given to others.

The Windamere Hotel is trying to hold the line. All around it, old Darjeeling may be dying or already dead. The Gymkhana is closed most of the time; the Planters' Club struggling. Electricity, water, forests, and land are in short supply. A Nepali nationalist movement, with its ubiquitous graffiti extolling a mythical Gorkhaland, controls the local government but has failed to win much support among its constituents or do much to improve the town, high on a mountain ridge in the eastern Himalayas. It was February, and fog, sleet, drizzle, and snow added to the gloom beyond the Windamere. Perhaps the atmosphere is less grim in other seasons—or so I said later, talking over my most recent visit with friends. Not at all, replied a journalist in Calcutta: "Be glad you weren't there in the summer, when you can't move around because of the crowds, the trash, the pollution." Unforgiving, these Indians can be.

"Life at the Windamere is warm, sedate, predictable," Hope Cooke wrote of her visit in 1959. Darjeeling proved a fateful detour that year on this American's first trip to India. It was there that she met the widowed crown prince of Sikkim, Palden Thondup Namgyal, and began the relationship that would make her the queen, the Gyalmo, of the second-last Himalayan Buddhist kingdom, just before it plunged into tragedy and was swallowed by India. A picture of the two of them, Hope and the prince, together in happier days, hangs in the Windamere, a hotel she remembered for its "brass-polish smell, grandfather-clock chimes, logs burning in fireplaces, chintz covers on freshly painted furniture." None of that has changed. There are still tea and sandwiches at four, a hot-water bottle in every bed at night, and a correctly spartan dining room that long ago made the serious mistake of building a cuisine around British cooking. (Fortunately, diners now have the option of asking for Indian food instead.) At Christmas, the last British tea planter in the neighborhood, H.H.E. Young—known as Teddy—dresses up in a Santa Claus suit and entertains fashionable guests and local children. Christmas and New Year's are very big events here and until not too long ago were also formal. The Windamere, however, is an island. On its own small ridge above the town, the hotel, presided over for decades by the Tenduf-la family, of Tibetan origin, can close its doors to the world and refuse to compromise. If you want television and a telephone that works, you will just have to go somewhere else, said Evelyn Shah, the hotel's classy vice president. Still, people clamor for rooms. It has that kind of reputation. Even if you might really not want to be here, it is the only place to be. This discomforts some people, like the Sikh gentleman I saw at breakfast wearing the headphones of his Walkman over his turban. Anything beats the British-style mealtime silence.

A few hours and hilltops away, the Himalayan Hotel in Kalimpong hews to similar standards, though in a far more open and casual way. Hotels can make a difference; they are often a reason for going to one place and not another. These two old inns, plus the unsurpassed views of some of the earth's highest peaks, combined with the Tibetan-influenced mountain cultures that distinguish this region from hill stations in the western Himalayas, are all reasons for persevering against the obstacles modern India puts in one's path to this distant corner. Darjeeling and Kalimpong are a special pair of hill towns that historically belong more to the Himalayan Buddhist world than to the flat expanses and plains people of Hindu India, at least before the British arrived. Their natural setting was once one of intense luxuriance, a palette of greens made more dramatic by the highest of icebound Himalayan peaks beyond. "Upon what a gigantic scale does nature here operate!" exclaimed the nineteenth-century naturalist Sir Joseph Hooker. "It is difficult to conceive a grander mass of vegetation, the straight shafts of timber trees shooting aloft, some naked and clean, with grey, pale or brown bark; others literally clothed for yards with a continuous garment of epiphytes, one mass of blossoms, especially the white orchids, which bloom in a profuse manner, whitening their trunks with snow. Perpetual moisture nourishes this dripping forest; and pendulous mosses and lichens are met with in profusion," he wrote of the scenery on his first ascent to Darjeeling.

Down below, the Indian state of West Bengal no less than the mountain forests seems nowadays to be fighting for its life. Arriving in Calcutta late at night in a battered taxi with one reliable gear still working, I plunged into a black squalor that assaulted all the senses. The once-quiet suburb of Salt Lake looked like a vast construction site; this is probably deemed progress. The sickly-sweet, putrid smell of the sewage of the shantytown clinging to the overpass near the city limits was, if anything, more penetrating. I remembered how, when I passed this way years ago, the stench drove one of my colleagues—a hardened, experienced journalist—to gag reflexively, uncontrollably. This time, I held my breath. Nudging aside a swarm of people walking the streets for lack of anything else to do, the taxi soon emerged into an open space where a new Science City gleamed. Incredibly, its signboard announced a meeting on infertility. Approaching Calcutta's center, the driver could barely see under dimmed streetlights the huddled forms camped at the curbs as he dodged ghostly carts and bicycles that seemed to have given up advertising their existence with bells or lights. Out of holes and dark corners along the wet streets, people and rats scurried along garbage-slicked pavements. At an intersection, caged chickens by the hundreds were being sorted or slaughtered for the morning market, adding feathers and blood to the hellish mix. This city will never make it, I thought. Calcutta is finally collapsing.

The truth, however, is that Calcutta is a daily miracle. When morning came, the city was transformed by its indomitable vibrancy. No place in India has more cerebral sizzle. It would be hard to find any other city in the world with so many bookstores and bookstalls—or a sidewalk book vendor who lays out his volumes to give prominence of place, among the cheap reprints of classic novels and science fiction, to a used copy of *Gray's Anatomy*. Bengalis are India's intellectual aristocracy: rational if disputatious, literate and learned, curious and nimble of mind, open, warm, generous, and always in search of a good argument. They are real urbanites, not village people camping out in towns like New Delhi or high-fliers perched tentatively in the towers of Bombay/Mumbai, but cosmopolitans living for generations in old apartments that, when they can be maintained, rival the mansion flats of London or New York City's Upper West Side. These are city people, and maybe it is this inborn urbanity that keeps Calcutta alive and gives energy and hope to activists of all kinds who do battle with a calcified political establishment that has let their city deteriorate and crumble.

Calcuttans may be the best judges of what has become of their hill stations of Darjeeling and Kalimpong, the closest high-altitude resorts to the great city on the Hooghly. The prognosis is not encouraging. In recent decades these towns, and nearby Kurseong, have endured not only over-crowding and the loss of natural resources but also the guerrilla war waged for the autonomy of Nepali speakers who call themselves Gorkhas—a variation of Gurkha, the spelling adopted by the British to describe the warriors of Nepal. To compound the assaults from within and without, the original hill people of the area, Lepchas and Bhutias, have forsaken many of their traditions for the "modern" life they see imported from the plains, symbolized by video shops and bazaars offering plenty of cheap imitations of Western-style clothes and shoes but very little traditional weaving or other crafts. The scene in Gangtok, nearby Sikkim's once-tiny capital, is pretty much the same.

Members of prominent Calcutta families and many other middle-class Bengalis remember different, better days because they have been regular travelers to these hill stations for generations and the life of the hills is part of local lore. If someone can't personally recall a detail or two of history, there are always the stories handed down to draw on. Because Calcutta was the capital of the British Indian empire for more than a century and a half, a substantial Indian professional class developed and grew around the city and in outlying towns. A strong education system turned out writers and scholars as well as *babu*s, the Bengali clerks and other officials so often wrongly caricatured as officious and faintly ridiculous native servants of the British Empire. Just like the British, Bengalis went to the hill stations for business and pleasure. Some "took a house" for the season; some settled there.

Darjeeling—the best known of a group of eastern Indian hill stations stretching as far as remote Shillong in the state of Meghalaya—was Bengal's Simla, a summer capital and year-round resort for East India Company agents and provincial government officials in the colonial era. Darjeeling once belonged to Sikkim, the independent Buddhist kingdom annexed by an imperial India in the mid-1970s. Kurseong, on the way to Darjeeling from the plains, was known for its schools and for its useful, way-station location. A natural overnight halt on the way to Darjeeling when the journey could take nearly a hundred hours, Kurseong is now a rest stop for motorists and a busy bazaar town that long ago lost its reputation for being "a clean and pretty little village," as one early traveler described it. Kalimpong, off to one side near the spectacularly beautiful Teesta River valley, has always been much smaller than Darjeeling and more a family town. Until the late nineteenth century, Kalimpong belonged to Bhutan, another Himalayan Buddhist kingdom and the only one to survive as an independent country. The drive from Darjeeling to Kalimpong ranks among the most pleasant in India, dropping over 6,000 feet from the monastery town of Ghoom along valleys with views of Sikkim to the spectacular Teesta River gorge before climbing 3,000 feet in the final ten miles to Kalimpong.

Darjeeling is, of course, tea country, producing India's most famous tea leaves—so famous that most of the tea sold abroad under its name is not from Darjeeling at all. Tea plantations, however, are not Darjeeling's most prominent natural attractions. Rather, Indians and tourists from around the world flock to the town in the hopes of seeing some of those awesome mountains. From the main ridge on which this hill station was built, Kanchenjunga seems to tower above the horizon at more than 28,208 feet. Mount Everest, 29,028 feet high, can be seen in the distance on a good day from Tiger Hill, about seven miles from the Darjeeling's Mall.

"Beyond all other mountain views is that first sight of the Himalayas," the American travel writer Eliza Ruhamah Scidmore wrote at the turn of the twentieth century. On a clear winter day at sunset, "the white peaks changed to gold, flame color, and rose-pink, blue and purple mists filled each ravine and valley." All along the Himalayas, there is no time of day when the mountains are not enthralling: bathed in a rainbow of light at dawn, crystalline and sparkling with perennial snows against a faultless sky by day, aglow at dusk long after the earth has given up its colors for the night, and finally shimmering in a ghostly silver-white under the moon. The trick in Darjeeling is to be there in the right season—usually spring or autumn—and on a good day. Stories abound of days if not weeks spent straining for even an outline of mountains through the clouds. On my last visit, I slipped and skidded to the top of Observatory Hill in the freezing rain and saw right away that there was not much to look at but the monkeys. But I have seen Kanchenjunga in other seasons on even brief visits, not only from Darjeeling but also from Kalimpong and Gangtok. Few vistas are more startling or exciting. One soon understands why some people are drawn back again and again, hopelessly and sometimes perilously enraptured by the Himalayas.

Like many hill stations, Darjeeling was built on land largely uninhab-
ited until nineteenth-century colonizers went looking for a place to cool
off. Darjeeling's name derives from *dorje,* the thunderbolt that is a central
icon in Himalayan Buddhism. A Buddhist temple once crowned Observatory Hill, and the rest was wilderness. The Gurkhas of Nepal, whose ill-
fated expeditions in the western Himalayas led to British annexation of
territory where Simla and Mussoorie were established, also played an un-
intentional role in the creation of Darjeeling. Gurkhas overran the region,
then part of the kingdom of Sikkim, in the early nineteenth century. All
of Sikkim might have remained in Nepali hands had the Gurkhas not
pushed the British a little too hard. Defeated in 1817, the Gurkhas were
forced to relinquish all conquered Sikkimese lands, which the East India
Company then gave back to the Sikkimese royal family. Little more than
half a century later, the Gurkhas of Sikkim would have their revenge,
aided by an expansionist India. But that gets ahead of the story.

By 1830, the British in Calcutta were looking for a hill station to equal
Simla, but a lot closer. After sending an expedition into the Darjeeling
area and finding it agreeable, the East India Company dispatched emis-
saries to the Sikkimese Chogyal, or king, to sound him out on granting
Darjeeling to the British for use as a sanitarium. Years of confusion about
who promised what to whom (and in return for what) followed, but the
British went ahead and built their hill station, paying the Sikkimese king
a modest sum for a while, then ending the grant after Sikkim arrested Sir
Joseph Hooker, the botanist, and Darjeeling's town superintendent,
Arthur Campbell, a physician by training; Darjeeling really did have a
large sanitarium, so it made sense to put a doctor in charge of the town.
Campbell was tortured by Sikkimese officials before the British sent
troops and the two were released. But the standoff did not effectively end
until the 1860s, when Darjeeling became for all purposes an integral part
of Bengal and its official summer capital. The issue of who owned Darjeeling still had explosive potential as late as 1966, when Hope Cooke,
then Gyalmo of Sikkim, wrote an article in the *Bulletin of Tibetology* arguing that Sikkim had never granted the British more than user's rights to
Darjeeling, and that independent India was repeating Britain's violation
of the agreement by assuming Delhi had inherited absolute sovereignty.
Many years later, she told me that this was not her opinion alone, but that
of her late husband, a tragic figure who lost his wife, his kingdom, and finally his life when Prime Minister Indira Gandhi and Indian agents engineered his overthrow, hounding him from his throne and leaving him a

broken man who died in New York of cancer, unable to the end to rally world opinion to his side.

From the colonial era on, Darjeeling has been awash with schools, educating Europeans, Indians, and relatively large numbers of students from Bhutan. Schools form an important part of the town's economy, I learned in the late 1980s, when parents had withdrawn children during a violent phase of the Gorkhaland campaign and shopkeepers complained bitterly about lost sales, especially in stationery and bookstores and snack shops. Kalimpong and Kurseong—also in the Darjeeling district of West Bengal—had schools, too, serving the Himalayas and the plains. In Bhutan, I kept running into public officials who had been pupils at Dr. Graham's Homes, despite its name, a school in Kalimpong. The experience was certainly life-altering. J. A. Graham, a former tutor to the second Bhutanese king early in the twentieth century—the "modern" monarchy was not established until 1907—was a Scottish Presbyterian who went on to become moderator of the Church of Scotland. His school on a hilltop in Kalimpong was populated by austere Scots missionaries who placed sanitation and book learning on an equal par. One of their most successful Bhutanese graduates is Pem Dorji, a regional administrator in Bhutan who never ceases to lecture his charges on the necessary humiliation of learning to clean one's own toilet in order to understand that keeping things tidy was everybody's job. When I met him in the Bhutanese hills, he was waging a one-man war against the introduction of a "sweeper" class of migrant Indians who would be happy to find even demeaning jobs in so pleasant a place.

In Darjeeling, there were two Jesuit schools, St. Joseph's College, on a hill called North Point, and St. Robert's High School, near Darjeeling's open central square, the Chowrasta. The Loretto Sisters from Ireland ran the Loretto Convent for girls, Anglicans had snobby St. Paul's, and Australian Protestant missionaries established Mt. Hermon. Thirty miles down the hill at Kurseong, there were more schools, where teaching was also in English (or Irish, which left its lilt all across northern India and Pakistan) or in Hindi. It was in Kurseong, at St. Alphonsus High School, that Father William Mackey, a Canadian Jesuit who became a legend in the Himalayas, began his Asian teaching career in 1947. Driven out of India seventeen years later, Father Mackey went on to become the first and only Jesuit priest to become a citizen of Bhutan, where he founded the country's first and only college at Sherubstse. A Bhutanese prime minister, Jigme Dorje, discovered Father Mackey at St. Robert's in Darjeeling, where the sometimes-contentious Jesuit had moved in 1959. About 80 percent of St. Robert's students were Bhutanese, among them a son of the prime minister. When Father Mackey ran into trouble in India, caught up in both Bengali-Nepali tensions and a wave of Indian nationalism that drove a number of foreigners (and the Peace Corps) out of India, Bhutan made an offer: Please come and teach, but no conversions. Father Mackey had no problems with that. "We would all be in trouble if we thought that salvation comes from a little bit of water being poured over your head," he told me later, a few years before his death at eighty in Thimphu, Bhutan's mountain capital.

The Bhutanese are still a presence in Kalimpong. I was reminded of this on arriving at Bagdogra airport from Calcutta. Leaving the terminal (an exalted description of a concrete box with stinking toilets and a corner newsstand selling old magazines, yellowed postcards, and "tourists' requisites"), I saw to one side of the extravagantly soiled cabin that houses the alien registration desk, a Mercedes with Bhutanese license plates. "The Rajmata," my taxi driver said. The "queen mother" of Bhutan, who spends much of her time in Kalimpong, had just returned from a visit to the doctor in Calcutta.

Nandini Ganguly, whose father was a prominent Calcutta lawyer, remembers how in the final years of British rule her family packed up every autumn for the *hawa badal*, or long puja, season when courts were closed for a long recess, to travel to the hills, including to Kalimpong, where they once rented a house for several months. Indians, even rich maharajas, stayed away from the few good hotels that the British made their vacation headquarters. I always got a sense that this distance was—and maybe still is—preferred by many Indians, in part out of fear of humiliation in colonial times and more generally because European life was and is, well, a lot duller. Not to mention the awful food. Caste considerations also separated the two societies; in many Brahmin families, dining with foreigners would be polluting.

"My father was a renowned advocate in the Calcutta High Court," Nandini Ganguly said when we met in Calcutta.

During the long puja season the English judges wanted to visit their country on home leave. The three months were well spent by the English, recapturing their culture and their way of life. The Indian judges and well-to-do barristers and advocates would leave for a hill station. The choice always fell on Darjeeling, Kalimpong, or Kurseong, all within easy reach, with no time wasted on the journey. Simla, a magnificent hill station, would take more time by train, and air service was not available. It could also be a hazardous trip. We Indians were happy to visit these Bengal hill resorts for their grand views of Everest and other mountain peaks and their salubrious climate and nature.

These hills stations were easily accessible overnight by the Darjeeling Mail, a prestigious train. In those days—about 1936—our traveling party comprised ten to twelve or more family members and relatives plus servants, helpers, cooks, and even ayahs for the children. The huge lot of portmanteaus, suitcases, bedrolls, tiffin baskets, lunch baskets, medicine chests, and a trunk full of provisions came with us. We spread our beds in the train, and our cook, Biju, served a sumptuous dinner he had prepared before we left Calcutta. Because labor was cheap and plentiful, we could carry as much as we liked. It was really a task to count the boxes and luggage at the station. Our eyes were most keenly on the big tiffin carrier, an enameled one from Holland for easy cleaning. We had to carry our serving plates and cups and saucers, also. We took all our cooking utensils in a wooden box, including a big Primus stove of Swedish make. In the hills, firewood was in plentiful supply. Nepali boys and girls, we called them *kancha* and *kanchi,* made a little money selling it to households.

The trip to the hills of West Bengal began much the same way when Elizabeth Sarah Mazuchelli—who was known as Nina—made the journey in 1872 with so much luggage that it had to come on a separate baggage train. Nina Mazuchelli, who wrote about the adventure under the pseudonym Lady Pioneer in a small book called *The Indian Alps and How We Crossed Them,* had to leave a servant behind at one point to round up the pieces of luggage when the baggage arrived at a transit point. A quarter of a century later, the remarkable American journalist and travel writer, Eliza Ruhamah Scidmore, described how annoying it was to travel with the British in India because they never traveled light. Leaving Calcutta after an overnight stop, she encountered a fellow passenger who had preemptively filled the railway compartment the two were expected to share with "the usual British impedimenta—tin steamer trunk, canvas hold-all, Gladstone bag, laundry bag, dressing-bag, tiffin basket, a roll of umbrellas, a tennis racket, a bag with her pith hat, a wicker chair, a collection of garments that hung from every available hook, and a large round-topped Saratoga trunk."

For the entertainment of anyone who has made an Indian railway journey of any length in the last decade or two, here is how a sharp-eyed local Anglo-Indian journalist, E. C. Dozey, remembered the Darjeeling Mail early in the twentieth century. "Those who now have occasion to travel to Darjeeling will appreciate the efforts of the Eastern Bengal railway in trying to provide for the comforts and convenience of its passengers," he wrote—and this was not sarcasm.

The Darjeeling Mail train is the fastest train in India, doing 50 miles an hour from start to finish. The comfort of the passengers has been the primary consideration, as evidenced by the numerous devices, though small in themselves but when taken collectively contribute not a little to our creature comforts. The bathroom, on the down journey especially, will be appreciated as in addition to the usual shower-bath it is provided with a spray-bath from jets along its walls. The electric fans are now placed over the heads of the diners instead of the center of the table, thereby adding to the pleasures of the meal. Another convenience is the electric cigar-lighter, which will save the loss of temper and keep the atmosphere from turning blue. The train is lit throughout by electricity, its lavatories are provided with paper towels (in rolls), while the basins are fitted with receptacles containing liquid soap. The guard's and luggage vans, and the dining saloon are furnished with fire-extinguishers, while an alarm communication is attached to each compartment.

Dinner was served in a dining car—read that and weep—and there was a very civilized 5 A.M. tea, an hour before arriving at Siliguri, where passengers met the toy train into the hills.

"The overnight train would transport us in the wee hours of the morning to Siliguri station, when light fog was still hovering," Nandini Ganguly recalled of her trip two decades later. "We all stayed awake to be the first to glimpse the mountains. In those days there were four classes of trains: first, second, intermediate, and third. First class was exclusively for foreigners, high officials, and aristocratic Indian gentry. Common people went by third class and comparatively rich people by second or 'inter' class." At Siliguri, passengers going to Kalimpong switched to road travel through the glorious Teesta River valley. Travelers to Darjeeling transferred—and still do now—to the little train from nearby New Jalpaiguri that climbs fifty-five miles into the hills on the tracks of the Darjeeling Himalayan Railway, one of the world's great rail journeys and probably the most enjoyable of all the hill station trains for its variety of scene. The hallmark precipices, ravines, switchbacks, S-curves, and enormous loops—four of them, the last at over 7,000 feet on an exposed plateau—are there for the train fans. But so are towns and villages and fields, where children run beside the small cars or jump out of their way as the train grinds along, sometimes at almost a walking pace. One can practically

shop as the coaches rumble through bazaars and along main streets at
Kurseong and Ghoom. The Darjeeling Himalayan Railway was built between 1879 and 1881, when the train Dozey described, which seemed state-
of-the-art to Europeans, ran directly to Siliguri from Calcutta. That line
is no longer open, the victim of the 1947 Partition, when East Bengal was
turned over to Muslim Pakistan; in 1971, it became Bangladesh. The border has long been a vexed one because of the flood of immigrants from
Bangladesh into West Bengal and the Indian Northeast.

From Bagdogra airport, I took the road to Darjeeling first and then
swung back a few days later along the mountain route to Kalimpong. A
sturdy Gurkha driver named Dilip was waiting for me at Bagdogra with a
small Indian-built van, sent down by the Windamere, a hotel that rarely
misses a beat when looking after guests. Racing to avoid a mountain
storm, Dilip proposed taking an old route to Darjeeling that was new to
me. This route, he assured me, was shorter than the more heavily traveled
one. That's true, but it is also true that the narrow road seemed to zigzag
straight up thousands of feet without a pause, as the small van strained to
meet steep inclines while dodging bigger jeeps on the descent. Fortunately, no trucks or buses use this route, which increases the odds of survival as well as the enjoyment of unobstructed views. Without trucks and
buses, there is no need for roadside foodstalls and huts offering other services. No guard rails or barriers here, either. The road was terrifying. It
was also a trip through forests I would not have believed still existed in
the Darjeeling area. It was probably the most spectacular drive, and least
environmentally degraded approach, I made to any Indian hill station.
Thick jungles of bamboo mixed with evergreens and countless plants I
could not identify closed in on the single-lane road. There were palms on
the lower ridges and giant ferns in the ravines. The Darjeeling area gets
very heavy rains, heavier than the hill stations to the west. This is part of
that richly endowed ecological zone that stretches into Sikkim and
Bhutan. Only in Bhutan, however, is this natural richness protected by
law and respected by a small population not driven by desperation to
threaten the jungles and forests in any significant way.

The shortcut to Darjeeling joins the more familiar route at Kurseong,
where a sleety rain was falling over the gridlock of train, cars, and people
in the middle of town when Dilip and I arrived. From here, we climbed
first to Ghoom, at about 8,000 feet and notorious for its dismal weather,
then descended toward Darjeeling, at its slightly lower altitude. Along the
way, poor children played or carried out their assigned chores barefoot in

the freezing rain and snow. In this weather, their small homes, some with door open to the elements, seemed no less uncomfortable or unhealthy. Across the Himalayas, respiratory illness is rife, often made worse by the smoky cooking fires that also provide the only heat, especially in higher elevations in Nepal and Bhutan, where wood is more plentiful. There are many treeless expanses along this route to Darjeeling, some of them natural open meadow and some the work of people. The British first stripped the environment hereabouts by tea planting. Wood was also cut to fashion the railroad ties for the little train. Most wild animals are now gone, no doubt a process that began long ago with the early loss of forests and an insane passion for hunting. Mark Twain—assuming this was not a tall tale—wrote that he shot thirteen tigers on his way from Calcutta to the Darjeeling hills in the 1890s.

When Dilip and I arrived at the Windamere, originally a town residence for planters, it was wrapped in a cold, thick, white, immovable mist. Inside, however, my room was ready, with a very effective coal fire blazing. Room 9 was a symphony of greens: walls, woodwork, bed frames and covers, even the bathtub. The bright kelly-green phone was accompanied by this helpful notice:

> Our telephone intercom service was Windamere's pride and joy when it was installed in 1950. It gave reliable service for twenty years and then went wrong. Several telecom experts in succession succeeded in making only patch-work repairs. The last expert, twelve years ago, did some serious repair work and, as a consequence, when certain numbers are dialled, three phones ring simultaneously in separate rooms, causing alarm to guests who value their repose. We have been keeping this deficiency in our intercom system under review and, meanwhile, crave your indulgence.

With the marauding electrical current of Mussoorie in mind, I asked for a transformer, and was supplied with one of those massive metal boxes that Indians have created to defy the worst of surges. It was placed at the edge of a riot of overlapping oriental rugs, safely out of the way, since tripping over it would be a serious matter. In an armchair near the fire, my laptop safe from zapping (though not blackouts), I thought what a perfect place this would be to write the whole book. The room was furnished with deep, wood-framed, cane-sided armchairs and a sofa with plump, flowered cushions. Nothing matched but everything worked together, in the same way that the decor of an English country cottage often blends a hodgepodge of disparate pieces into a harmonious collection. Two sturdy wardrobes and two huge built-in wall closets were evidence of the days people came to stay a while.

The Windamere, it must be said, is a rather formal and self-important hotel with numerous rules and an almost determined air of not caring too much about the contemporary world. Year-old copies of the *Economist* are piled on reading tables with newspapers at least a week out of date. Ladies are asked not to wear "slacks or nightgowns" to dinner. Men are to avoid "shorts and pyjamas." But there is the grace and good manners to make exceptions. A late arrival gets food, for example. A jogging suit passes muster in the dining room on a cold, wet night. One of the nicest touches is the selection of postcards left on the table for guests, with international airmail stamps affixed, ready to be dropped in the old red British pillar mailbox by the front door. At the Windamere, boisterous behavior just does not happen. I never heard voices raised anywhere in the hotel. No one in authority shouted at the staff. The noisiest interruptions at night sounded like monkeys throwing things on the galvanized iron roof, though there were also fireworks for the Buddhist new year. Life outside intrudes, however, in the signs reminding visitors that Darjeeling is short of water. Firewood is also scarce. On Darjeeling's narrow byways, women and children, bent under the weight of large baskets, plod up hillsides carrying twigs and sawed-off sections of logs.

The Windamere is now one of several "Heritage Houses of the Himalayas," a worthy cooperative effort among the keepers of traditional inns who want to help each other preserve a style of hill station tourism that is under threat from newer hotels. At the Windamere, I heard about the Himalayan Hotel in Kalimpong, another Heritage House. With Dilip at the wheel again, I left Darjeeling through shady groves of cardamom and descended along a valley rim dotted with small Buddhist villages identifiable by the traditional prayer flags of the Himalayas flapping over neat little houses with bright cloth hangings for doors. There is a Teesta town, named for the river, at the low point on this route, altitudinally speaking. It is suddenly warm at river level, and Teesta town, with wonderful views of the gorge and a new bridge across it—the third since the colonial era—seemed to be thriving. Here a traveler can choose among roads: to Sikkim or Bhutan, higher in the mountains; to the plains towns of Siliguri and Bagdogra; or to Kalimpong, at only 4,100 feet. This area is an especially lush part of the Himalayan hills. Rhododendrons big as trees once blanketed whole hillsides. Pine, wild roses, wild strawberries, blackcurrant bushes, and peach and apple trees grow here. Wildflowers, when unmolested, spread everywhere. There were, until very recently, many wild animals. Nandini Ganguly remembers the abundance of Kalimpong in the 1930s. "We enjoyed shopping every day for fresh vegetables in the market. The forests were full of wild animals then. One day the cook brought down a bear cub to show the children. Our father was angry, because he was afraid that the mother would follow the scent. He sent the cub back to the woods."

Kalimpong once stood at the end of one of the great trade routes from the Tibetan capital, Lhasa, passing through Gyantse and the Chumba Valley. Another caravan route went westward to Ladakh via Shigatse; two routes led into China proper. For the British, who set up rest houses along the Kalimpong-Gyantse road, this route was the most important, and closest to the East India Company headquarters in Calcutta. After the end of the British Empire in India, until the Chinese takeover of Lhasa in 1959, Kalimpong continued to be the center of the Indian wool trade with Tibet. Trade first brought David Macdonald to Kalimpong at the turn of the twentieth century. The Himalayan Hotel, with its solid oak ceilings and supporting pillars made of teak, was his family home. His grandson Tim inherited it and gave up a planter's life to run it with the help of his wife, Nilam, a teacher by profession. David Macdonald, a fluent Tibetan speaker, was the interpreter for the ruthless 1904 British military expedition to Lhasa led by Sir Francis Younghusband. The adventurer Younghusband conspired with the viceroy, Lord Curzon, to attack Tibet to thwart an apparently exaggerated Russian bid for influence there. This was an eastern version of the long-running political tournament known as the Great Game. The British government did not approve of the mission, which accomplished little more than creating sympathy for Tibet and the then Dalai Lama. Britain did get the right, however, to establish a trading post in the Tibetan town of Gyantse, and David Macdonald served there and at Yatung, where he once hid the thirteenth Dalai Lama's chief lieutenant, Chensal Nangang, in a storeroom during a crisis. Macdonald also helped that Dalai Lama flee a Chinese assault in 1910 and find asylum in Kalimpong and Darjeeling, pursued by a band of unsuccessful Chinese assassins. The thirteenth Dalai Lama's flight was in a sense a prelude to the fourteenth Dalai Lama's escape from Tibet in 1959, again in the shadow of a Chinese invasion. The thirteenth Dalai Lama was able to return triumphantly to Lhasa in 1912, however. China seems in no mood to let his successor do the same.

David Macdonald, who also had served as the British government's representative in Sikkim, turned his Kalimpong home into a hotel after

his retirement in 1924. He began to write, and completed two books—
Land of the Lama and *Twenty Years in Tibet*—while his three daughters
took over the running of the inn. The Himalayan Hotel played host to a
stream of famous guests, most of whom loved it. But Nilam and Tim
Macdonald still smart a little over some unkind comments made by John
Kenneth Galbraith, who visited the hotel in 1962 (before their time),
when he was American ambassador to India. Galbraith described it in
Ambassador's Journal as "an exotic and highly uncomfortable hotel run by
three sisters of Indian, Tibetan, Scotch, and possibly other ancestry
named Macdonald." The blunt ambassador had heard that Kalimpong
had "a famous reputation as a resort of spies, thieves, smugglers and multi-
purpose rascals," which he thought was probably an exaggeration. Even
the town did not make the grade.

The Himalayan Hotel is timelessly magnificent. Tucked into a steep
hillside terrace above the main town, it is a solid two-story stone house
with wide verandas on both levels, overlooking a small lawn with tables
and umbrellas and, in the distance, Kanchenjunga and other mountain
peaks. For the Lepcha people, who believe they are indigenous to this region, Kanchenjunga is the source of their creation. The story is that God,
Rum, took two handfuls of snow from Kanchenjunga's summit and made
a boy and a girl of them. Though they were created brother and sister, the
inevitable sexual attraction brought them together as father and mother,
and they produced dozens of children who became the Rong-pa or Rong-
folk, as the Lepchas call themselves. Kalimpong, like many Himalayan
foothill towns, especially in the Darjeeling district, is now dominated by
ethnic Nepalis—the Gurkhas—and this is reflected in the staff of the Himalayan Hotel.

The hotel's rooms are huge but bare-floored and heated only by a small
fireplace for which wood is brought in small installments by a new generation of Nepali boys and girls, more than half a century removed from Nandini's *kancha/kanchi*, who tend the fire solicitously, returning at intervals
with long, ineffectual sticks. One evening, when I was down with something like the flu and trying to read in bed, the knocking on the door never
seemed to stop: Someone brought tea, the fireplace tender came and went,
and then a completely surprising stranger arrived. He was a very old man,
wrapped in the proverbial shawl over his copiously wrinkled cotton
trousers and shirt, and he carried in his hands a wooden box full of grimy
bottles. He knew one word: massage. I acted out that I didn't feel well:
cough, cough. He mimed a chest and sinus rub, pointing to something that
looked like motor oil in one of his bottles. I declined. He was back the next

day, and the next, slipping without a sound along the wide wood-floored corridor, looking so hopeful when I opened the door. It seems that trekkers had found his muscle-relaxing techniques commendable, and since there were no trekkers in residence, he was looking for other business. Curing colds would do. "I guess his crankcase oil wouldn't have hurt you," another guest remarked on hearing the story. I'll never know.

I got to know my room well, as I retreated there with my fever, cough, and books every evening. The furniture was old-fashioned simplicity: a table and chair near the fire, another by the window corner; a dressing table, a wardrobe, and two beds, and still there would have been room to hold a party. The starkness accentuated the old home's rich wooden frame and beams, a very pleasing sight. The one nicely cluttered room in the hotel was the long ground-floor gallery, with a dining room at one end and a cozy (there is no other word for it) bar lounge at the other. This space was full of craft work and family memorabilia. Important to this eleven-room hotel is its location, in one of the last undeveloped corners of Kalimpong, a town with a few surpassingly ugly commercial streets leading to and from a central bazaar area of no great charm. In 1916, the journalist-cum-timber expert E. C. Dozey described the main street as "laid out in the correct boulevard style with rows of trees." None, apparently, survived. The town, centuries ago the center of a Lepcha kingdom regularly pillaged by both Sikkimese and Bhutanese, seems to have been strangled by its recent popularity. The saving grace is that Kalimpong is still relatively small in geographic size, and it has some fine bookshops, the best of them Kanshi Nath and Sons, where a traveler can find something to read in the garden or on the veranda or in some other peaceful corner of the Himalayan Hotel.

Across town on a distant hill was Dr. Graham's Homes, a rather forlorn collection of buildings because students had left the school for a winter break when I visited. But there I met an extraordinary British scholar, R. K. Sprigg, who has retired to Kalimpong with his wife, an Indian citizen. Sprigg, a linguist of international renown, has known Kalimpong for half a century and mourns its transformation from a village of great charm and grace to the dirty and overcrowded town it has become. A bagpiper, Sprigg recalls piping out the last British planter, a man named Stroud, in 1974. He told the story over his lonely lunch in an otherwise barren and chilly dining room of the house on the school's property where he now lives. His lunchtime companion was a cat who was not averse to tackling the tough pieces of meat that humans couldn't manage. We—Sprigg and I, not the cat—shared an aperitif. He had made a rule that he never drank alone, so he was always happy to welcome a guest. Sprigg has never lost his fascination for the mountain cultures and their Tibeto-Burman languages. This has led him into a study of Lepcha history.

Sprigg's life in the hills is not without antecedent. Other British scholars brought to the Himalayan foothills by British colonialism stayed on and died in India. The most famous—as far as the Lepchas are concerned—was George Byers Mainwaring, who was born in India in 1825 and later rose through the ranks of the British Indian army to become a lieutenant general. He was also a linguist. As a lieutenant colonel he was sent to the Lepcha region to compile a dictionary, a rather unusual military assignment, but one he obviously relished. Unlike Sprigg, resplendent in tweeds even when not expecting company, Mainwaring (whose name was pronounced Mannering) was given to showing up in local bazaars and government offices in Lepcha robes. Rumor has it that he took a Lepcha wife, a priestess who was his tutor and collaborator in the dictionary that was published after his death in Bengal in 1893. Mainwaring tried and ultimately failed to nurture native Lepcha scholars, sending at least one to England for a university education. Nearly a century after he was gone, Lepchas in Sikkim established an annual literary award for the best creative work in the Lepcha language. They agreed unanimously to name it for the Sahib Mainwaring.

Maybe it was the Sprigg lunch, served in such austerity, or unseasonably cold nights in Kalimpong, when hotel guests shifted their dining room chairs closer to the cauldrons of coals that kept our feet warm, that made me think about the differences in Western, especially American, expectations about old inns in the Himalayas. In a generation or two, old hotels in what was once colonial America—New England, Pennsylvania's Bucks County, and the Eastern Shore of Maryland, for example—have become luxurious. Designer sheets and weightless duvets under canopied four-posters, freshly baked muffins and fancy coffee for breakfast, drinks by an evening fire—all of these have disguised frontier life under a cloak of cozy charm. Not so in the Himalayas. Life here is still authentic, and perhaps a good deal less sybaritic than it was in colonial times. People came to the hills then for the bracing air, the hikes, the summer-camp atmosphere. Those who understand that, and expect that, are happy. But those who anticipate a stay in an English country hotel or an American bed and breakfast inn that just happens to inhabit a very old house will be bemused by the Himalayan experience. Nilam and Tim Macdonald have become resigned to encountering the odd misfit in their hotel. Nilam recalls the visit of two British women, mother and adult daughter, who arrived on a special quest. They wanted to experience what a father and grandfather had found compelling about Kalimpong many years ago when he lived in the hills as a planter. The daughter, apparently already traumatized by the knife-edge Indian driving style of the taxiwala who had deposited them on the doorstep of the Himalayan Hotel, took one look at the grand but appropriately unadorned room assigned her, with its cold, cavernous bathroom, and—without more than a second's pause—screamed.

KODAIKANAL AND OOTACAMUND

All the great hill stations of India have their individual personalities and histories, but one of them is very different indeed. Kodaikanal, in the Palni Hills of Tamil Nadu, was founded by Americans, and their influence pervades it to this day. For many years, a good choir concert drew a crowd as big as any that turned out for Gilbert and Sullivan. At the heart of the town is the famous Kodaikanal International School, established for the children of American missionaries and still very American in its style and curriculum. The town of Kodaikanal draws artists, intellectuals, and environmentalists from those Indians in the growing and diversifying contemporary middle class who are not wholly preoccupied with getting rich and building eco-hostile palaces of consumption. Like-minded foreigners enjoy living here and seem to have a hard time leaving. The school attracts adventurous teachers, whereas leftover Western hippies hang out on the fringes of the friendly town, camping at Fairy Falls, taking nourishment at the Big Belly Vegetarian Restaurant, and outfitting themselves in cheap cotton clothes from street markets around the Seven Road Junction. Some years ago, a German jumped his tourist visa, chucked his passport, stayed for twenty-five years, and died here. Townspeople, worried that somewhere there was someone who cared, gave him a simple funeral and then went about tracing his mother in Europe to tell her of his death.

"Kodai is a bit of home to us all," Charlotte Chandler Wyckoff, the best-known colonial-era historian of the town and its people, wrote in the mid–twentieth century. "To the Scot it is a reminder of mountains and lochs and glens; to the English of trim box hedges and rolling downs; the Australian owns the tall blue-gums that bend in the monsoon winds; the Scandinavian chooses the steep hillside where the pines grow; the American sees the Blue Ridge or the Sierras or the Adirondacks in every turn of the trail."

One element in the atmosphere of Kodaikanal would by itself distinguish it from strictly British hill stations: a strong egalitarianism. American and, later, European missionaries not only largely built the town but also dominated its early life. There was no official British presence except for the ubiquitous government representative known as the Collector and some civil servants on leave. There was no military cantonment. Nora Mitchell, the British-born chronicler of Kodai, put it politely in a geographical research study she wrote for the University of Chicago in 1972: "As the first permanent houses were built by missionaries, who outnumbered the government officials, they were justified in feeling that the center belonged to them. Furthermore, as the early missionaries were American rather than British, they were probably less sensitive to the innate rights and privileges of the British upper class."

In other words, the snobbery and rank that decided one's place at the dinner table in Simla did not count for much here. There always was and still is an easy social mix of Indians, other Asians, Americans, and Europeans in Kodai. Foreigners have stayed on and retired here, though perhaps not as many as would have liked to, since India—or more accurately, some Indian politicians, have a way of making outsiders feel a little insecure and unwelcome. And only Central Intelligence Agency operatives, real or imagined, are held in higher suspicion than foreign missionaries.

The missionaries who built the first houses in Kodaikanal in 1845 belonged to the American Madura Mission, a Congregational outpost established in the South Indian temple city of Madurai in 1834. At least some of the missionaries had moved into South India from the Jaffna peninsula of Ceylon, where American mission schools would educate generations of Tamils in the nineteenth and twentieth centuries. Inadvertently, the American mission schools would thereby also play a role in modern Asian history by turning out better qualified graduates than many institutions elsewhere in Sri Lanka attended by the majority Sinhalese, who came to resent the successful Tamil minority. There were two results of this enmity: a Southeast Asian diaspora of educated Jaffna Tamils in the professions, often law or medicine—and civil war in Sri Lanka. The climate of Jaffna had apparently been much kinder to the American missionaries than that of Madurai, where six of their number died within a decade. Malaria may have been the culprit, though this is not clear, because the disease was one of a number of lethal fevers around at the time. But what struck next was certainly cholera; of that there seems to be little doubt.

The missionaries, relying on the medical knowledge of the period, thought it might be wise to buy a ship to ferry the weaker of their number back to Jaffna for recovery. The British had been shipping the infirm and convalescent out of India to Indian Ocean islands or South Africa for years. In the long term, a ship would provide the American missionaries a ready means of escape if needed during an epidemic; at other times it would serve the Lord's servants as a floating health resort. Bracing sea voyages were thought to be restorative in themselves, and Jaffna was known to be a relatively salubrious place to land. But finding a home port on the Coromandel coast and maintaining a ship would have been a major expenditure for a mission. That idea was doomed.

Since this was the dawn of the hill station era, there was an alternative. The mission could build a mountain retreat. Ootacamund, across the state, had already established itself as a hill station for the Madras presidency, the East India Company region into which Madurai also fell. One or two of the American missionaries had been sent there to recuperate in 1840. But Ooty, more than 7,400 feet in altitude, was too far away. Closer to Madurai were the Sirumalai hills, with several peaks over 4,000 feet and a generally cool climate. The American Mission built a bungalow there in 1844. But unaware that the altitude of the Sirumalais was not adequate to deter mosquitoes, the missionaries were struck again by a powerful fever, probably malaria, and there were more deaths.

In the 1840s, the world was still almost half a century away from learning that the malaria parasite was carried by the anopheles mosquito. There was only a dimly comprehended and probably exaggerated relationship in colonial minds between clean, cool air and physical wellbeing. The instinct to climb was the right one, but people living in the tropics did not know that the hills had to be very high, preferably over 5,000 or 6,000 feet above sea level in most places, to get out of the mosquitoes' range. They also did not know that altitude and cold air were not enough to prevent outbreaks of cholera or other epidemic diseases, which sooner or later struck hill resorts for the same reasons they afflicted the plains. Poor sanitation, contaminated food, and dirty water became more common as hill towns grew and Indians from the lower altitudes built bazaars and villages around the edges. But in the 1840s, the American Mission in Madurai had only one thought in mind: Its community was being devastated and it had to find a way to stop the loss of life.

The Americans went to the British for advice. A British surveyor, Lieutenant B. S. Ward, had visited the Palni Hills, about seventy miles northwest of Madurai, in 1821, at the time that Simla was taking shape in North India. But nothing came of Ward's visit or that of another party of British officials in 1834, though some accounts say that one of the later visitors built a collector's cottage about six miles from the present location of Kodaikanal. A 1909 guide to the town credits a botanist, Robert Wright, with leaving the first permanent record of what he saw there, largely an account of the bountiful natural setting. He was able to collect over a hundred plant specimens in fifteen days. The hills were then known as the Varahagiri, or Hog Mountains, because of a local legend about an ancient holy man who turned twelve insolent children into pigs. Stone monoliths of a vanished ancient civilization are scattered around, but the people who erected them left no recorded name for the place. This eastern section of South India's mountainous ghats appears to have taken its name, the Palni Hills, from Palani, a large town on the north side of the mountains, or from early inhabitants called the Paliyans or Puliyans.

As for Kodaikanal, there never has been a consensus on what that means. Kanal is not the problem; it means "woods." But Kodai has at least half a dozen unrelated meanings, from "end" to "umbrella." Since one definition seems to be "vine" or "creeper," local historians settled on "forest of creepers" to define the town's name; it is certainly apt, in the parts that have escaped deforestation. Kodaikanal's historians have been frustrated over the years by the secrets the hills have kept. "Did none of the subjects of the kingdom of the Pandyar, described by Marco Polo as 'the finest and noblest province in the world,' pause while bathing at dawn in the Vaigai to gaze at the hills seen so clearly in a blue horizontal line against the sky?" Charlotte Chandler Wyckoff asked half a century ago. "Did none feel the urge to visit them?"

The American Mission eventually came to rely for information on a British entrepreneur, a Mr. Fane, who had explored the commercial possibilities of the area and built godowns. He obviously was persuasive. The Americans decided to take a chance on Kodaikanal. When the first two American houses, Sunnyside and Shelton, were built, the ever-obliging Fane helped the missionaries round up and transport the construction materials and was full of ideas for other development projects, which the cautious missionaries put to one side. Looking for a site among hills that rise to 8,000 feet, the Americans decided to build not on a ridge but in a grassy basin averaging about 7,000 feet high. Whether Fane and the Americans were aware of it or not, their undulating, high-altitude grassland was sheltered by hills from the worst of both monsoons that sweep

India every year, one from the southwest, the other from northeast—though Kodai has been devastated occasionally over the years by exceptionally powerful storms. The town grew up and down hills, but most are not precipitous, so bungalows, churches, and schools could be graced with lawns and gardens. Walking in Kodai is strenuous exercise, but not so challenging as the virtual mountain climbing often demanded of hikers in India's northern hills. There was room for playing fields, a golf course sheltered by woodlands, and a large lake.

Kodaikanal grew slowly, even though several British officials, among them a retired judge and a former Collector of Madurai, built residences, encouraging other Britons to visit. The 1879 *Murray's Guide* described Kodaikanal as a settlement of "only 10 to 15 small ugly houses." But by 1909, when the *Guide to Kodaikanal,* whose author was identified only as E.M.M.L., was published, there were 151 houses, "most of them anything but small and ugly," and a number of public buildings, including a post office, churches, clubs, schools, and shops. Perhaps the greatest individual promoter and benefactor of Kodai was Sir Vere Henry Levinge, an Irish baronet who retired from the Madras Civil Service in 1867 and lived in the town until his death in 1885. Spending considerable amounts of his own money, he built roads and contributed generously to the construction of the bund that turned a swampy depression with a meandering stream into the lake that is still the town's natural centerpiece. A memorial to his civic-mindedness was erected near the post office. He was, it said wordily, "A true friend to the poor, no one ever appealed to him in vain, while his upright character, his love of justice, and his kindly heart, endeared him to all classes of the community, European and native. And thus he bore without abuse the grand old name of gentleman."

In 1845, six pioneering American missionary families spent April and May, the South Indian summer, at Kodai in the mission's two new houses. "Each year thereafter, till more houses were built," said Wyckoff, "the missionaries came up by turns, sending all the children with the first to go, and leaving them to come down with the last to depart." By 1853, Kodai's summer residents had begun planning the first church. It was finished in 1858, with some Rube Goldberg touches. The roof was made of flattened Huntley and Palmer biscuit tins. A bell from America was installed, just before the whole building collapsed in a severe storm. A visiting Swedish ship's carpenter was persuaded to stay long enough to build a new steeple after the congregants had restored the rest. The town's first cemetery was established in the churchyard; among the graves were many where children were laid to rest, often victims of cholera. That interdenominational Church Under the Hill served all the Protestants of Kodai for a quarter of a century.

The missionaries on vacation thus established a "spiritual season" in April and May, precisely the time of year when other hill stations were at their most frivolous. Not that the missionaries did not have fun. They rode horses, played tennis and by the 1990s were enjoying the socializing at Tapp's Dairy, Bakery and Tea-Room, with its honeysuckle-draped outdoor pavilion, where strawberries and cream were a specialty. Picnic hampers were available, and lucky children had birthday parties at Tapp's. At home, women pressed wildflowers and learned to decorate their otherwise conservative dresses by transferring the patterns of a silver-powdered fern directly to cloth. Nonetheless, a wag writing in the Calcutta *Pioneer* remarked later in the century that "during the months of April and May—the missionary season—black-coated padres fill the air with the odor of sanctity. When Kodai Spiritual departs, the Kodai Carnal season commences with the rains." Missionaries did make the rules, frowning on Sunday activities unless they were church-related. The Kodaikanal Club got its land near the lake on a promise that there would be no barroom. Kodai's busiest club was the Kodaikanal Missionary Union, which still has a very good library, though it is no longer a hub of social life.

Kodai must be the only hill station in India that greets the visitor from the plains with a steady stream of Christian graffiti. On various boulders and a rock wall beside a waterfall on the road into town from Madurai, I noted the following hand-painted offerings: "Jesus Loves U," "Jesus Is Lord," "Everything Is Passing but Jesus." On the other side of town, toward Palani, pious graffiti artists had contributed, in very large letters, the exhortation to "Join Jesus" and the warning that "Jesus Is Coming Soon. Repent." The graffiti is in flawless English, of course, because the standard of English usage is very high in South India, most of all among those educated in Christian schools, Roman Catholic or Protestant. South Indians, who speak Dravidian languages that are very different from the Sanskrit-based languages of North India, have never been prepared to accept the northerners' Hindi as the lingua franca. In Tamil Nadu, they demonstrated soon after independence that they were prepared to fight for their linguistic rights, and won for themselves a Tamil-speaking state. Forced to choose a national language, southerners generally like the neutrality and increasing usefulness of English, which is now Asia's common language. The South is home to a lot of India's high-technology industries, with many links to the United States. Much to the chagrin of many northerners, English is also the de facto common tongue of India's Parliament. On a trip south with an Indian prime minister some years ago, I shared a taxi in Madras with two journalists from the North, neither of whom spoke English very well. As we careened around town trying to catch up with the official motorcade, my colleagues shouted instructions at the driver in a mix of Urdu and Hindi, which he either genuinely could not understand or refused to acknowledge. In the end the foreigner and the Tamil driver conducted all our collective business in English, leaving the driver's fellow Indians out of the conversation.

Like English, Christianity has deep roots in South India, but they go back much further into local history. Christians in South India believe that St. Thomas, one of Christ's apostles, took to heart the command to "go therefore and make disciples of all nations, baptizing them in the name of the Father and of the Son and of the Holy Spirit" and came to India to do his part. Legend says he reached the Malabar coast of southwest India about A.D. 52 and made some conversions in what is now Kerala. Then (although there is no documentation to support this) St. Thomas is believed to have moved eastward, toward Madras, preaching and converting. About twenty years later, he was stabbed by an outraged Hindu in Madras, where he was buried. "He, like his master, sacrificed his life yielding to the Father's will," wrote the Reverend K. V. Mathew in his *Faith and Practice of the Mar Thoma Church,* which, as the reformed branch of the oldest Christian community in the country, the Syrian church, safeguards the Apostle's legacy.

The story of the congregations St. Thomas is credited with founding in South India remained largely unheralded until the Roman Catholic Portuguese arrived on India's west coast in the fifteenth century and found Indian Christians celebrating their religion with Syrian rites. Those Malabar Christians had apparently maintained links with Syrian, Persian, and other Middle Eastern and West Asian pockets of Christianity. Later, factionalism would rend the fabric of Indian Christianity, which always remained a minority religion in an overwhelmingly Hindu nation. Some Indians became Roman Catholics, others continued to follow various Eastern rites, and still others eventually joined Protestant, even charismatic and evangelical, churches. The Anglican church, now the core of a broadly based Church of South India, has over recent decades brought a number of Protestant denominations into its fold, though not the charismatic churches.

In South India more than in any other part of the country most Christians consider their religion wholly indigenous and not the by-product of Western culture or the offspring of Western missions. South Indian Christians point out that their ancestors were Christians before the conversion of northern Europe and centuries before the Reformation. In Bangalore, George Ninan, a retired advertising executive who is a member of the Assemblies of God, told me he knew about Jesus long before he ever heard of America. His India had no need of imported preachers, and he opposed efforts of American evangelicals to establish a foothold here. Thus the Protestant missionaries who pioneered Kodaikanal found an understanding environment, if not exactly enthusiastic welcome, in South India, where Western Christians eventually became best known and most appreciated for their hospitals, schools, and colleges. Kodaikanal International School, no longer serving a missionary community, has become part of this legacy, transforming itself into an Indian school it calls Christian and multicultural, with students from India, other Asian countries, and the West.

Kodai school opened in 1901 in a hotel called Highclerc that was rented at off-season rates until the school could buy the property. The first principal was an extraordinary American woman, Margaret Norton Eddy. Born in Ohio but raised in Kansas, where she went to school with Buffalo Bill Cody, Eddy got her first job as a teacher at the age of sixteen. Her intention was to save for college, and she entered Vassar in 1868, but had to leave because of a vision problem that was not yet correctable. She married a pharmacist and had three children before being widowed at the age of forty-six. By then a grown son, Sherwood, had gone to India in missionary service. She decided to visit him.

Eddy arrived in India in 1900, just as the missionaries in Kodaikanal were casting about for someone to help them open a school for their children, who might benefit from the healthy atmosphere of the hills more or less year-round. Eddy became not only the principal and housemother to the first boarders but also a formidable fund-raiser. In the early years, she returned to the United States to find $10,000 to buy Highclerc and give the school a permanent home. When ill health forced her to leave India, she went right on creating new challenges for herself until her death in her eighties. Late in life, she moved to New York City to take classes in its universities, vowing to memorize a piece of literature every day to keep her mind at work. When she died, someone found a confession she had written about herself, listing her faults: "being impatient, failing to keep drawers and boxes in order, and spending too much time on newspapers instead of better reading material."

The Protestant missionaries who founded Kodaikanal International School were not the first to establish an educational institution in Kodai. The Jesuits had opened a seminary more than thirty years earlier and soon also built a network of schools for local Indian children. The Jesuit fathers took an interest in the prehistory of the Palni Hills and established a museum at their headquarters, La Providence, to house a collection of natural and historical exhibits. In 1916, another Roman Catholic order, the Sisters of the Presentation, opened Presentation Convent, also an English-language school. By then, Kodaikanal had become a center of learning that drew families to the hill station for substantial portions of the year. Europeans—Swedish and German missionaries—also built schools.

During World War II, an interned Italian, Maria Montessori, taught and trained teachers for two years, spreading the Montessori system through India. Montessori was one of many internees the British exiled to Kodaikanal. Among them, though much earlier, were a couple of potentially troublesome Afghan princes, Akram and Azam, along with their mother. Britain also used its colonies to scatter prisoners of war and sometimes put them to work on public projects. The lake in the Burmese hill station of Maymyo was excavated by Turks taken prisoner in World War I.

Like the Woodstock School in Mussoorie, the Kodaikanal International School survived Indian independence with only a few adjustments. But given the general deterioration in the level of Indian politics by the 1990s, it was perhaps inevitable that sooner or later the unusually untroubled relationship between the Kodai school and India should have been most severely strained by politicians. In July 1991, while the school was on vacation, gangsters wielding knives seized Loch End, a part of the school's property across the street from the main campus, and drove away some staff members living in cottages there. Six years later, the mess was still in the courts. In a generally deteriorating ethical environment, it appears that an ordained pastor who was an officer of the Indian Evangelical Lutheran Church Trust Association had conspired with politically well-connected developers to sell the land without notifying the church or the school, which was technically a tenant of the religious organization. Like many other missionary establishments, Kodai school had been transformed into an Indian institution, its directors thinking that in that way nationalization or other political problems could be avoided. The aston-

ishing level of corruption that swamped state politics in Tamil Nadu by
the early 1990s could hardly have been foreseen.

The "buyers" of Loch End apparently intended to turn the lakeside
property into a tourist hotel, even though the church trust was pledged to
maintain Loch End for Christian educational purposes. The case symbol-
izes—apart from the politics of a larger-than-life film star turned chief
minister, Jayalalitha Jayaram—the intense interest in hill station development everywhere in India among politically well connected people who
see a growth industry and therefore a way to make easy money. Not far
from Bombay, developers were recently found to have coerced poor farmers into parting with their land to build a hill resort. The same developers
were also working on a much larger "planned" hill station in the same region in defiance of environmental protection procedures. The magazine
India Today, noting allegations that billions of rupees had changed hands,
said the developers were promising a town of 250 mansions, four or five
lakes, a helipad, an eighteen-hole golf course with night lighting, shopping malls, a cable car, and a convention center with videoconferencing.

In Kodaikanal, the school seemed to have a clear case against the trust
because no one doubted that the transfer of property was not only illegal
but also violent. But nothing is ever that straightforward or easy in India. In
Madras, the Indian newsmagazine *Frontline* reported that the school was
told it was pointless to complain to the police or government officials because "people in high places" with the power to close the school were back-
ing the developers. It took a change in state government in Tamil Nadu to
reopen the case, by which time the school had been forced to build new ele-
mentary classrooms. But six years later, there was still no resolution.

Indians of all faiths historically had mixed relations with Western
Christians. Tensions erupted early, as soon as the first Europeans arrived.
The Portuguese pushed conversion too far here, as they also did in Ceylon. Although many Indians were already Christians of a sort when the
Portuguese arrived in the fifteenth century, the Portuguese tried to wipe
out Syrian rites by imposing and enforcing Roman Catholicism. In a
demonstration of continued defiance in 1653, about 25,000 Syrian Christians, led by 633 priests, marched on Cochin Fort, then a Portuguese outpost, and took a public vow never to become Roman Catholics. They were
in essence the aristocracy of Indian Christianity, and their influence was
critical both to reaffirming the position of the Indian church and to the
later social development of South India. South Indian Christians opened
schools for boys and girls, putting education—and educational equality—

at the heart of policies that would help make the South Indian states, especially Kerala, the country's most progressive region, with the best-educated women. South Indian Christians laid the foundations for literacy levels twice as high as the national average and for near-universal health care, legacies that would be built on later by enlightened maharajas and Marxist-led state governments that added a dose of political equality, giving lower castes a shot at power.

After foreign missionaries became part of the Christian mix in India, large numbers of outcaste or very low caste Hindus began converting to Christianity to escape the stigma of being born untouchable or otherwise lowborn. Most numerous in North India, they became known as "Indian Christians," a nomenclature with a very specific meaning in a country where the "old" Christians and "new" Christians are often widely separated by caste. Among St. Thomas's earliest converts, according to their descendants, were Brahmins, the highest caste, and one with priestly and scholarly functions. Their attitudes toward low-caste Indian Christians have not often been charitable. "Indian Christians," however, took readily to education with no less enthusiasm than the upper castes.

The first American missionaries to escape the plains for Kodaikanal in 1845 seemed to have left all such problems behind, along with their fevers. They gushed over the trip to the hills and the quality of life they enjoyed, however primitive the accommodation. "Our stay of two months on the hills was exceedingly pleasant," one wrote. "Especially did we enjoy the wonderful scenery on the ascent; grandeur beyond anything we had witnessed before." These pioneers were made of sturdy stuff. The ascent to Kodaikanal was not a joyride. Whether the trip began in Madurai—or, later, at the railway stop between Madurai and Dindigul named Kodaikanal Road, though more than forty-five miles from the hill station—the first part of the journey, to the foot of the Palni Hills, was made by bullock cart through most of the nineteenth century and into the early years of the twentieth. An essay apparently written by a pupil or teacher at the Kodaikanal School in about 1910 described the trip as a "jostling overnight journey" for which travelers were advised to bring rugs and blankets to cushion themselves against the hard wooden floor of the primitive cart, called a transit, whose boards were barely softened by a layer of straw.

From the foot of the Palnis to Kodai is about thirty miles by the modern highway. Before that, the shorter but more precipitous route—rising 6,000 feet in the last twelve miles—was up the Coolie Ghat, a dirt track too narrow and steep for wheeled vehicles. The climb began at a point known as the Tope, the boundary of Raja Kistnamma Nayak's estate, where carts were abandoned for horses, hill ponies called tats, canvas sedan chairs, or boxlike palanquins known here as doolies. Travelers called the sedan chairs *hon-go-gum*s because of the chant of the four coolies who carried them: *"Ha-ah-ho; hon-go-gum. Ha-ah-ho; hon-go-gum."*

It was necessary to get away from the Tope as quickly as possible because malaria lurked there, travelers were told. And it was important to keep up a smart pace on the ascent because of predatory animals. Travelers were urged to make a lot of noise to deter the unseen beasts, which were known to seize cows and other domestic creatures accompanying the migrating families, if not the people themselves. With relays of fresh porters to carry the luggage, bicycles, and what have you, and coolies to transport the doolies and chairs, the trip from the Tope to Kodai could be made in about six hours. It all added up to a punishing journey of up to twenty hours just from the Kodai Road railhead.

We made the trip all the way from Madurai to Kodai in two and a half hours, the Kandaswamy family and I. One never has to go far in India to experience extraordinary hospitality. Even by those standards, this trip was exceptional. V. Kandaswamy, who had recently retired from the United Nations, is a friend of Secretary General Kofi Annan. In the course of a party one evening in New York, I told the secretary general that I was taking time off to revisit the Asian hill stations. He remembered that Kandaswamy and his warm and generous wife, Rajalakshmi, had a summer house in a hill station whose name he had forgotten. It turned out to be Kodaikanal. Two days later, Kandaswamy, then in Princeton, called to say he would like to arrange my visit to Kodai, starting in Madras, where he lived in retirement and where I would arrive from Colombo. Marshaling the extended family, we flew to Madurai to be picked up by the driver of a nephew who lives there and taken to a wonderful South Indian breakfast of dosa and idli at his home.

J. B. Shankar, the nephew, managed a steel mill. But he wanted to talk about issues of international policy, not business. He was a reader of *Foreign Affairs*, the *Asian Wall Street Journal*, and the *International Herald Tribune*, when he could find them. Because we were on our way to Kodai and I mentioned the International School, he recalled his own secondary education at Christian schools in India and Sri Lanka. Though a devout, even ascetic, Hindu all his life and a Brahmin, he said about his Christian schooling that it "made me look more deeply into my own religion." He was impressed with the moral lessons of Christianity, even though they were not always followed. I asked about their equivalents in Hinduism, and he said that he thought one could find them in the teachings of the Ramakrishna mission, founded on the reformist and universalist teachings of a nineteenth-century Bengali mystic whose movement was brought to the West by the Swami Vivekananda. Anyone who has lived in India a few years knows that it is impossible to have a boring dinner party or leave any group gathering without some new intellectual stimulation. Here we were at breakfast in Madurai and already I had been forced to confront the relative merits of ethical systems. I had a head full of things to think about on the way to Kodaikanal. Naturally, we went in one of Shankar's cars.

Out of Madurai, the highway to the hills passes through flat agricultural land with vast fields of sugarcane and rice. The narrow road is made even narrower in rice-harvesting seasons, when farm families use one of the two lanes as a threshing floor. After the Kodai Road station, as the hills loomed nearer, we passed under a canopy of tamarind trees, a tunnel of leaves that blocked the piercing sun. Early accounts of this journey mention that the trees were planted along the road to shade the carts making their way back to base in the heat of the day after the overnight trip from the train to the Tope.

The climb to Kodai is not among the worst that hill stations have to offer. The road is good, with low, whitewashed walls on the outer side to prevent plunges. As with the road to Nuwara Eliya, the Sri Lankan hill town, much of the altitude is still achieved in the final miles. Flowering vines brightened the undergrowth along the shoulders, where work crews were hacking back an unruly jungle trying to reclaim the road. A few times we passed a dry pocket, and there were incongruous cactuses. The Kodai road is famous for the fruit stands set up at bends or on small patches of flat space at the shoulder. These offer whatever produce may be in season. On this trip in January, it was mostly oranges. Rajalakshmi Kandaswamy, who has spent part of every year in Kodaikanal since her childhood, remarked that the quantity and quality of fruit and vegetables from this region had declined with the recent tourist boom in the town. She laughed sort of sadly at the thought that she more often brought produce to Kodai these days instead of buying it here to take home to Madras.

As we neared Kodai and passed some bald hills baking in the sun, she also spoke about how thickly forested this terrain once was. On empty hillsides, dozens of small houses and huts were being built on treeless plots, not a very attractive entrance to what is, nonetheless, one of the more pleasant Asian hill stations. Nearer the old town center, the stone walls and cottages from earlier years softened the impression of runaway development. Some of the newer houses were built in harmony with this style, including the Kandaswamy family retreat, which had stone walls and made much use of rich hardwoods. Concerned citizens try hard to control development through zoning, but some critical battles and a great deal of virgin land have already been lost.

Two Kodai houses came to symbolize for me what made this hill station architecturally superior to many others. One, tucked in a grassy crevice overlooking the lake, is set aside for the principal of the Kodaikanal International School. It is a rambling bungalow built entirely of stone, fronted by a veranda where flowers in pots bloomed on every available ledge or sunny nook. Paul Wiebe, the current principal, invited us in for a look and a chat. The comfortable rooms inside are finished in beautiful dark wood, to which the Wiebes have added colorful accents with rugs and textiles. Outside in the garden, there are an arbor for climbing plants and hedges that give the cottage a sense of seclusion.

A similar atmosphere pervades the old stone house where the writer Zai Whitaker lives. The cottage, part of an old missionary compound, has an enclosed front porch with a potbelly stove, a warm room that Whitaker has furnished with her desk, bookshelves, and a few comfortable chairs for friends. Sun filters in through old-fashioned, small-paned cottage windows as she serves tea and cakes she has baked. Beyond this cozy porch are dark, high-ceilinged rooms not very easy to warm in this cold climate, she said. Whitaker, who teaches English as a second language at the Kodaikanal International School, has written a guide to the town as well as a novel, *Up the Ghat Road*, and a book about the work of her herpetologist husband, Romulus Whitaker, called *Snake Man*. Romulus Whitaker, an American who became an Indian citizen, lives on the Coromandel coast south of Madras with his reptiles; she stays in the hills with her books.

Zai Whitaker is gloomy about the future of Kodaikanal, where she said the long walks she loved were no longer possible and the silence of her lakeside compound was often shattered by the entertainment at the town's largest hotel, the Carlton, a concrete extravaganza that filled the lakeside site where a smaller old hotel by the same name once stood. I knew what she meant; I was staying at the Carlton because I love hotels and wanted to sample what tourists came here to enjoy. The night I arrived, a cricket-equipment convention was in full swing, and a long green carpet with a wicket at one end stretched across the lobby. Grown men were running around in various stages of intoxication or hyperventilation with fluorescent green orbs attached to their shirts. Those not wearing them were pursued by a fellow with a plastic bag full of the things, glowing like freak limes out of science fiction. There was a lot of noise, even before the music started. At the reception desk, a fussy, frazzled clerk insisted I pay for bed and full board, although I didn't want to eat there.

The Carlton gets frequent complaining calls from Zai Whitaker, she said, but her protests have limited effect. Calling the police is not much help. When she had her house burglarized, the policeman who came to inspect the damage stole the valuable fountain pen on her desk, which the thieves had overlooked. Whitaker, who was working on another novel about Kodaikanal when we met, said that the price of property has been rising so quickly, beginning in the 1980s, that local people can no longer afford to buy even a small piece of land. This, plus the tourist influx, has changed the character of the town.

It is hard for an outsider to say, "Wait, it may not be that bad." I found more to like about Kodaikanal than in some other hills stations. I had walked the length of the golf course past a dense virgin woodland called a *shola*, from which wild buffalo emerge at night to drink at a stream crossing a fairway. I had strolled along the lake just after dawn and seen the fifty-mile view at night from the Arulmigukurinji Andavar Temple on its lone hilltop outside of town. I had been driven into the surrounding hills to meet a reclusive artist one day and eat at a homestyle Italian restaurant in a farmhouse overlooking meadows the next. This unlikely trattoria, run by an Italian settled here with his Indian wife, had only a few tables, and meals were ordered a day or more in advance to be cooked to order. I had met people like Zai Whitaker and an energetic couple, Girija and M. S. Viraraghavan, who are very active in the Palni Hills Conservation Council, with its range of projects to reverse ecological destruction. In Kodaikanal a lot of people seemed aware that the environment was threatened and wanted to do something, despite a political and commercial atmosphere not generally friendly to their cause.

Yet even a visitor who sees a hill station more or less intact cannot ignore the busloads of tourists arriving on weekends for a few hectic hours of taking in the sights: Pile out for a bit of breakfast—some do their own cooking and dump their garbage right on the lake shore, which is also used as a communal bath and toilet—and then back on the bus for a five-mile spin out to Pillar Rocks, three granite cliffs 400 feet tall, obscured only by the roadside vendors selling cheap souvenirs and all manner of snacks. Take a few photos and back on the bus to Suicide Point (now Green Valley View), where there are more vendors, begging monkeys, and a sign announcing euphemistically in three languages that "Mocking of Ladies Is Punishable." More photos. Then maybe another meal and it's time to return to the plains on a lurching bus that will (with the help of the greasy fast food) make a number of them miserably sick on the way home.

At the height of the tourist season, which is at its peak from late March through June, an astonishing 10,000 people may be visiting Kodai on any given day, some residents say, nearly doubling the year-round population. The narrow roads are choked and the lakefront is ringed by their dented and dusty coaches. Most will not stay overnight; they don't have the money and the town hasn't got the beds. Conservationists are not insensitive to these day-trippers. They recognize the great social and economic progress in India that the boom in tourism signifies. At the Kodaikanal International School, Nancy Garrison, then acting deputy principal, reminded me that Thomas Cook got his start selling day tours to Britons. Indians were always great travelers in their own country, she said. Trains have been full since the moment the British built the railways. Millions of Indians believe life is not complete without pilgrimages to great religious sites, and even the elderly make punishing journeys to complete the circuit before death. Now that there are nearly a billion Indians, the numbers of tourists on the roads and in the hills can only mushroom on a horrific scale. The problem is management.

"The health of the hills is the wealth of the plains," said M. S. Viraraghavan, when he and his wife, Girija, came to lunch at the Kandaswamy home. The Viraraghavans settled in Kodaikanal when he decided to retire early from India's administrative service and dabble in horticulture. They are not only among the leading environmentalists of the Palnis but also successful breeders of roses. Mass tourism worries them if it means more ecological change. "Not hurting farmers on the plains must be more important than the rights of tourists," Viraraghavan said. To illustrate his concern, he noted that in only eight years between two surveys made by India's National Remote Sensing Agency in 1972 and 1980, the Kodaikanal region had lost 25 percent of its forest cover. These tropical forests, Viraraghavan said, do not regenerate as easily as temperate forests, and they are being leveled for tourist development on top of the damage caused by the introduction of water-guzzling trees during the colonial period. The blue-gum eucalyptus, for example, was used in Australia for draining swamps; the British brought it here as an ornamental tree. Other trees were introduced for industrial use, such as the wattle for viscose. Grasslands in the hills also retain water, though more briefly, before sending it on to the lower elevations. But the grasslands that remain in the Palnis are now almost entirely given over to commercial agriculture, which consumes virtually all the available water for crops.

Ecologically, Kodaikanal Lake, Viraraghavan said, is also in very bad shape. Two luxury hotels, the notorious Carlton and the sprawling Sterling Resort, dumped raw sewage into the lake before a citizens' protest forced them to treat it. But even treated sewage is not free of the nutrients that feed algae. Sooner or later, eutrophy—the loss of oxygen—sets in. That is where Kodai Lake was when I saw it. The Palni Hills Conservation Council sends local schoolchildren out in boats to monitor the water quality in the hope of broadening public awareness. A lack of awareness, I recalled—or maybe it was a case of profit over preservation—caused Srinagar's Dal Lake in Kashmir to die years ago, weighted down with the sewage of several thousand houseboats. Only a guerrilla war for Kashmiri independence may, ironically, save it by scaring off tourists for long enough to allow the lake to return to life.

Back at the Carlton, I was delivered a lesson in appreciation by the staff. My $55 room, I was told, could have gone for as much as $400 a night by India's newly inflated standards, so I should be lucky there was a vacancy. The Carlton, however, was not an Oberoi. There were too many rough edges here. I wouldn't call the room totally clean. I sent back the hairy pillow cases. The bathroom towels may have been washed, but just. They were stained and had an unpleasant smell. Breakfast at the Carlton reminded me of a brilliant if brutal essay by Duncan Fallowell in the London *Spectator* of August 9, 1975. Writing about Ooty, Fallowell, whose visit became tangled on all manner of thorny impediments, reached the sad conclusion, "This country never gives what you expect." At the Carlton, instead of the sumptuous breakfast by the garden, there were significantly stained tablecloths on the breakfast buffet table in the indifferently designed dining room. But did I notice the stains because so little food was where it should have been? When the dishes arrived a little behind schedule, they were depressingly familiar to anyone who has done time in innumerable bed-and-breakfast houses (not inns) in England: pasty oatmeal, limp cereal, and baked beans (toast on request). The waiters, as always in India, fussed over male guests—a throwback to the sahib-raj? No one mentioned that there were dosa or eggs for those who wanted them. I ordered a bottle of water and asked that it be put on my bill. The waiters had written down my room number, since no one gets to sit still for more than a minute without being accosted by someone wanting to be sure you belong. Then why, I wondered, when I was back in my room writing, with a "Do Not Disturb" sign on the door, was someone pounding away, shouting that I did not sign for the water I took? Not much class here.

What saves the Carlton is the lake, which glittered in the sun across the lawn from the terrace outside my room. On the lake shore, the town (and the hotel itself) is forgotten, at least on weekdays. Except for the odd motor scooter buzz or the whine of a bus horn drifting down from town, all is birdsong. The air is clarity itself. Tourists are warned repeatedly, almost proudly, about the dangerous sunburn the thin air can foster at this altitude. From my room, I could see the ponies forming up under the sign that says "Horse Riding Hire Particulars." The rates for rides in every direction are very specifically stated, followed by a warning painted in red capital letters that "extortion of money is punishable."

A short walk from the Carlton is the Seven Roads Junction, where a turn to the near right leads to the Kodaikanal Club, still known as the English Club, apparently to distinguish itself from American organizations. We all combed the library here on my behalf and found it adequate for short stories, novels, and mysteries but devoid of history about the club or the town. The club has a number of forlorn, spartan lounges. The TV room seemed the liveliest place, with rows of gray plastic chairs arrayed for the likes of a cinema audience. There is great cocoa and tea to be had at the club, an agreeable place for conversation. Photographs and plaques on the walls of the Kodaikanal Club and the Golf Club tell the story of the gradual replacement of one elite, foreign, by another, Indian. The transition was civil and predated independence in Kodai. In 1942, Captain B. R. Dorai, the rajah of Pudukottah, was the first Indian elected president of the Kodaikanal Club. The last Englishman, J. Shackleton, served in 1962–1963.

In a sense the transition is still going on, as the generation of Indian gentlemen who slipped effortlessly into the postcolonial social leadership retire or die. Sitting outside the Golf Club in the morning sun, I watched the rich young men—never women—of the next generation come and go from the fairways, dressed in the latest and most expensive clothes, fine leather golfing gloves, and the best studded golfing shoes. They are self-confident, sometimes arrogant and dismissive, as they deal with their caddies or the boys who serve the coffee or cold drinks. They were born when colonialism was already history, so no one could accuse them of mimicking the sahibs.

Still, Kodai had a good feel about it, much more so because at every corner there were those watching its every change, blowing whistles to sound alarms. Ooty is another story, I was told again and again. Ooty is held over Kodai as the specter of what can happen if those who care about a hill station let down their guard or retreat behind walls. When I spoke with Nora Mitchell, now retired in London, about what she thinks of Kodai three decades later, she said she worries "that it will go the way of Ooty." The Viraraghavans, monitoring the environment day to day, know exactly what she meant.

"All the orchids in the Nilgiris forests around Ooty have been eliminated," M. S. Viraraghavan said.

The combination of emissions and drying out of the woodlands eliminate orchids first, then the ferns. Many species of plants in the Western Ghats have been drastically reduced. In Kodai, 60 percent of the land is still forest, and a lot of it is protected government land. Forests have a stabilizing effect, even when they are the wrong kind of forest, the wrong kind of trees. But Ooty—I shed tears over how badly ravaged it is. One hates to say it, but I think Ooty is beyond redemption.

And so I left Kodai, down the other side of the hills to the town of Palani, past more Jesus graffiti, to have a look at Ooty. Or Ootacamund, as the British knew it. Or Udagamandalam in its latest incarnation. The trip down from Kodai has certainly improved since 1933, when Father C. Leigh, a Jesuit, did it on foot. He arrived "after untold difficulties, the feet wounded, the temples throbbing, the body jarred in every nerve." Cicadas and noisy waterfalls taxed his brain as he stumbled along, "taking care not to sprain an ankle, or trip on the loose jagged stones, or go too far and shoot headlong into the abyss." And then, plodding out of miles of the furnace heat of a gorge, he hit the "torrid plain." I did it a lot quicker by road, but arrived in Ooty in about the same condition, sans cicadas and waterfall damage.

In the southern hill stations, imported air-conditioned cars were still a distant luxury, so I made the trip in a kind of Indian station wagon with the windows open. The road journey of about 120 miles from Kodai to Ooty, which took more than seven hours, dipped down to the plains and passed by the city of Coimbatore to Mettupalayam, at the foot of the Nilgiri Hills. Until I made that trip from hill station to hill station, I thought people who warned me about breathing in India today were exaggerating. I had lived there several years not so long ago with no apparent ill effects. But at the end of that day, I had absorbed enough fumes, dust, and whatever else pollutes the Indian air (perhaps as in Mexico City, it is dried fecal matter) to give me a respiratory infection it took weeks and a ticket out of India to cure.

After Palani, a big town with a well-known Hindu temple and a raucous, prosperous business life, the road toward Coimbatore crosses flat agricultural land. There were grazing cattle herds, some tobacco farming, and plantations of a palm grown for the lumber of its tall, slender trunk. I saw prosperous towns with huge new textile plants. India has lately been fighting for greater access to Western markets for its textiles, and there is an irony in this. In the nineteenth century, textile imports from Lancashire mills flooded colonial India, wiping out weaving in a number of places. Indians then had no right or power to put up the kind of barriers Europeans now erect against them.

The climb to Ooty does not begin until about twenty-five miles from the town, and the road is one of the best to any Indian hill station. Improvements were going on, among them widening of the road and building new parapets along dangerous edges. Traffic was heavy for an off-season weekday. Still, there were stretches of deep green jungle, with vines, ferns, bamboo, and flowers. Tea plantations suddenly appeared at Coonoor, a hill station in its own right, with a skyline of church steeples above piles of concrete baking in the sun. No Jesus graffiti on this secular route. But there were a couple of other exhortations: "Speed is a five-letter word. So is the death," followed a few miles later by the mysterious "Speed is a five-letter word. So is the life." Reasonably large industries in this area make both Coonoor and Ooty more commercial and businesslike than many other hill stations. I passed a needle factory and a cordite plant near Coonoor. Ooty has Hindustan Photographic Films.

Just outside Ooty, a developer has raped a mountainside to spawn the Royal Castle time-share flats, a glaring white incongruous pile of cheap ornamentation over third world cement. That apart, Ooty looked pretty wonderful at the end of that journey, environmental warnings to the contrary. Especially welcoming was the Savoy Hotel, which India's Taj group has made comfortable without sacrificing any of its style or history. Trellised doorways, white wicker, flower beds, birds, and lunch in the sunny front garden are all there to be enjoyed, as they must always have been. The Savoy Hotel is hill station life the way it should be. Each room is a cottage opening out to a lawn, and cottages are grouped into clusters with names: Villa Flora, Iris Cottage, the Chalet, Sunny Side. My little home had a tiny front parlor, a big bedroom, and a spacious old bath. There was both a working fireplace and satellite television. I watched Bill Clinton's 1997 State of the Union address live. Outside, shrill British voices—Home Counties tourists?—kept the past alive.

Little in Ooty's neighborhood escaped the attention of the British, who had made Ootacamund the official sanitarium of the Madras presidency by 1827 and an official summer capital later. The rolling hills over which Ooty and its 80,000 or more people are now spread were wrested from Tipu Sultan, the heroic ruler of Mysore, who was defeated in 1799 at the historic battle of Sringapatnam. The collapse of Tipu Sultan's sustained resistance to foreign domination opened new territories to the East India Company in South India, just as the defeat of the Nepali Gurkhas had in the north, making the establishment of Simla, Mussoorie, Darjeeling, and other hill stations possible in the Himalayan foothills.

In the South, the Nilgiris, literally Blue Mountains, were inhabited by several indigenous peoples, among them Badagas, Kotas, Kurumbas, and Todas. The Badagas were pastoral herdsmen, according to local accounts; the Kotas were known for their craftsmanship and the Kurumbas for their skills at sorcery. But the group that has attracted the most interest from Indian and foreign anthropologists are the Todas, whose thatched village huts known as *mund*s were thought to have given Ootacamund its first modern name. This may be a myth, like so much about the indigenous peoples of the Nilgiris. Sir Frederick Price, writing a history of Ooty in 1908, confidently ascribed the name of the town to the Badaga people. Price was a refreshing and comprehensive myth buster. He also did not believe that John Sullivan, the British Collector of Coimbatore, was the initial discoverer and founder of Ooty, though most people before and since continue to say so.

Sullivan was certainly the first European householder in what was then a place called something akin to Wotokymund, according to Paul Hockings, a British anthropologist who more than likely knows more about Ooty's history than any Indian scholar. A census taken in 1821, two years before Sullivan's house was finished, listed only 222 Todas, 317 Kotas, and 3,778 Badagas in residence. Hockings credited Sullivan, the son of a Persian translator and negotiator also in East India Company service, with a natural instinct for development and an unusually respectful and helpful attitude toward the indigenous people of the Nilgiris.

Sullivan also generously augmented his own salary over the years by building and renting properties to East India Company convalescents, and it got him into some trouble, but that is another story. Though he may have exploited his employer, he did not abuse the local people who lived in the way of his grand designs for the Nilgiri Hills. Instead, he introduced them to modern agriculture, protected their land rights, and demanded compensation for them when grazing lands were given to British settlers. Although Sullivan was largely successful at promoting Ooty as a sanitarium and agricultural experimentation station, he suffered repeated tragedies in his personal life. His wife and two or three of their children died there, more evidence for skeptics who doubted the health-giving promises of the hills.

Among the indigenous people, the Todas' unique language and their religion, based around their herds of milk-producing buffalo and the dairies that are revered as temples, have made them especially fascinating to outsiders since these people were first encountered by a Portuguese priest early in the seventeenth century. A legend grew up asserting that the Todas were a lost tribe of Syrian Christians. The formidable Helena Blavatsky, a founder of Theosophy, was among those who pursued the stories of the hill people of the Nilgiris and rhapsodized over the glorious landscape they inhabited, where "eternal spring reigns." Blavatsky did have a tendency to get carried away. She exclaimed how after a shower "everything on these summits seems to be born for the very first time." But that's not far off the mark. Such a vivid taste of unspoiled nature is an even rarer delight in India now.

Like indigenous hill people almost everywhere in Asia, the original inhabitants of the Nilgiris are now mostly marginalized. But more has perhaps been written about them than many other people in similar circumstances around other hill stations, and their presence in local history is bizarrely safeguarded: They have become tourist attractions. A model village is preserved for visitors at the edge of town and quite a number of shops tout tribal crafts. One forlorn little hut rests uneasily in the Botanical Garden, where souvenirs are sold when it is open.

Ooty's churches were built very early in this hill station's life. St. Stephen's, most famous as a landmark near the center of the official quarter of town, was ready for worshippers in 1832, more than half a century ahead of the Ooty Gymkhana's decision to lay out polo grounds. The church provided the town a lot of unintended entertainment, Price told us in *Ootacamund: A History*. St. Stephen's was a hotbed of parish politics from the day the doors opened, perhaps reflecting the officious nature of the town. Every renovation, the placement of an organ, the handling and disbursement of offerings from the collection plates—they all provoked prolonged and acrimonious arguments. In 1867, a bold vicar scandalized the conservative congregation by introducing a new hymn book, *Hymns Ancient and Modern*, which was replacing the Islington hymnal among Anglicans at home. On a Sunday morning soon after, an enraged lay trustee marched toward the altar, threw his copy of the offending hymn book into the baptismal font, and stormed out of the church. The choir resigned en masse.

The cemetery behind St. Stephen's Church was filled to overflowing and closed to further burials in 1881; a cholera epidemic in the late 1870s had contributed to the overcrowding. Burials thereafter took place at St. Thomas Cemetery some distance away, where the sign says simply: "At the going down of the sun and in the morning we will remember them." At St. Stephen's the old graveyard is now dank and densely tangled in grasses and vines that make deciphering the tombstones of empire difficult. But inside the church is a plaque collector's paradise. Apart from the memorial to the unfortunate Lieutenant Colonel Ouchterlony, who fell to a jungle fever, there is the tribute to the Reverend William Sawyer, "who having laboured with diligence and zeal for six years as a missionary to the heathen at Madras died in the faithful discharge of his duties as chaplain of this station." That was 1832, and he was only thirty-five years old. Then there was Richard William Preston, captain in the First Bombay Grenadiers, who in 1895 "drowned in the Kromund River while out hunting with the Ootacamund Hounds." Given the rather more horrendous forms of death that stalked India, his epitaph concluded rather lamely: "Thy will be done." In the absence of foxes, incidentally, the hounds chased jackals.

St. Stephen's, in its quiet garden flanked with flowers, looks across sternly at the red-brick Collector's office, library, and courts that still anchor the official town. The Ootacamund Club was not far away, and around it were scattered the white-trimmed terracotta bungalows of the Raj, bearing bosky, genteel names. A list of residences in 1905 includes The Cedars, Birdwood, Glenburn, The Laurels, Ivy Bank, Apple Cottage, Primrose House, and, most intriguing, Hopeful Cottage. A gingerbread palace, now the Fernhill Hotel, was built by the maharaja of Mysore. And of course there was the Savoy. All this comprised the snootiest of Snooty Ooty, and St. Stephen's has not forgotten its place in that world. When I asked the church caretaker whether services were now in Tamil as well as

English, he recoiled. "Oh, no," he replied and pointed to a smaller chapel across the road. "Tamil is over there."

It appears that just about anyone with literary credentials in the British Empire came to Ooty—or felt free to comment about it even without seeing this widely known hill station. It became a very worldly place in many ways and manages to maintain a certain cosmopolitan air today. Not everybody liked Ooty, of course. Sir Richard Burton, the nineteenth-century explorer and scholar, trashed the place. "Is there a theater, a concert room, a tennis, racket or fives court? No, and again No!" he wrote. "Then pray, what is there?" Thomas Babington Macauley could answer that question. "Such beautiful English rain," he wrote of his monsoon visit. "Such delicious English mud."

More than 125 years later, the British journalist James Cameron, noting that Sir Edward Lear had compared Ooty with the Surrey town of Leatherhead, ventured that it was more like "an embryonic East Grinstead," with its gabled suburban Victorian villas. "One knew without looking that behind the mock-leaded windows would be chintz and cretonne, and doubtless ceramic ducks," he wrote. Cameron was astounded to discover in 1971 that the Indian establishment had picked up where the Raj left off. Gardens were still cultivated in English style. Military officers sitting under hunting scenes and views of England regaled each other over billiards with phrases like "jolly good show." That gentleman's army is less in evidence now, a quarter century later, after bruising confrontations with Indian separatists on restive frontiers and an ill-planned venture into Sri Lanka in the late 1980s. But the formal demeanor of an Indian officer class still bred in old traditions has not totally disappeared. The Indian officer corps at its most polished is a very impressive collection.

Malcolm Muggeridge, who spent holidays in Ooty in the waning days of the British Empire, could also not resist comparing this proper British hill station to the Home Counties when he described the clattering arrival at church of the British governor of Madras. "His grey frock-coat and topper somehow failed to suggest majesty, reminding me more of a Worshipful Mayor than an Excellency," Muggeridge observed. "The Indian princes at least had better props and costumes; highnesses all, and sometimes Serene ones, with their jewels and elephants and dancing girls and dusky, self-indulgent faces, they belonged to the Indian scene, whereas the Governor seemed to have strayed out of Croydon Town Hall."

Then a teacher at a Christian college, Alwaye, in Kerala, Muggeridge boarded in Ooty with a pious benefactor named Miss Hopwood, who sub-

sidized the vacations of missionaries by charging a pittance for accommodation. In return, the boarders were expected to participate in acts of worship beginning with prayers at breakfast, when all would kneel by their
chairs amid the toast crumbs. Except for the occasional bishop, Miss Hopwood's guests, Muggeridge found, tended to be "wild American evangelists
ready at the drop of a hat to show lantern slides of their work among head-
hunters on the Burmese frontier; tough maiden ladies who had travelled
prodigious distances in bullock carts, and live in remote places among fero-
cious tribesmen; stubborn fundamentalists who had acquired immense
erudition through translating the Bible into obscure vernaculars."

On the whole, however, Ooty entertained more socialites than servants
of the Lord. It was, moreover, a base for tea planters from the surrounding
hills who would come to town now and then for a little club life and the
company of Europeans. As in Malaya, planters around Ooty were known
for crossing racial divides to ease their lonely lives on the plantations.
Sometimes they were also a little rough cut, adding to the exotic image
that could be publicly condemned while secretly admired by the ladies
and gentlemen of Ooty as they went from party to party without so much
as a frisson of other excitement. Military officers were always in abundance, to judge from Cameron's accounts and memoirs of the colonial era.
There was a major British military base nearby at Wellington as well as
the usual complement of men at arms needed for ceremonial purposes at
official hill stations. And since Ooty had been founded as a sanitarium,
convalescent officers and troops were always part of the mix.

Because Ooty proper is spread out over a large area, as hill stations go, it
is still possible to get a sense of the town in walks and rides on the bilious
little scooter taxis that have migrated here from lowland cities. The
process of following the footprints of history can begin even earlier, down
on the plains, with the small blue-and-ivory train that has been carrying
passengers up from Mettupalayam since the early twentieth century. On a
journey of just over four hours, the train passes through Coonoor, with a
picturesque station, before reaching Ooty, where donkeys sometimes have
to be shooed off the tracks. It carries real commuters, students and workers going to and from home, as well as tourists, making it less a theme
park ride than it might otherwise have become.

Ooty's lake has deteriorated badly. It seemed all but dry in large patches
when I saw it in February, still months away from the monsoon rains. The
contrast with Kodaikanal was stark. The shrinking of the lake has been in
progress for a long time, however. In 1908 Sir Frederick Price included in

his history of Ootacamund pictures from 1875 and 1905 that showed that much of the lake had already been filled in for development. Boating was no longer as pleasurable and had declined considerably. At the commercial center of town, crowded shopping streets have now added all the confusion, cacophony, and squalor of bigger towns. Price thought the streets were "filthy" as early as the turn of the twentieth century.

But there is more to Ooty. Past Charing Cross, where the town traditionally began after the ascent from the plains, is the spacious Botanical Garden, one of the finest public parks to be found in any hill station, though its plant collection seemed a little meager, a not uncommon problem in today's straitened times. Families roam the lawns, bundled in hats and scarves against weather that is downright balmy to those of us from temperate climates. Parties of schoolchildren and groups of teenagers cavort on the grass, taking pictures of one another with their inexpensive locally made cameras, a sign of new affluence among the children and the proliferation of consumer goods industries. More formal are the honeymoon couples being recorded by professional photographers, now and then on video. In India, that stock character of a resort town, the untutored itinerant photographer with his ancient camera, may soon be facing hard times.

I spent most of my days in Ooty around the cluster of official buildings, a short scooter ride from the gate of the Savoy, on Sylk's Road. The Savoy was once Sylk's Hotel and before that Dawson's Hotel, which opened in 1841. What is now the main building, with a dark, tapestried dining room and an open-air reception area, was built in 1829 as a school. Its ceiling beams, like those of St. Stephen's, were hauled up by elephant from Tipu Sultan's palace. The Savoy is such a faithful period piece that it is used as a backdrop for films about the Raj. In fact, a local guidebook titled *The Nilgris* says that no place in India is used so often as a cinematic backdrop as Ootacamund.

My goal was usually the Nilgiri Library, a private institution in a marvelously ornate gothic structure resting on an overgrown patch of green space up the hill from the Collector's office and St. Stephen's Church. The library and the church face each other across a small sea of red brick that fills the dip between them. This little neighborhood has not lost its aura of authenticity. There is Mohan's departmental store, with remarkably (if unintentionally) old-fashioned-looking wares displayed in wood-framed glass cases. Nearby is Higginbotham's bookstore, a cool cavern of volumes of every imaginable kind: bloodthirsty stories from Hindu mythology for children, the latest novels, and new reprints of valuable old gazetteers and histories, along with maps and guidebooks. Higginbotham's sits in its own dusty compound away from the street and, for India, empty. In a country where every available centimeter of commercial space soon sprouts the carts and makeshift stalls of vendors, this patch was more than quaint.

The private Nilgiri Library, in its spacious though unkempt grounds—not to be confused with the public library closer to Higginbotham's—was also uncrowded if not empty most days. Its chapellike reading room was big and airy, its massive wooden tables covered with periodicals from around the world. Big, comfortable chairs invited reading. The books I needed were locked in a cabinet in full view of Sandia Kumar and Daphne Samson, the librarians. A trustworthy but slow-moving retainer was available to send away for photocopying somewhere in town the pages I selected from the most cherished volumes.

One of the sequestered books was Molly Panter-Downes's classic *Ooty Preserved*, a work out of print and no longer found in stores. Like other classic books on Nilgiri life and history, it had become an endangered species. Panter-Downes (who paid five rupees to become a library member in the 1960s; I paid twenty) described in great detail the very room in which I sat to read her book. I looked around. It was almost all still in place: five tall arched windows, eight rectangular tables, the comfortable chairs. The moth-eaten mounted heads of a bisonlike wild gaur and a stag still watched over us. Only the portraits of Queen Elizabeth II and Prince Philip, the Duke of Edinburgh, are gone, along with the English ladies Panter-Downes observed as they dropped in to gossip before tea. Of course, the reader's right to browse freely among the enticing volumes on the shelves had also vanished.

I didn't know until much later, when I returned to New York, that Mollie Panter-Downes, long a correspondent in Britain for the *New Yorker*, had died in London barely two weeks before I sat down in a big leather chair to read her *Ooty Preserved*. Her spirit was certainly still alive at the Nilgiri Library. Every mention of her book brings instantly to mind its agreeable reading room.

Leaving Ooty by car for Bangalore, I found pleasant surprises. We passed through the Mudumalai Wildlife Sanctuary, which, with the Bandipur Tiger Reserve, Nagarhole National Park, and Wynaad National Park, form one of the largest protected woodland areas in India. Mudumalai is on a high plateau, with tall grass and teak forests where the gaur lives among tigers and panthers, bears and hyenas. These animals are elusive and require hours of patient watching and waiting to sight. But even just passing through, I saw herds of spotted deer and elephants coming out of the jungle to visit a feeding station. There are rest houses for human guests, and elephant or jeep safaris for better animal watching. The jungle animals of India are under tremendous strain from human over-population and loss of water holes and natural food supplies. Wildlife and wild places always seem more precarious here than in Africa.

But that said, the drive through Mudumalai was delightful, and the scenery all along the route out of Ooty—at least until Mysore loomed—was enthralling. Long stretches of road passed under canopies formed by giant banyan trees. In some places these old sheltering friends had been gravely wounded, their branches hacked away for wood and their attempts to throw down new roots from the branches above—the banyan's special trick—thwarted. Elsewhere, they had been left alone or even cared for. I later read in *India Today* that a woman in Karnataka, the state we were passing through, had been given a National Citizens' Award for looking after no fewer than more than 280 banyans along three kilometers of country road for more than forty years. Her name was Thimmakka, and she was born low-caste. She calls the trees her children, and recalled how she first covered her saplings with thorny branches to keep away ax-wielding villagers and tree-climbing youngsters bent on destruction. Environmentalism in India is not the sole preserve of the middle class.

And then came Bangalore and another Indian reality. Bangalore, not too long ago a graceful city with extraordinary public architecture, shady streets, civilized shopping, and relaxing cafés, had become manic. I hardly recognized the city behind the forest of scaffolding as new buildings rose where trees once stood. The city center was in gridlock; the density of traffic and the level of noise would make Bangkok proud. My taxi, a plump little Ambassador, crawled, at last, to the airport—well behind schedule. Not to worry. The flight to Calcutta was at least three hours late.

4

✻

Sri Lanka's Tea Country

Nuwara Eliya

Schoolchildren climb the tea gardens of Kandipola

$\mathcal{S}$RI LANKA IS SO DIFFERENT from India in so many ways that one could easily be led to believe that this extraordinary island off the southeastern Indian coast had drifted to its mooring from some other place. The majority of its people are Buddhists, unique among South Asian nations, save for the distant Himalayan kingdom of Bhutan, where Tibetan-style Mahayana Buddhism is the state religion. A less colorfully extravagant, more scholarly Theravada Buddhism prevails in Lanka, and its holy sites, relics, monuments, and libraries draw Buddhists from Southeast Asia, Korea, and Japan. This is an island of unsurpassed beauty, from its beachfront coconut groves to hill roads with hedges draped in honeysuckle and morning glory to cool, gentle mountains carpeted in tea bushes. Shallow terraced rice fields flow lazily down its sloping valleys, looking like emerald rivers under a brilliant sun. A nineteenth-century writer called Ceylon, as it was known until 1972, "one huge tropical garden." Its people are, on the whole, more literate than their neighbors and correctly old-fashioned in their manners. In the morning, the street cleaners in quiet residential neighborhoods of the seaside capital, Colombo, sweep away more fragrant fallen flowers than trash. "Dear me, it is beautiful!" Mark Twain exclaimed when his ship reached Ceylon during a voyage around the world in the 1890s. More than a century later, an arriving airline passenger descending over velvet mountains and quilts of coconut plantations and pineapple patches might well say something very similar.

Of course no country or its history can be free of ironies and paradoxes, and here they are so shocking that they have to be confronted without delay. In this earthly paradise that Arab traders called Serendip, "a pleasant surprise," ethnic rebellions and the savage retaliations they engendered, both distinguished by mindless brutalities, have killed and maimed tens of thousands of people, warped a generation of youth, and all but robbed a centuries-old civilization of its traditional gentility and repose. Terrorism seems always to lurk around the corner, even when periods of peace prevail. One might wonder why, given this uneasy environment, tourists have been flocking here. The grand old hotels of Nuwara Eliya, the hill station high in the central mountains, are often besieged by more visitors than they can handle. Perhaps one explanation is that there are some countries so hauntingly beautiful that their sins are tolerated or overlooked, if not forgiven, like the misbehavior of attractive and clever people. For more than a century, travelers have made much of the second stanza of a missionary hymn by the Reverend Reginald Heber, which seemed to suggest its people were the island's fatal flaw. In 1819, promoting vigorous conversion in a hymn known to generations of Protestant churchgoers in the West as "From Greenland's Icy Mountains," he wrote:

> *What though the spicy breezes*
> *Blow soft o'er Ceylon's isle,*
> *Though ev'ry prospect pleases,*
> *And only man is vile. . . .*

The problem with reading too much into the opinion of the good Mr. Heber, who went on to become bishop of Calcutta a few years later, is that he had never been to Ceylon when he composed his complaint about the recalcitrant heathen who "bows down to wood and stone." Wood and stone could hardly be considered a description of the country's magnificent temples and religious art. Mark Twain, who was critical of missionaries—and annoyed at how their schools forced the lithe bodies of little local children into awkward Western clothes—made a point of accentuating the positive in Heber's verse. In the book he wrote of his round-the-world lecture tour, *Following the Equator*, Mark Twain found the line about spicy breezes very evocative of a place he thought was wrapped in "tropic deliciousness." Ignoring the blinkered missionary's condemnation of the heathen, Twain was taken by the people, the formality and propriety of life and felt in his bones that this was truly an exotic Oriental land.

Mark Twain never got to the hill station of Nuwara Eliya, which is endlessly and boringly described as a bit of England, as if that were all there was to it. To be fair, Nuwara Eliya, the "city of light," is a relative newcomer to the map of a nation whose origins are lost in mythology. Legends about Sri Lanka's past abound. Did Ptolemy, the ancient Greek geographer, first map the island and mistake its Mahaweli River for the Ganges? Is the port of Galle the Tarshish of King Solomon's time? Did Adam, cast out of Paradise, really take his first step on earth on the peak that bears his name? Or could that giant footprint belong to the Lord Shiva? Or the Buddha? So real is the Ramayana story to many South Asians that the contemporary nation of Sri Lanka is still the Lanka of old, where the evil king Ravana, having stolen the flawless Sita, wife of the Indian prince Rama, hid her in a cave in the hill country. One of Nuwara Eliya's waterfalls is named for Ravana, who is believed to have bathed in its cascade, and visitors to the botanical garden at Kakgala are told this was once his outdoor pleasure palace, as if he had been a historical figure.

Sri Lanka's history has a fabulous quality about it even in verifiable, recorded time. By the first century A.D., hydraulic engineers with a level of knowledge unprecedented in the region had created vast reservoirs and irrigation systems that were a wonder of their age. Devout Buddhist monarchs commissioned soaring stupas they called *dagoba*s, some as large as Egyptian pyramids, to be erected at their holy city of Anuradhapura by the second century. Overpowering, mammoth statuary made another early cultural and political center, Polonnaruwa, one of the world's great monuments to Buddhism. Deep in Sri Lanka's classical history can be found the first chapters in the sad, long-running conflict between Tamils and Sinhala people, which erupted again in our time with such renewed ferocity. The majority Sinhalese, largely Buddhist and of northern Indian origins, and the Tamil minority living around Jaffna, mostly Hindus who came from South India, have been battling over this Indian Ocean island for 2,000 years.

By the time the first Europeans arrived—the Portuguese in 1505—there were numerous regional kingdoms, but a great deal of royal power was concentrating in a Buddhist monarchy based in Kandy, far from the coast and very hard to reach. The pale Portuguese were an odd sight. A spy sent by the king of Kotte, a once powerful ruler now reduced to controlling little more than a city-state near the coast, reported back that the intruders wore metal hats and coats, ate what looked like hunks of stone, and drank blood. Because commerce seemed to be what the Portuguese were looking for, the Kandyan court saw no harm at first in granting Portugal, which already had a port in Indian Goa, the right to land and establish a trading post on the shores of Ceylon. Later Portugal brazenly added fortifications that became the heart of old Colombo, but this caused no undue panic. When the Portuguese turned their attention inland, however, and began to harass Kandy, the Kandyans made common cause with the Dutch, who were happy to help disrupt Portugal's commerce and stop its imperial expansion.

The Portuguese were finally displaced by the Dutch in the seventeenth century, but they left behind a series of ports around the island, its name of Ceilao or Ceylan, numerous Roman Catholic converts, and families with Iberian surnames that are still in common currency: De Silva, Rodrigo, and Fernando among them. The Dutch also were active missionaries, converting their share of Ceylonese to a Calvinist Protestantism while adding to the island's ethnic mix. The descendants of colonists from the Netherlands (along with other Europeans) became known as Dutch

Burghers, still a distinct though dwindling Sri Lankan ethnic group. A nineteenth-century traveler passing through Colombo on the way to the hills, seeing a lake "fringed with people of every hue," marveled at the diversity of the Ceylonese. Like the Portuguese, the Dutch were at first content to stay near the coast, building their sturdy homes, churches, courts, offices, and plantations in or around Colombo and a few other port towns. They were intent on dominating and virtually cornering the regional spice trade, especially in nutmeg and cinnamon, which grew wild and in great abundance on the island. One of Colombo's most fashionable residential neighborhoods, Cinnamon Gardens, was once an experimental spice plantation that tried but failed to tame the cinnamon tree. Ultimately, however, the Dutch too quarreled with Kandy. Britain was next.

The British, who defeated the Dutch at the end of the eighteenth century (here and in Europe) and made Ceylon a crown colony separate from India in 1802, finally brought down the Kandyan kingdom in 1815 and opened the way into the hills for Europeans. There was not general jubilation when this news reached London. The overthrow of the Ceylonese monarchy was berated by some, including members of Parliament, as having no purpose beyond an imperial urge for conquest. Henry Marshall, a British military doctor in Ceylon who wrote a history and description of the island in 1846, was harsh in his judgment of colonial behavior there and in neighboring India. "The doctrine of our right to seize a territory which suited us, provided we could only find an excuse for quarreling with those who ruled over it, has seldom been publicly avowed, however frequently it may have been acted upon," he wrote, accusing the British of maneuvering the downfall of the last Kandyan king by playing off rivalries and intrigues within his court. "But there seems to be a propensity in the Saxon race to seize or acquire the possessions of contiguous estates, without much reference to consistency, justice or good faith."

Marshall flatly rejected the notion that the last king, Sri Wickrema Raja Sinha, was a despot who had to be removed for the good of his people. He suggested that it would have been better to let the king "be judged by the standards of his own country." The thoughtful doctor could not resist describing the atrocities that civilized monarchs of Europe had been known to indulge in, lest a reader assume the superiority of European example. Sri Wickrema Raja Sinha died in Vellore, in southern India, in 1832. He had been a British prisoner for seventeen years, during which time British troops in Ceylon laid waste villages, crops, and people to pre-empt any moves to restore the monarchy and to put an end to lingering, sporadic rebellions against colonial rule. More than half a century later, the sentiments of Marshall seemed to echo in George Orwell's *Burmese Days*, when a fictional character, Flory, summed up British imperialism in Burma this way: "The official holds the Burman down while the business-man goes through his pockets."

The road most frequently traveled to Nuwara Eliya passes by Kandy, a city of 100,000 people that is still the Sri Lankan—or at least Sinhalese—cultural capital and a kind of lower-altitude hill station itself, at about 1,600 feet above sea level. The Kandy Road was one of Britain's first big engineering projects in Ceylon. Before the British arrived, there were no highways of any account anywhere on the island. Roads made controlling the population easier for the military. But road building also had other, more benign results, observed John Ferguson, a British resident of Colombo in the late nineteenth century. "As in India, so on a smaller scale in Ceylon, it is a recognized fact that there is no more effective preventa-tive of famine than internal means of communication, whether by road, rail, canal or navigable river," he wrote in 1887 in *Ceylon in the Jubilee Year.* (The jubilee was Queen Victoria's fiftieth year on the throne.) Ferguson was even more enraptured by the beneficial effects of railways, also built by the British.

"The railways in India and Ceylon are doing more in these modern days to level caste and destroy superstition than all the force of missionar-ies and schoolmasters," he concluded. By the time Ferguson wrote his ac-count of development in Ceylon, the British had constructed more than 3,000 miles of roads on the island, with dirt tracks "too numerous to men-tion" and more than 180 miles of railway. On an island 140 miles wide and 270 miles long, that was a fairly comprehensive transportation network, and Ferguson thought it a "great educator" of the Ceylonese people.

The Kandy Road opened the hill country to plantation crops, especially coffee, which the Dutch had tried, also unsuccessfully, to introduce in the lower coastal areas. It was evident early that coffee would do well in the hills around Kandy. But until there was a way to transport the crop to Colombo, there was little reason to plant coffee or anything else on a large scale. The Kandy Road solved that problem, and the economy of the hills began to grow rapidly. In 1832, the Reverend Miron Winslow, an Ameri-can missionary based in Jaffna who was on his way to Nuwara Eliya, noted a large coffee plantation where cocoa was also grown by an Eng-lishman, a Mr. Bird. Until a fungus devastated the coffee plantations in the 1870s—after which the planters turned to tea—the crop was a major money earner for the island and made a number of families rich. Most of the planters were British, but their coffee groves, warehouses, offices, and homes provided jobs for many Ceylonese in service industries and crafts. Thousands of additional laborers were recruited in South India to pick the crops and tend the fields. These Indian plantation workers established a second Tamil concentration on the island. Unrelated by history or caste to the Jaffna Tamils of northern Sri Lanka, traditional rivals of the Sinhalese, the later immigrants became known as Indian Tamils, and they still form the majority of the peaceful working population of the hill country.

Before the Kandy Road was built—a task that consumed more than five years, from 1820 to 1825, with paving added in 1843—it could take troops six weeks to march the seventy-odd miles to Kandy in single file through vine-snarled jungle, even with hundreds of coolies to hack open a path and to carry the gear. By the 1840s, mail coaches could make the trip in little more than twelve hours, though this service was short-lived because of the opening of a railway line from Colombo to the hills. Today, the drive along the two-lane road takes little more than two hours by car, though there is always so much to see that stopping along the way is a frequent temptation.

Over the years, I had made the trip a number of times and always found some new distraction. On this most recent visit an abundant pineapple crop lined both sides of a long stretch of the road with heaps of the fruit, graded by size. Large placards advertised the prices, so that drive-by competitive shopping was possible. The driver of my rented car, who like others had his favorite vendor, filled a burlap bag with fruit for his family and seemed to think I might want to do the same. Farther along, some villages specialize in cashews, cane furniture, baskets, musical instruments, flower pots, or king coconuts, though drivers seem to prefer shopping for those along the coast road down to Galle. Individuals sometimes come out to try their luck at assorted entertainments in the hope of raising a little cash, though far fewer of them than in India, where there is always somebody around hauling a burlap sack who wants to show you the cobra within. That's why I was taken aback to see a Sinhalese man and boy posing gamely for photographs with two enormous porcupines outfitted with leather harnesses and leashes. I couldn't resist.

A popular detour on the Kandy Road begins near the town of Kegalla, where a turn leads along a country lane to the elephant orphanage at Pinawella. Abandoned or injured baby elephants are raised at the orphanage to become work animals or temple mascots with ceremonial duties. Between towns and villages along the Kandy Road are those brilliant green rice fields and farmsteads that form one of the earth's most soothing landscapes. The area gets the benefit of two monsoons, from the northeast and the southwest, permitting two rice crops and all manner of other harvests year-round. The variety of trees and flowering plants has been noted by many visitors to the island over the centuries. Passing through one small village, my driver was on the lookout for a gigantic talipot tree that he heard was in full flower. He was as delighted as I to find it. This extraordinary palm, whose huge leaves were the umbrellas of the Sinhalese when the first Europeans arrived, towers above most other trees in this part of the country. It can live fifty or sixty years or longer, but in its lifetime each talipot produces only one huge yellow, crowning bloom up to twenty feet high, in effect announcing its impending demise. When the golden spray arrayed like fireworks atop the crown of leaves shrivels and dies, so does the tree.

Just before Kandy comes the hard choice of whether to detour into town or head directly to Nuwara Eliya, another couple of hours away and nearly 5,000 feet higher. Either way, there is much to see. Kandy is best known for the Temple of the Tooth near Kandy Lake, where Sri Lankans believe a tooth of Gautama Buddha, smuggled to fourth-century Lanka in the hair of an Orissan princess from India, is stored away in multiple caskets of precious metals. Once a year, for two weeks in August, a replica of the Tooth Relic's *dagoba*-shaped container (it is considered too risky nowadays to bring out the real thing, whether or not what's inside is indeed Buddha's tooth) is paraded through the streets of Kandy in one of Asia's most spectacular festivals, the Esala Perahera. Dozens of elephants robed in brilliantly colored and gilded caparisons (some illuminated by strings of electric lights) march in procession through the town, accompanied by classical dancers, folk entertainers, and officials of the temple. One special elephant bears the golden canopy sheltering the symbolic Tooth Relic. When the festival is over, Kandy returns to its normal life as a relatively quiet and pleasant city in the hills, rich in museums, temples, monasteries, and the occasional church and stately bungalow.

The through road to Nuwara Eliya also has its temptations. About four miles from Kandy is Peradeniya, the home of Sri Lanka's largest and most highly regarded institution of higher education, the University of Peradeniya. Nearby, in a U-shaped bend in the Mahaweli, the country's longest river, are the Peradeniya Botanical Gardens, established by 1821, six years after the British deposed the last Kandyan king. So famous were these gardens that when the duke of Sutherland organized a yachting party to Southeast Asia in December 1888, he made a stop in Colombo on the return journey four months later to give his guests the opportunity to visit Peradeniya. His traveling companions, already on sensory overload from the wonders of Malaya and Siam, had no trouble raving about the 140 acres of gardens at Peradeniya, where the spices and herbs of the island, above all cinnamon, grow amid royal palms, orchids, and ferns. A visiting Italian called it "the heart of Paradise."

Peradeniya has always been a practical research station. At the gardens, botanists first experimented with tea and cinchona, from which quinine is extracted, as replacement crops for coffee. This research would later salvage and transform the plantation economy of the island when coffee was struck by a blight. Peradeniya is one of three large botanical gardens in Sri Lanka. Hakgala, near Nuwara Eliya, and a third at Henaratgoda, in the western lowlands, complete the trio. It was at Henaratgoda that rubber was introduced to Asia in 1876. A British agent had smuggled tens of thousands of rubber seeds from Brazil to London's Royal Botanical Garden at Kew, where enough of them sprouted to send about 2,000 plants to Ceylon. At Henaratgoda, they took root and thrived, so much so that from that patch trees were sent as far afield as Malaya and Indonesia as well as to India, creating a new and very lucrative plantation crop.

Florence Caddy, an Englishwoman in her fifties with a great interest in botany, who was in the duke of Sutherland's yachting party, was ecstatic as soon as the train from Colombo pulled out of the town and entered a lush landscape "absolutely laughing with cultivation." Caddy was entranced by the people, too. When the train taking Caddy to Kandy slowed to a stop at a station en route, she fixed on the "lovely male creatures, mahogany-colored, with red, scanty skirts" who sold fresh pineapples, bananas, and coconut water to passengers. Caddy's account of her visit to Peradeniya was included in her book *To Siam and Malaya in the Duke of Sutherland's Yacht Sans Peur*, published in 1889, the year she returned to London. "Here at least was no illusion dispelled: The garden is a Kew palm-stove magnified and glorified; every tropic tree and plant that I know spindling, drawn up and skied to hot-house roofs at home are here displayed in full girth, grace and development," she wrote, and then rambled on for hours, and pages, over the wonders of the bamboos, palms, ficuses, raintrees, fruit trees, medicinal plants, vines, and flowers. She was deterred from wandering off the paths into patches of adjoining virgin jungle only by the possibility of encountering a cobra. "This delicious island has been a dream, an oasis of rest," Caddy noted as the party left Kandy.

The Duke had vetoed a visit to Nuwara Eliya because he had heard that the weather was too cold at that altitude. Had the party decided otherwise, they would have traveled along roads that are in themselves pathways through botanical wonders. The missionary Winslow, traveling to Nuwara Eliya in 1832 to ask the British governor for permission to open more American religious outposts, described the country as "wild and mountainous." Work was then under way on a road from Peradeniya to Nuwara Eliya, which would broaden and pave the narrow dirt track. After a miserable night at a mud rest house at Pussellawa, the halfway mark, Winslow plunged into a dark, deep forest. When he reached the highlands, he was stunned by "the grandest mountain-scene I have ever witnessed." He had arrived at the tree line near Ramboda Pass, where the unexpectedly dramatic skyline of the hill country comes into view. He looked into a valley he thought was 3,000 feet deep and saw no fewer than five waterfalls. "God appeared to be speaking in those cataracts, and to be exhibiting the emblems of his power in those deep vallies and everlasting hills," the missionary wrote in his journal, extracts of which were reprinted in the fascinating anthology compiled by H.A.I. Goonetileke, *Images of Sri Lanka Through American Eyes.*

Nuwara Eliya, which he reached the next day, was largely undeveloped in 1832, except for a sanitarium and the British governor's hot-season residence. Winslow described the site as an undulating plain, with flowering rhododendrons the only trees. Only a few houses had been built: "They are most of them like neat cottages in temperate climates, with chimneys, floorboards and glazed windows." In the garden of the governor's residence, he saw "American" flowers, roses and carnations, and vegetables and fruits from home. The temperature was 42 degrees Fahrenheit, and he was invigorated—"so different from the languor felt below," he observed.

It was January when I last made this trip described by Winslow, and wildflowers of every color were in bloom along the road, taking the sting off the warning signs announcing "verge failures" where shoulders had collapsed into the abyss at the outer edge. Hedges of luminous red hibiscus and poinsettia swayed and bobbed, and in the ditches, flaming canna lilies bloomed. Children stood at the roadside, offering mixed bouquets from fields and gardens for sale to passing motorists. After about fifteen miles of hairpin turns that enliven the latter part of the journey, the landscape begins to broaden, with less verdant hills now scantily marked by pine trees. Then, at the Ramboda Pass, where Winslow saw only barren pasture or some rice cultivation, vast tea estates are all around.

Other hill stations have tea plantations, but nowhere is tea so overwhelmingly a presence as in the hill country around Nuwara Eliya—even more so along the less well known route to the town from Colombo through Hatton and Nanu Oya, a trip I have come to prefer for its scenery to the Kandy-Peradeniya road. The train from Colombo also approaches Nuwara Eliya on this side, stopping at Nanu Oya. For miles and miles in every direction, green carpets of uniformly trimmed tea bushes in shades of green roll on to the horizon, punctuated only by the factories that process the fine Ceylon tea leaves within hours of harvesting and the nearby "line cottages" of the plantation workers, some looking like rows of slave quarters from the pre–Civil War American South. The bright clothes of the tea pluckers, all women, sprinkle color along the rows of bushes. Here and there, a Hindu temple, extravagantly decorated, keeps these transplanted workers in touch with their South Indian Hindu legacy.

Tea picking goes on year-round, and these plantation workers are not migrant labor. But neither are they true Sri Lankans. Though many families have lived here a hundred years, the Tamils of the plantation country, organized by the redoubtable Savumiamoorthy Thondaman and his Ceylon Workers Congress, have been waiting more than half a century for the right to Sri Lankan citizenship. No Sinhala-led government, which is to say all of them since independence, has worked up the courage to make the Indian Tamils full-fledged Sri Lankans. It is a wonder that they have not been tempted to make common cause with the Jaffna Tamils. Of course, Thondaman's enforcers would see to it that they do not; one of them told me years ago that if anyone shows up to talk revolution on the plantations, he is swiftly turned over to the police. Thondaman's political influence in Colombo, where he has been a member of cabinets led by both major parties, has depended on his ability to deliver up the hills when it is time to vote and to keep them quiet between elections.

A greater threat of terrorism in the plantations has come from another quarter, the Sinhalese radicals of the Janata Vimukti Peramung, the People's Liberation Front. The supernationalistic JVP—fueled by a combustible mix of Buddhist fanaticism, xenophobia, muddled leftism, and hatred of Tamils, of India, and of all those who truck with either—have twice in the past half century terrorized large areas of the hills and the coastal areas to the south and southeast. Vulnerable plantation workers in their isolated cottages on huge tea estates live in unending dread of another JVP resurgence.

Long before tea and ethnic politics, Nuwara Eliya was chosen by the British as the highest and healthiest place to establish a convalescence center, because with the conquest of Kandy, the interior of the island was now accessible. Henry Marshall, the British army doctor who had questioned the motives of the colonial establishment in its war with the Kandyan king, thought Ceylon was a particularly unhealthy place for Europeans. In wet weather, soldiers who spent much of their time in jungle areas were routinely attacked by leeches that could penetrate clothing by day and seek out the face and gums of men sleeping at night. Marshall pulled as many as eighty leeches off the body of a single soldier once, trying to clean the skin as he worked. He knew that the wounds would fester or ulcerate quickly when soldiers were back in the field without adequate sanitation. Many lives were lost among the troops and the work gangs of coolies that accompanied them. Numerous endemic fevers, intestinal complaints, and liver disease weakened and killed not only soldiers but also civilians who ventured into the interior. Mercifully, sunstroke was rare. But smallpox and cholera were recurrent plagues, though they were not so prevalent among Europeans as among the Ceylonese, the doctor decided.

Among the fevers, malaria was a constant. By an accident of history, Nuwara Eliya owed its early development to that disease more than any other malady. Sir Samuel Baker, a British explorer of the Nile, spent several weeks in Nuwara Eliya in 1847 recuperating from a malaria attack and was so taken by its setting in a wet, high-altitude valley two miles long that he decided to settle there and build "a little English town around my own residence." Sir Samuel did not think small. "Why should not the highlands of Ceylon, with an Italian climate, be rescued from their barrenness?" he asked rhetorically—or so he later wrote in his account of what followed, *Eight Years in Ceylon.* "Why should not the plains be drained, the forests felled, and cultivation take the place of rank pasturage, and supplies be produced to make Ceylon independent of other countries? Why should not schools be established, a comfortable hotel be erected, a church be built? In fact, why should Newera Ellia, with its wonderful climate, so easily attainable, be neglected in a country like Ceylon, proverbial for its unhealthiness?"

Sir Samuel went back to England and thought about this plan. Always the hunter of game large and small, he also recalled the opportunities the

Lankan hills would offer for sport. A year later, he had put it all together. He bought a large tract of land from the colonial government, hired an English bailiff, and looked for other emigrants willing to sail with him to the Indian Ocean island. Nine volunteered, among them a blacksmith, important since Sir Samuel was a great horseman and horses would provide the settlement's only transportation. Methodically, he bought and prepared for export a ready-made rural town: seeds, farm implements, sawmill equipment, a cross-bred Durham-Hereford bull and a Durham cow, sheep, a thoroughbred horse, a pack of foxhounds, and a greyhound. Sir Samuel's family, his brother, and his wife and children also sailed for Ceylon. The explorer himself had gone ahead of the others—"as Noah's dove," he wrote—to pick a place to build his new world. Lord, did it rain. He had arrived in a monsoon season when the ground turned to swamp and local labor could not be found except at very high wages. Meanwhile the ship bearing the flora and fauna of his experiment, and its inhabitants, was sailing closer. Fortunately, the sky cleared in a few weeks, and he was able to construct "neat white cottages" for one and all.

When his ark, the ship *Earl of Hardwicke,* docked in Colombo, Sir Samuel had to find a way to transport the menagerie to the hills. He contracted with a wagon maker to build a cart for his precious cow, fearing that the fat animal could not walk the distance in the heat. The cart was constructed to bear the weight of an elephant, but when the sturdy Durham climbed on board, she fell straight through. Like the other animals, she had no alternative but to begin a walk of more than a hundred miles to her new home. To save the livestock, the pace was set at ten miles a day, but even so the poor cow did not make it through the steaming lowlands. It took four elephant carts to carry the machinery and a number of smaller wagons pulled by bullocks to ferry other equipment into the hills.

A horse-drawn coach conveyed the immigrants; Sir Samuel's family had a new carriage called a *clarence.* An elephant was to follow with their personal baggage. All of this might have gone smoothly if Baker had not included among his emigrant colonists a groom of intermittent sobriety named Henry Perkes. When the traveling circus reached Ramboda Pass, about fourteen miles from Nuwara Eliya, the going got too steep for the new carriage. The horses had to be unhitched and ridden the remaining distance; the carriage was left at a rest house to be picked up later. After the party reached its destination, Sir Samuel sent Henry Perkes back down the pass with a pair of horses to bring up the carriage. The groom was also in charge of the elephant, which was to fetch more baggage.

The next day, Sir Samuel recalled, he received a "dirty looking letter" that is now part of Sri Lankan folk history, even if its contents were later reconstructed and often embellished since in the telling of the story. In short, it was a note from Perkes announcing that "the carrige and osses has met with a haccidint and is tumbled down a preccippice and its a mussy I didn't go too." The pair of good Australian horses "is got up but is very bad" and the new carriage was overturned about 80 feet below the road, resting on the mountainside. Sir Samuel rode down to the scene and found one horse so badly injured that it had to be shot; the other died in a few days. The carriage was a wreck, but he hoped to salvage it with the help of his blacksmith. Perkes had been drunk when he raced the carriage around the sharp bends of the pass, and one bad corner was his undoing. But there was more to come.

Perkes was sent back to the site with an elephant to help haul the carriage back up to the road. Against the anguished pleas of the elephant's mahout, the dim-witted and pickled groom thought it would be sport to ride the animal down the pass at a trot and then race it up the final incline to the bend where the accident took place. As the mahout, without elephant, later told the story to Sir Samuel, Perkes, fueled on brandy and water, literally rode the animal to its death. Meanwhile, Baker got the news that the Durham cow had died barely forty miles out of Colombo, dashing his hopes of breeding a good cattle here. He seems to have taken the death of the cow harder than the loss of his carriage and horses. Macho as he was—when he wasn't colonizing, he was shooting anything he could—Sir Samuel had a warped admiration for Perkes. He last saw him being rolled around Nuwara Eliya in a wheelbarrow, too drunk to walk, and later heard that he had left Ceylon and found work as a groom in Madras. Perkes, who wore a black patch over an eye kicked out by a horse, "was perpetually making successful love to the maid-servants, and he was altogether the most incorrigible scamp that I have ever met with, although I must do him the justice to say he was thoroughly honest and industrious," Sir Samuel later wrote. Moreover, "he had the satisfaction of knowing that he was one of the few men in the world who had ridden an elephant to death."

Coming through Ramboda Pass last time, I could see that the spirit of Perkes still haunts it. A cowboy driver with a van full of passengers took an inside bend too fast and tumbled into the tea. Luckily, no one appeared to be seriously hurt, but true to history the van was upside down. And there were no elephants or tow trucks to rescue it.

The footloose adventurer Baker, who had such high hopes for Nuwara Eliya, stayed eight years and suffered many disappointments. Many of his valuable animals died. The soil needed manure (or a fertilizer that had not yet been invented). Elk and wild hogs ate the crops that flourished. Three acres of potatoes were consumed by grubs. But there were successes: vegetables produced harvests to rival those of Europe, and when the potatoes were not attacked, they became a very profitable crop. In farming, Sir Samuel developed a powerful appreciation for an animal that normally did not pull an English plow or harrow, the Asian elephant. These huge animals, which modern Sri Lanka has gone to great efforts to save—a passion that is evident not only in the Pinawella elephant orphanage but also in game parks— are as intelligent as they are strong. Baker wrote of his farm elephant, who was also put to work building a dam: "She was a very large animal, and it was beautiful to witness her wonderful sagacity in carrying and arranging the heavy timber required." The elephant, he found, could lift immense logs and then apparently think about their perfect placement. "She rolled them gently over her head, then with one foot, and keeping her trunk on the opposite side of the log, she checked its way whenever its own momentum would have carried it into the stream." Everywhere in Asia, the working elephant is in peril. In Thailand, they beg for food on the traffic-clogged streets of Bangkok. In the forests of Vietnam, they have all but disappeared.

Sir Samuel Baker saw Nuwara Eliya bloom before he left. His surviving ram had fathered a flock of strong sheep. His bull found other cows. An "extremely pretty church" and a library were built. There was time to explore the countryside, starting with the island's highest mountain, Pidurutalagala, which rises from the Nuwara Eliya valley to a height of 8,300 feet. Sir Samuel waxed poetic on its sublime peak, with nothing but "the dusky arch of heaven" above him. Down in the valley, he reveled in the transformations. "Here, where the wild forest stood, are gardens teeming with English flowers; rosy-faced children and ruddy countrymen are about the cottage doors; equestrians of both sexes are galloping around the plain, and the cry of the hounds is ringing on the mountain-side." There was also a brewery.

Many colonial pioneers in Asia must have shared Sir Samuel Baker's emotional attachment to a place where he knew every footpath and natural landmark. But few wrote with such profound feeling, and so little cynicism, about it. Perhaps it was the nature of his life to move from one passion to another. But he thought there was more. He concluded before the end of his life that there was something hesitant about the English colonist, a reticence not shared by the French. An English settler, he wrote in *Eight Years in Ceylon*, always thinks of himself or herself in temporary exile. The French, in contrast, say good-bye to home with an "eternal farewell" and throw themselves into an adopted country, building and planting for children and grandchildren. His remarks about the British did not ring true of settlements in North America, nor did they account for the substantial building that went on in India, Burma and Malaya. But his basic intuition may in the long run have been proved true by the longevity of the French and their culture in Africa and to some extent Indochina or the Iberians in Latin America long after the collapse of empires.

As time passed after Baker's departure, Nuwara Eliya went on growing. A collection of stately mansions and grand old inns was crowned by one of the finest planters' clubs in Asia—the Hill Club. Although the British colonial government did not move here in its entirety in the hot months of March, April, and May, high officials had begun spending the season here as early as the 1820s, more than two decades before the arrival of Baker, when Governor Sir Edward Barnes built a residence. The president of Sri Lanka now has a home here, and Barnes's rambling mansion has become the Grand Hotel. Having tried the Hill Club and found it less than cozy on previous visits, I had planned to stay at the Grand on the last trip, but arrived in time to be swamped by European tour groups ebbing and flowing through the lobby, to and from the garden and dining room. My reservation had mysteriously been lost. But serendipity kicked in and I was better off for it, though I would like to have had the chance to experience the Grand, with all its red velvet and brass. I knew there was an alternative, apart from the Hill Club and the St. Andrews Hotel, another old building in lovely grounds, but across town close to a noisier quarter just off the main shopping street.

On the way down from Delhi to Colombo a few days earlier I had read in Air Lanka's in-flight magazine about a bold new hotel recently created within the skeleton of an old tea factory—not a plantation house, but the factory itself. It was called just that; the Tea Factory, and it offered a new perspective on Nuwara Eliya as a community at work, not play. Thinking back over years of staying in Asian hotels, I could not remember another conversion so imaginatively conceived and skillfully executed as this. There could not have been a better setting for experiencing the planter's world. Quick tours of working factories, encouraged by tea estates eager to promote their brand names, are useful to understanding the process of tea making, but living on a barren rise amid the tea bushes is something else.

About seven miles from the center of Nuwara Eliya and 600 feet higher, at Kandapola, the Tea Factory stands surrounded by acres of tea interspersed with fields of vegetable crops. Only a narrow, winding dirt road leads in and out of the plantation. Guests are told it is prudent to return from a day's activities early because late every afternoon, like clockwork, a chilling mist rolls in and the universe disappears. The Tea Factory, on its lonely hill, stays wrapped in cold fog until sometime during the night or early morning. There are no neighbors save for the resident plantation manager in an old planter's bungalow and tea pickers' families in the line cottages, now apparently shared by some hotel workers.

This factory, on the Hethersett Plantation, was built in the 1930s, although the plantation itself was created in the 1870s, about thirty years after a Scot, James Taylor, planted the first tea seedlings on land that later became the Labookellie Estate. Ceylon tea had a worldwide reputation for excellence by the end of the nineteenth century, with Nuwara Eliya producing some of the more delicate flavors. By 1968, after many tea plantations were nationalized and consolidated, the Hethersett factory was closed and eventually abandoned. Hethersett's high-quality tea leaves were still plucked but were sent to other factories in the Concordia group, which had taken over this estate. In 1992, a chance visit to Kandapola—serendipity again—by the hotel magnate G. C. Wickremasinghe, chairman of the Aitken Spence company, led to the factory's surprising rebirth. Wickremasinghe, whose hotels are the cream of Sri Lankan coastal resorts, happened to see the silhouette of the old building through the mist and got to thinking. He called in the Sri Lankan architect Nihal Bodhinayake, a wise choice, and took a chance.

Sri Lankan tea factories are invariably big rectangular, barnlike buildings with very clean exterior lines, rows of large, regularly spaced windows for light and ventilation along the sides, and a sloping roof. Factories sit atop hillocks among the tea-covered slopes, open to the breeze on all sides. Inside, there were usually four or five stories of workspace with a central open atrium through which hot air was pumped to upper lofts to "wither" but not dry the tea leaves spread on burlap stretched over racks. The leaves are then crushed and allowed to ferment very briefly (less than two hours) before being dried in machines, sifted, graded, and packed. The whole operation can be completed in under twenty-four hours.

By the time the Tea Factory hotel was conceived, much of the old machinery had been removed or destroyed. But the building, with a new interior steel framework (left exposed and painted deep red) was strong enough to be converted into a hotel without losing the industrial atmosphere. The withering lofts became fifty-seven guest rooms, with original pinewood floors and, naturally, tiny tea chests in every room, with a choice of blends and an electric teapot for round-the-clock brewing. The five-story central atrium has been left open and two large withering fans are still in place on its walls. These drew the hot air from the dryers to the lofts. The lobby, restaurant, and bars have been finished with brass-pegged wood flooring to maintain an industrial look. Seaworthy tea chests hold up the restaurant's buffet table; an old copper tea dryer hangs overhead. At night, the factory, even now, is wrapped in the utter silence in the hills. In a week, I heard only a very occasional gunshot to chase marauding animals away from vegetable crops or the plantation workers' gardens, or so I was told when I asked.

At daybreak, I commuted from the Tea Factory to Nuwara Eliya town to visit the sights as a tourist rather than a journalist, and to explore the library and look for bookshops. The latter was easy: There weren't any, at least none with history books. The librarians showed me what remained of their collection: not much. They seemed proudest of a glossy pamphlet printed in color to commemorate the town-twinning of Nuwara Eliya and Uji City, near Kyoto in Japan, which is known for its Uji green tea. In the great tradition of American higher education, someone had carefully sliced out of books on Sri Lanka the pages on Nuwara Eliya that a traveler might find useful. But somewhere in what material was left, I came upon the name S.A.W. Mottau, who seemed to be an accomplished local historian. The librarians thought he was still around town but did not venture a guess where I might find him.

It was a short walk to the famous Victorian post office, so I went looking for the postmaster to ask if a person was permitted to request an address. A confab of employees produced a Mottau who fit my description at 21-upon-9 Upper Lake Road. One thing journalism teaches is the insouciance to arrive unannounced at a private home. Just before lunch, I startled Mottau in his garden, where he was seated in his lawn chair, dressed in blue-and-white striped pajamas and nursing a shot of gin. "Bit of tummy trouble," he explained. He also told me he was tired of talking about Nuwara Eliya. But being a gentleman he invited me inside to look at copies of articles he had written and books he had collected.

S.A.W. Mottau—he said he was ninety-five years old and of Bavarian-Burgher descent—was not just a local historian. This unassuming man had been director of the National Archives in Colombo. Nuwara Eliya was his retirement home; he had come to its history late, more interested in the Nuwara Eliya Golf Club, of which he was the only life member. But he was very concerned about the town's future, a theme that was clearly going to run through conversations with anyone who remembered hill stations in their less overcrowded days. "The place is now highly commercialized," he said of the town center, a few blocks of tatty shops and an ugly two-story market jammed together between the post office and a church that mark the extremities of Old Bazar Street. "In the old days, you had more people of culture here, or people with a cultural education. And those who came here in the season were more interested in cultural amenities; that's what they wanted," he said.

His adopted retirement home was noticeably warmer in winter than when he settled here, he noted. But at least the water was still good enough to sustain the brewery. In most other hill stations, the early breweries have long gone. "The water in the hills is pure. That's the thing." Mottau has clipped numerous articles that mourn the destruction of local landmarks or the development of another piece of land. To the outsider, modern Nuwara Eliya, now scattered over several valleys between 6,000 and 7,000 feet above sea level, still has a lot of small-town charm, especially around its old hotels and churches. But Mottau and others who have watched the town transformed, say this impression is deceiving.

Warming to his topic, and saying he was feeling much better, he suggested books to read and people to meet who would set me straight, if I had time in Colombo. He fumed over his failing memory when he tried to recall the names of the last two British planters remaining in the nearby hills. But he shared the view of others who thought that the nationalization of the tea plantations in the 1960s under Prime Minister Sirimavo Bandaranaike, at a time when neighboring India was also infatuated with socialist formulas for economic development, altered the social patterns and traditions of the plantation country for good, not because foreign owners left Sri Lanka (a process hastened by land reforms a decade later), but because private Sri Lankan planters would become mere businessmen in the employ of the state and not men of substance, philanthropic activism, and social importance. Ironically, it was in the 1960s that the venerable social fortress of the planters, the Hill Club, was just opening to Sri Lankan members.

Leaving Mottau to the lunch his daughter had prepared for him, I went to the Hill Club for mine. About the time the club, once the preserve of only British or other foreign planters, opened to Sri Lankans, it also be-

gan admitting women and foreign tourists for meals and club events. I
had remembered endless evenings of formality over dress, drinking hours,
and dining room regulations that ended with deeply disappointing meals,
after which there was nothing to do but face up to a freezing room with
no light properly placed for reading. But this was a beautiful day for
lunch, so I went back, paid my temporary membership, and, clad in a
dress for the first time in many days, crept into the dining room.

Mendelssohn's *Melody in F* was on the tape deck. The lighting was sub-
dued. The silver shone. The enormous vases around the room were filled
with fresh flowers. Some things did not change, or so it seemed. When I
sat down to order, there were only three other people in the room, a
woman and her husband on holiday from London and their apparently
new acquaintance, a British woman who lived in the Middle East. The
man was telling her that he had been a tea taster for Twinings for forty-
two years in London and had come to see the old plantations. Their conversation was just getting interesting when a van pulled up outside and, to
the amazement of all of us, disgorged a very noisy, casually dressed gang
of French tourists, complete with travel bags that they piled on the floor.
They were followed by a busload of Germans in Bermuda shorts, who
trooped in and out of the room, visiting the rest rooms and overpriced
souvenir shop. I could see I was wrong about the Hill Club. It was different, at least at lunch. Except for the food. That was still awful.

5

FORGOTTEN BURMA

Maymyo

Morning in Maymyo, in the Burmese hills

*I*N BURMA, ASIA SHIFTS GEARS. To the west lie the countries of South Asia, perforce in orbit around the overwhelming power and dominant land mass of India, soon to become the world's most populous nation. To the east are the less harsh, tropical nations of Southeast Asia. Whether Buddhist, Muslim, Confucian, or Christian, Southeast Asians have created usually (though not always) less violent, certainly more egalitarian, societies than that of technically secular, but profoundly Hinduized, India, with its pervasive caste distinctions. Burma has been part of both worlds in certain ways and at different times. In antiquity, the country that is now Burma felt the influence of Hinduism from South India and the Mahayana form of Buddhism that flourished in North India, the Himalayas, and Tibet. Eventually, Theravada Buddhism, to which most Burmese now adhere, became entrenched through contact with both the Mon people of the Siamese border area to the southeast and the formidable monasteries of Ceylon to the southwest, where monks and scholars safeguarded and refined the early Buddhist texts written in the classical Pali language. Much later, in the nineteenth and early twentieth centuries, Burma was administered as a part of Britain's Indian empire. Indians migrated to Burmese towns and cities, along with Indian food and odds and ends of Indian languages. Then, after independence in 1948, and a long spell of strict neutrality and isolation, Burma began to look eastward, turning its back on South Asia and lobbying to become a member of the Association of Southeast Asian Nations (ASEAN). It was not only the economic miracle of ASEAN that attracted Burma's military rulers, but also the limits on political action and free speech that all but two Southeast Asian nations—Thailand and the Philippines—have imposed, wrapped in transparent theories about "Asian" values. To the west, the countries of South Asia are more rigorously, noisily, and successfully democratic—not a club the Burmese rulers who first named themselves the State Law and Order Restoration Council would want to join.

There is still much about Burma that links it westward to the British Empire in India. But, leaving aside military rule, there is perhaps a great deal more in its society that gives this Buddhist nation a natural affinity to civilizations to the east. Had a succession of military dictatorships not strangled its potential, Burma—with high literacy, a sophisticated and intellectually vibrant religious life, and considerable economic promise—could have ranked prominently among Southeast Asian nations. Compared with India, the atmospheric difference is palpable. In Burma, there is no permanent degradation of the lowborn that consigns most of them to perpetual poverty and humiliation, despite the political success of low-caste politicians. Although an international boycott of Burma after the suppression of Aung San Suu Kyi's democracy movement hurt in important ways, creating, for example, a shortage of petroleum fuels, the country still has the feeling of a place blessed by nature, where there are always things to eat or sell and the means to live in dignity. "We have everything in Burma: food, teak, jade, silver, rubies, lead," a teacher said. "That's why our governments can talk rude to everybody in the world."

Substantial, mostly Asian, investment in Burma's tourism industry is adding to the national coffers, though not as much as the government hoped. Nevertheless it is not dreams of hard currency that keep the bitter Burmese on an even keel, but something of the character they share with many other Buddhists. Buddhism may have displayed flaws and short-comings over recent decades in Cambodia, Sri Lanka, Thailand, and indeed Burma, but it remains an individualistic faith with a practical philosophy to live by. Buddhists can incorporate modernity or reject it, without a spiritual struggle. Believers can somehow be at peace and at ease within the Buddhist fold, however inhumane the government that overshadows them. There is an evenness of temperament. What may be in shorter supply, of course, are the explosive, expressive, creative flashes of South Asian vitality and genius. "Buddhists have no guts," a Hindu Tamil living in the Burmese hills said emphatically as he offered his take on recent history.

The British Empire came late to Burma, a kingdom united only to greater or lesser degrees throughout its history. The country was buffeted by invasions, including a punishing sweep by Kublai Khan's forces in the thirteenth century, but it also enjoyed periods of strong temporal power that made the ethnic-Burman-led armies the scourge of Siam, a traditional enemy. The British, when they did finally arrive, did not stay long. Not much more than half a century passed between the final conquest of Burma in 1886 and the restoration of its independence in 1948. There had long been a lively trade, however. Among other commodities transported to the Sub-continent, Burmese teak built the mansions of colonial India. Long before the fall of the royal capital of Mandalay to Queen Victoria's troops, British trading houses flourished in Rangoon, a cosmopolitan city that attracted other Europeans and the Armenian merchants and developers who also played a significant commercial role in the Straits Settlements of Malaya. An Armenian family, the Sarkies brothers, built not only Rangoon's Strand Hotel but also the Eastern and Oriental in Penang and the Raffles in Singapore. In any case, among the glorious gilded pagodas, monasteries, and royal monuments of Burma, the imprint of imperial Britain was overshadowed in most places. Maymyo is an exception.

On a golden morning in February, when the nights were cold and the days balmy, before the heat of a Burmese summer reached the hills, I cycled out of the gates of my small hotel in Maymyo and pedaled into a bit of British history. Along the quiet, tree-shaded roads of the old imperial quarter—where the only other vehicles were the bicycles of schoolchildren who shouted, "Good morning!" and "Where you come from?"—the scene had barely changed in half a century. Deep in their gardens and lawns, some grown very unkempt with the passing of time, magnificent half-timbered English country houses sheltered among the towering hardwoods in a neighborhood older residents still call Forest Road. A turn toward the town center, with its chiming clock tower, brought into view the solid but graceful government offices, the churches and a hospital, all part of the legacy of Maymyo's years as the summer capital of British Burma, and all still in use for the same purposes by new masters. Scattered through the town are old hotels, some in former official residences, their high-ceilinged rooms paneled in silk-smooth teak, their restaurants struggling to maintain the formality of yore in the face of group tours. The halls are hushed; the sound of a crackling fire or the weak ring of a "shambolic" telephone at an empty reception desk the only distractions.

Maymyo, which Burma's military government in its zeal to wipe out foreignness formally renamed Pyin Oo Lwin—a pre-British name meaning something like "a pleasant hilltop meadow"—has probably changed less than most Asian hill stations, and certainly less than other Burmese towns that tourists visit. The extraordinary pagoda city of Pagan, once crumbling and almost ghostly on its sun-bathed plain, is now restored and expanded into a comfortable, fashionable town bustling with tourists. Parts of Mandalay were beyond recognition to me when I returned after a decade. Burma's newly rich and their Chinese counterparts who find it convenient to park some of their wealth across the border in Burmese cities are racing to copy the obscene concrete mansions of Thailand with their incongruous arches, balustrades, balconies, and windows of every size and shape thrown in with no reference to a unifying design. The conspicuous consumption of the wildly affluent in Southeast Asia has nothing to do with that useful bugbear "Westernization." The old Victorian-Tudor British houses and offices of Maymyo are far more at home in the Burmese landscape than a bank with flashy, mirrored, bright-blue plate glass windows or a huge, two-level concrete shopping center with store rents too expensive for the stall-holders in the streets. Especially in Burma, where traditional architecture is so fine and enduring, the proliferation of vulgar, slapped-together buildings is a depressing phenomenon. Construction is predictably shoddy. In Mandalay everyone was talking about the new hospital for eye, ear, nose, and throat specialists that had recently collapsed, crushing an unknown number of patients. "You won't read about that in the newspaper," someone said. "But we all know what is going on." Money laundering and corruption is what he meant. Cutting corners for profit has become a way of life. By contrast, the new stone gates and buildings of the Defense Services Academy in Maymyo seem as solid as granite mountains, constructed to last a thousand years.

"Maymyo is particularly well fitted to be a hill station," the 1901 *Gazetteer of Upper Burma and the Shan States* recorded only a few years after the founding of the colonial town.

> There is abundant room for house-sites, and considerable level spaces occur. The plateau has now been cleared of the denser jungle, and the low hills that encircle it are covered with picturesque thin oak forest, over an undergrowth of bracken fern. With the opening up to passenger traffic of the Mandalay-Kunlong Railway, Maymyo will be placed within twenty-four hours of Rangoon. There can then be no doubt that, for many years at least, Maymyo will remain the hot-weather residence of the Lieutenant-Governor.

Surveyors of the time noted the abundance of bamboo and teak and observed that experiments with pine looked promising.

The trip to Pyin Oo Lwin, which many people still call Maymyo, is an easy one, about on a par with the drive to Murree in warmer months, though the Burmese roads are not up to the Pakistani standard. There is also a train, as the gazetteer predicted. In a good car or bus, the climb to Maymyo from Mandalay, a distance of forty-two miles, should take no more than an hour and a half. My slightly longer journey had to do with Nan Mon Khan, the inventive and very competent day receptionist of Maymyo's Royal Park View Hotel. Since the journalism police of the State Law and Order Restoration Council, who turned down my first request for a visa, waited until the last minute to respond favorably to my appeal and reverse themselves, I arrived in Burma from India via Singapore with the remains of an Indian dysentery attack and no hotel reservations anywhere, least of all in Maymyo, where I had also never been. A traveler approaches this hill station with but one universal piece of advice:

Go to the Candacraig. This monument to Maymyo's brief encounter with the British Empire is thought to be the hotel most reflective of the town's history. In Mandalay, where I spent the first night, I tried to phone the Candacraig, now a government-owned inn known officially as the Thiri Myanmar. Name changing must have been a major project for the folks in SLORC, as the Orwellian State Law and Order Restoration Council was known. (Eventually it changed its own name: In late 1997 it decided to remake its image and became the State Peace and Development Council.)

No one answered the phone at the Candacraig. I later understood why; there is often no one in charge at the front desk, where the light is so low the receptionist needs a candle to complete his transactions. The phone book did not offer many other choices in Maymyo. But there was a number for the Golf Club, and that seemed a likely place to find someone who also knew the Candacraig. This golf course, I later learned, was the one where early visitors to Maymyo quipped that a wood-ax would be more useful than a club or putter in playing a round. The Golf Club manager, U Khin My Aye, was very helpful. He told me not to bother with the Candacraig, which had "gone down" and had electrical problems. There was a much better hotel nearby, the Royal Park View. It was brand-new, he said. Brand-new was not what seemed right in Maymyo, but I called anyway. Nan Mon Khan answered, and after that, I was in her hands. First, she told me her hotel was full the following day, but if I really wanted to try the Candacraig, she would book me there for a night and then squeeze me into the Royal Park View for the rest of my stay. She didn't tell me then that her "new" hotel was a remodeled British-era bungalow and privately owned, which would have made me a little less hesitant. Her offer sounded good, so I signed up for her first opening and asked about transportation to Maymyo. The hotel in Mandalay was asking $80 for a private car with a driver. Most people did not stay in Maymyo, the hotel clerk said a little dismissively, so for just getting dropped off, I would have to pay the round-trip price. Nan Mon Khan took about two minutes to find me a car that would come down to Mandalay to fetch me for 1,500 kyat, about $10. Less than an hour later, she had also maneuvered me a reservation in her small inn. I never really wanted to know which of the fussy French tourists who checked in just after me had to double up.

That accomplished, I was free to enjoy an evening in Mandalay, a much glossier town these days, with its magnificently restored palace walls and moat—regrettably rebuilt by forced labor, a money-saving abuse. Mandalay Palace, constructed of teak in the mid–nineteenth century, is gone,

destroyed by fire during a British attack on Japanese troops holed up in it
during the closing days of World War II. Burma, a channel between the
Western allies and the Chinese trying to reverse a Japanese occupation,
endured some of the worst fighting during that war and produced some of
the most heroic feats by American and British forces and their Asian allies. The names of men like Field Marshal William Joseph Slim, Joseph
Stilwell, and Orde Wingate will be forever associated with the Burma
campaign.

Destruction was widespread in Maymyo and Mandalay. But with
tourism a high priority now, a lot of restoration and new construction is
taking place. At last, Mandalay has some new hotels, first among them,
the Novotel. From my overpriced room there, I had a view of Mandalay
Hill and its numerous pagodas, whose domes were set aflame briefly by
the setting sun. As darkness fell, strings of lights came on to illuminate
pagodas on the nearby slopes and across the more distant horizon. It is a
magical display, staking out the reassuring presence of Buddhism in every
direction. Never mind that some pagodas have added strips of colored
neon to their pinnacles or that across the way by the wall of Mandalay
Palace a very large billboard tells us that the *tatmadaw*, the Burmese army,
is tirelessly looking after the interests of the people. The army uses the
palace grounds as a base.

Down on the terrace around the Novotel pool, with its open-sided
Thai-style pavilion, which serves as the stage for entertainment, the hotel
staff was preparing for one of those inevitable Southeast Asian buffet dinners for tourists, where waiters keep appearing at the table to ask if you
have a coupon. Few encounters set an independent traveler afire as fast as
hotels unable to deal with anyone not on a package tour. The Mandalay
version of the Saturday night poolside buffet looked pretty good. A band
was setting up in the pavilion. Then, as a reminder of how close we were
to India, one of the band members, in jeans and a camouflage jacket,
leaned over the exquisitely carved wooden railing and raising two fingers
to his nose, blew out the copious contents toward the wall a few feet from
where dinner tables had been lavishly laid. People who ridicule Lee Kuan
Yew for outlawing spitting in Singapore should be sentenced to a few
weeks on the slimy, betel-stained streets of Delhi, Calcutta, or Rangoon, I
thought, as I headed for the indoor coffee shop instead.

Next morning, I was off to Maymyo in a well-worn Toyota station
wagon of unknown vintage and uncertain performance, courtesy of Nan
Mon Khan's network. We passed through cool villages of thatch-covered

homes with gardens where mounds of brilliantly colored bougainvillea tumbled over fences and arbors. There were hamlets of bamboo weavers, who split the canes and fashioned panels that, combined with local hardwoods, build pleasing houses, open-fronted restaurants, and small-town public buildings. As the road began its climb, and the orchards and banana groves gave way to harsh, dry, denuded hills, the old Toyota started to cough and buck. The driver bailed out. "Please wait," he said, as if I had a choice. He opened the hood and then rummaged through supplies in the trunk for a part. I thought of those helpful hints on road maps in India that urge drivers setting out on a serious journey to take along more or less the components of another car in order to avoid grief en route. "Filter too long," the driver explained a few moments later, as he jumped back in after replacing the offending, worn-out piece. The engine almost purred. Not another hiccup was heard for the remainder of the trip.

But now the driver was hungry, "very hungry," he said. This was to prepare me for the ritual stop at the 21st Mile. This is midpoint on the Mandalay-Maymyo run, and a long row of roadside restaurants, kiosks, and an occasional engine-repair shop have sprung up to serve travelers. The roadside activity was reminiscent of any number of service towns in provincial Thailand. These Burmese cafés were clean, appealing places, where whole families, down to the babies, were in attendance to provide a quick hot meal and a drink from a glass-fronted refrigerator or shelves where bottles of Johnny Walker Black Label stood next to containers of motor oil. The ubiquity of Johnny Walker scotch in Asia is legendary. Not all of it is real, of course. In India it was confidently said that more "Johnny Walker" was sold there alone in a year than the total output of the Scottish distillery. At our open-fronted café, with its wooden tables and small stools, a molting pet parrot worked the floor, squawking as it looked for scraps. From a room in the small house next door drifted the sounds of a youngster taking singing lessons from a patient teacher who repeated a tricky phrase again and again in a rising and falling voice: "bim, bum, bim, bum." While we ate, a few trucks packed with soldiers rolled by, no doubt in search of ways to advance the interests of the Burmese people.

The journey to Maymyo was a lot more arduous a century ago when Beth Ellis, a young Englishwoman intent on visiting a sister whose husband was in the Burmese colonial service, rode into the hills on an obstinate Burmese pony. The book she wrote in 1899, *An English Girl's First Impressions of Burmah*, stands as one of the most complete, if not only, accounts of daily life in the new hill station in 1896, before it was officially named Maymyo in honor of a Colonel May of the Fifth Bengal Infantry, who commanded a garrison there in 1886. The garrison took his name first, and then the town, but not until 1897. At that time, Pyin Oo Lwin was known as a trade-registration post whose officers monitored goods moving between Mandalay and the Shan States. When Beth Ellis visited, before it was officially called Maymyo, she referred to the hill station as Reymyo, but I have yet to discover why.

Riding her recalcitrant pony, Ellis arrived in Maymyo, as she wrote, "grasping in one hand the pummel and in the other my large green sun umbrella, for the sun was terribly hot." She also had with her more than a hundred strawberry plants for her sister's garden; only one survived. Emerging from the jungle, she saw less a town than a construction site, including a very British Circular Road.

> There is something infinitely pathetic to my mind about this poor new road, wandering aimlessly in the jungle, leading nowhere and used by no one. At regular distances there stand by the wayside tall posts bearing numbers. The lonely posts mark the situation of houses which it is hoped will, in the future, be built on the allotments they represent. In theory, the Circular Road is lined with houses, for Reymyo has a great future before it; but at present, the future is travelling faster than the station.

Like the road, she said morosely, the new railway station was left "sitting sadly expectant in the jungle, waiting patiently for the arrival of that future which alone is needed to render them famous."

For most of the trip to Maymyo now, the road rises gently through land so parched in winter that even the bamboo had turned brown. The jungle of Beth Ellis's day is completely gone. The driver, putting the best face on it, said that this landscape came to life quite miraculously with the monsoon rains. That seemed a sight worth seeing. Meanwhile, we hit a patch of brush fire that had jumped the road, blowing bursts of searing heat into the car from both sides as we raced between the flames. Then, suddenly, the ascent grew steeper, and at about 2,450 feet, the air was instantly cooler, the landscape green. George Orwell, who as a young man served for seven years in the 1920s in the imperial police in Burma, took the train to Maymyo; more than a decade later, while fighting in the Spanish Civil War, he recalled "this rather queer experience." It came to mind, he wrote in *Homage to Catalonia*, when he was considering the odd dissonance between embarkation and arrival on a trip between the war front and quieter Barcelona. In his imagination, he relived the trip to Maymyo.

You start off in the typical atmosphere of an Eastern city—the scorching sunlight, the dusty palms, the smells of fish and spices and garlic, the squashy tropical fruits, the swarming dark-faced human beings—and because you are so used to it you carry this atmosphere intact, so to speak, in your railway carriage. Mentally, you are still in Mandalay when the train stops at Maymyo, four thousand feet above sea-level. But in stepping out of the carriage, you step into a different hemisphere. Suddenly you are breathing cool sweet air that might be that of England, and all around you are green grass, bracken, fir trees and hill-women with pink cheeks selling baskets of strawberries.

At roadside stalls three quarters of a century later, fair Shan women with healthy complexions sit among buckets of fresh flowers worthy of an Impressionist's palette. Others sell coffee beans and, lately, shiitake mushrooms. Horticulture is an important business around Maymyo. In the cool morning hours, small trucks and motorcycles laden with bundles of buds and flowers bump down the hills to Mandalay to sell blooms that will soon reach the hotels and flower shops of Rangoon. The success of other crops has been mixed, however, residents of Maymyo say. They scoff at the town's government agricultural experimentation center, perhaps a little unfairly, since the acres of grape arbors I saw seemed healthy enough. Wine making has begun to attract some private investment in Maymyo, barely 3,500 feet above sea level in most places and with a warm enough daytime sun to encourage the growth of grapes, if the composition of the soil is right. Here, as everywhere they went in the Asian highlands, the British promoted experimental crops in the hope of supplying their hill stations and lowland cities with fresh food.

Maymyo still feels like a town with space to grow, not a common attribute of hill stations on more dramatic terrain. And because it is no longer an administrative hub, it has lost the tensions and pretensions that once repelled some thoughtful and sensitive Britons in colonial service. Maurice Collis was one of them. A brilliant writer with an intense fascination for and extensive knowledge of Burma, its people, its history, and its languages, Collis instinctively hated Maymyo at first, as he admitted in his autobiography, *Into Hidden Burma*. Some of this disdain may reflect the confident snobbery of an insider, a man able to move beyond the margins of safe colonial society with great ease and therefore one who could have cause to feel superior. But whatever the reason, Collis soon found another hill station he liked better, Kalaw, in the southern Shan State—and still a favorite of foreigners who know Burma intimately. On a break between assignments (and after a substantial promotion) in 1920, Collis once escaped to Kalaw, in a pine woodland 3,000 feet in altitude, to stay with friends.

"Before setting out, it would have been a prudent move to show my face in official circles," he wrote.

> Almost any other Civilian in my position at Mandalay, with a few days' leave due before he assumed charge of his first deputy commissionership, would have slipped up to Maymyo close by, called on the Lieutenant-Governor and the heads of the departments who were all in their hot weather quarters, made himself pleasant to their wives, stood drinks at the club bar, asked senior officers for their advice, and, if he did not play polo and tennis, at least have played bridge with the right people. Instead, I had gone to Kalaw, an unfashionable hill station that no Civilian ever went to, there consorted with Burmans and pro-Burmans, and talked about art, poetry and the like. I wanted to get on, but that was not the way to do it in the Burma of the 1920s.

Later, when he was based in steamy, mildewed Rangoon—more an Indian than a Burmese city—Collis would have kinder words for Maymyo and its cool, refreshing air. But by then, Maymyo society may have seemed slightly less claustrophobic than official Rangoon, where he longed for the countryside and missed friends he had made in smaller towns and cities. Collis was gratified about his position, saying "My duties in the secretariat were of such an impersonal nature that any unorthodox leanings I might have were not noticeable." It should come as no surprise that Collis, now dead, is still a favorite of many Burmese, who see him as a Briton who could truly cross into their culture and appreciate it, despite the depths to which Burmese royal life occasionally sank.

The history of Burma—or Myanmar under its military rulers, who apparently drew on the "Mranma" or a variation thereof in use in Burmese antiquity to describe the land—is a tragic story full of bloodshed, torture, and abuse. Attacked by the Mongols, under perennial threat from neighbors, especially the Siamese, and always in the shadow of China, Burma also was victim of its own rulers' excesses. Very early, patterns of repression were established that have reappeared repeatedly down to the present day to inflict sorrow and to take a great toll on life and liberty. Forced labor for construction projects and porterage for the military are not new. Nor are the ethnic conflicts among Burmans, Shan, Mon, Arakanese, or other components of this fragmented nation. The Muslim Rohinga refugees who periodically flee Arakan into Bangladesh have their histori-

cal antecedents. Burman kings pursuing such exiles two centuries ago inadvertently laid the ground for British intervention, since incursions into
what was then East India Company territory were not to be tolerated.
The breathtaking scale of Burmese atrocities was noteworthy in Southeast Asia. Take these examples: In 1782, King Bodawpaya replied to a relatively harmless guerrilla attack on his capital by killing and burning every
man, woman, child, animal, and plant in the town that had harbored the
plotters. In 1846, King Pagan Min did away with 6,000 wealthy subjects in
order to confiscate their riches. In 1879, dozens of members of the royal
family were slaughtered by a new king, Thibaw, and his wife, Supayalat, as
insurance against rivalry from within the palace. In the light of these stories and others retold by D.G.E. Hall in his *History of South-East Asia*, the
worst excesses of European imperialists dim by comparison.

Only the fierce and persistent love that the Burmese of many (if not all)
ethnic groups had for their homeland and the pride they felt for its people
would cause them to put aside this legacy of factionalism and terror long
enough to mount a sustained campaign for freedom from Britain in the
early twentieth century. Independence, sadly, did not mean the end of
cruelty. Even before freedom could be fully savored, assassins jealous of
his authority murdered General Aung San, the hero of independence and
the father of Aung San Suu Kyi. He died with six members of his cabinet—in effect, the core of what would have been Burma's first elected
government after independence. Since then, modern military governments may not have condemned people to be trampled to death by elephants, in the style of kings, but a succession of generals can and do
frighten and stifle the spirit of a devoutly Buddhist population and its
gutsy monks. Knowing I was a journalist, almost no one wanted to be
named in anything I wrote, even if he or she was only relating local history with no politics involved and though I persistently argued that this
was only a travel book. It took days to persuade anyone to come to tea or
join me for a walk. Every day, the official media shrieked warnings about
traitors who consorted with foreigners.

The British were snooping around Burma unofficially by the turn of the
seventeenth century. European merchants of various nationalities found
the place enticing because of its possibilities as a gateway to China, despite periodic fighting among ethnic armies that made the traveling too
dangerous at times. Border trade is still important, though its most lucrative commodity these days is narcotics. Officially, the British government
in India did not decide to annex any Burmese territory until 1826, after a

war provoked by an impetuous Burmese court whose forces had been threatening the British on several fronts around Bengal and the northeast frontier of India. During the fighting, which began in 1824, British troops captured Rangoon, then a major trading city but not the Burmese royal capital, which was then at Amanapura, just south of Mandalay. After the Burmese military commander, Bandula, was killed in an unsuccessful battle to dislodge the British in 1825 and it seemed clear that British troops could now march to Amanapura without much difficulty, the Burmese were forced to cede territory to stave off worse humiliation. In the 1826 Treaty of Yandabo, Britain got the southern coastal provinces of Tenasserim and Arakan, along with unchallenged sovereignty in Assam and Manipur in the Indian Northeast. In 1862, the British, having conquered Pegu, combined its administration with that of Tenasserim and Arakan and made Rangoon the capital of British, or Lower, Burma.

Nearly a quarter of a century passed before Britain attacked Upper Burma, completing its takeover of the country and deposing the last king, Thibaw, in 1886. The move followed decades of squabbles with the court, then in Mandalay, over commercial and political relationships between areas controlled by the king and those under the British. Under Thibaw, the Burmese wanted to deal directly with London and Queen Victoria, not with British India. Ominously for Britain's economic interests, the Burmese were also negotiating with the French for various commercial concessions. When the British struck back, it was comprehensive. Not only was the Burmese monarchy abolished but the king was also sent into exile, as Ceylon's last king had been sent off the field seventy years earlier. The administration of the country was reorganized, Rangoon became the capital, and Mandalay, with its fabulous pagodas and palace barely a few decades old, was on the way to becoming a tourist attraction. Created by King Mindon, a Buddhist scholar, in 1857, Mandalay remains a powerful religious center and national symbol for the Burmese, and its monks have from time to time been a political force to be reckoned with.

With the British swarming Mandalay, the hills beyond naturally beckoned. Within a decade of the British conquest of Upper Burma, colonial officials had looked at several potential hill station sites. One was Taunggyi, the Shan State capital and a well-known resort today, and another around the gem-mining region of Mogok. What would become Maymyo was at first regarded as too troublesome a place because resistance to the British was strong. But by 1896, this seemed the best choice, and construction of a summer capital was well under way, just as Beth Ellis was arriving. Units of the Indian army were based there, since Burma was then administered as part of India, not to everyone's liking, Burmese or British. Britain did soon raise the rank of its senior representative in Burma from a commissioner to a lieutenant governor. And in 1923 Burma got a full-fledged governor, Sir Spencer Hartcourt Butler—for whom Maymyo's new lake, built by Turkish World War I prisoners, was eventually named. But it was not until 1937 that Burma was detached from India to form a separate colony. This gave the Burmese confidence that they could not easily be claimed by a future independent India. Indeed, in 1947 Indian nationalists assumed the right to inherit all lands and people imperial Britain had ruled in their name. Some Hindu nationalists still argue that Burma as well as Pakistan and Bangladesh should one day revert to a Greater India.

Oo Chit Swe, a Maymyo journalist who compiled a commemorative volume of writings about the hill station in 1996 for its hundredth birthday, said when we met over drinks at my hotel that social and recreational institutions were established very quickly. Without the steep cliffs and deep gullies of many other hill stations, development in Maymyo was relatively easy. The town soon had a golf course and polo ground as well as a gymkhana for other sports and recreational activities. There was an imposing club, even when Beth Ellis visited. "I verily believe that when the white man penetrates into the interior to found a colony, his first act is to clear a space and build a club house," she observed tartly, adding that since it was off limits to women, the club house might as well have been a sepulchre to her. The nearby Ladies' Club was no more than a hut, she wrote with some disgust.

Because of the space on Pyin Oo Lwin's plateau, avenues could be broad and lawns wide. Maymyo always was, and still is, a healthy place to live, said Oo Chit Swe. In this pleasant environment, schools were soon built, the most famous of them St. Albert's High School for boys and St. Joseph's Convent for girls. Although St. Albert's, where Oo Chit Swe was a student, is now a government school, a group of its old graduates still meet every year for a cozy reunion. "Cakes and tea in the afternoon and dinner at night," is how another alumnus described it. Maymyo is a place many people do not want to leave, and so a sense of community is strong and lifelong residents of the town have friendships going back to colonial times. There seems to be time to visit friends and take walks in Maymyo, where there are no day-trippers in buses or sidewalk shantytowns that signal the press of population in many South Asian hill stations. I seemed to spend a lot of time at small outdoor noodle-and-rice restaurants, under signs advertising a beer from Singapore: "Get that man a Tiger."

Maymyo, mostly flat and with roads not choked with traffic, is a great town for bicycling and for the *myin yahta,* a small horse-drawn carriage that Americans would describe as a miniature stagecoach. The four-wheeled carriages, a world away from the two-wheeled tongas of the Northwest Frontier of India and Pakistan, were introduced by the British, who by that time had a knack for matching the right transportation to whatever Asian terrain they encountered. Smaller-than-average horses seem capable of pulling these little carriages with ease on the relatively level ground of Maymyo, even when the load was a cargo of wood or pipes or a whole family on a shopping trip. The first *myin yahta* I hired, to take me to the botanical garden and the golf club, was a riot of color—sea green, red, and flamingo pink body with solid brass fenders over the bigger rear wheels. The decoration applied to these eye-pleasing carriages was always individualistic. From the little veranda of my room, with its view of the road, I watched them go by and saw, among others, a deep olive green buggy with a carefully understated touch of gold trim and then a slightly Wild West version in red and white whose driver sported a cowboy hat. In town, I hailed a lovely pale blue model with doors and back panel adorned with very skillful and delicate paintings of local birds. But that one had stainless steel fenders, a cut below my first *myin yahta* with its shiny brass.

That carriage had not only a driver but also a footman, an apparently unemployed buddy, who rode on the roof and jumped down to open the door in the best Jane Austen fashion at every stop, solicitously making sure that my foot didn't slip from the tiny wrought-iron step between carriage and road. The two of them, dreamily silent as we clopped along, horse bells jingling, became a talkative pair when it came to negotiating a fare. Long conversations ensued when I wanted to change direction and could round up an English-speaker to intercede and renegotiate. But the bottom line, despite all the hard bargaining, was always surprisingly modest. As we jangled our way to the botanical garden, past Butler lake, I saw a row of expensive mansions under construction for Rangoon business tycoons. I went back later by bicycle and, while searching for the home of the writer Ohn Pe, managed to get a look inside one of the new houses. With some pride, the workmen showed me the teak floors, stone fireplaces, and marble baths. The house may have been ostentatious, but it was not in bad taste, a relief to those who fear that the architectural character of Maymyo is doomed to destruction as money, especially Chinese money, moves in. Some old British houses were being restored reasonably faithfully elsewhere in town. But questions still hang over other homes and public buildings that have deteriorated badly and could face demolition by buyers with little interest in their historical value.

The botanical garden was a treat in its near-empty serenity, though it was a little short of plants to match the ambitious placards scattered around the grounds. The blossoming season for trees was ending and summer flower beds were still dormant, but the rolling lawns crisscrossed by paths made for a nice lonely afternoon walk. A few families came to have their pictures taken together under the sun, then strolled to a pagoda on the ornamental lake while children ran off their energies on the grass. An elderly resident of Maymyo told me he had always been too afraid of the British, or had felt too unwelcome, to visit the botanical gardens as a child. His boyhood was in any case interrupted when the Japanese took the town in 1942. At only eight years old, he was put to work dismantling machinery of all kinds taken from British properties. Some parts were recycled and others melted down, he said. After the war and independence, when Maymyo was still recovering from the damage of World War II, he was able to spend many hours in the gardens. He remembers how the protected forests that formed part of the conservancy still had tigers and had snakes large enough to kill and swallow a small deer. The woodlands are a lot tamer now and much reduced in size. The tigers are long gone, along with the bragging about encounters with them. Beth Ellis soon decided that tiger stories were the fish stories of the Asian colonies. But for an outsider, the woods are dense and diverse enough to suggest what so much of the Maymyo area must have looked like when the British began to build the town.

Spoiled by the plentiful reading material available in English on the hill stations of South Asia, I was not prepared for the dearth of books, even basic guide books, in Burma—and the disappointment continued almost all the way through Southeast Asia, until I found time to browse in Kuala Lumpur and Singapore. Cycling to every bookshop I could find in Maymyo, I sifted through piles of old books and shelves of new ones, but old Maymyo seemed to have disappeared without a written legacy. There was no library like those I had used in India and Sri Lanka. Bookstores could offer only English texts for school courses and examinations, books with intriguing phrases like "Hla Tin put the dead baby in the fork of a tree" or "U Soe riding could hear the warning of spirits in the forest." Not a word of local history. No bird books or wildlife guides. No maps of any account, though one sales clerk was pleased to produce an old street map of Mandalay.

I enlisted the energetic Nan Mon Khan and her colleague Nay Lin Tun at the Royal Park View Hotel, where I had decided to stay put, since the Candacraig, lovely as it was, had the air of a place run by bureaucrats and the food was close to inedible. The Candacraig, which was built as a rest house—a bachelors' "chummery"—for the Bombay Burma Trading Company, had flower gardens and a wide veranda with comfortable chairs, but its big rooms were not quite as luxurious as those of the Nan Myaing Hotel on the other side of town, where guests of the British governor once stayed. My Royal Park View was not in that class, but it was friendly and well situated and the gang of young people who ran it were enthusiastically helpful. They soon produced a clutch of writers and their books, all of them in Burmese, of course. The authors marked passages I might find most interesting, and I brought them back to New York to be translated. It was Aung Myint, the hotel's manager, who actually went around in his van and collected his old friend, Oo Chit Swe, the author of the commemorative volume.

Years ago, climbing a hill to a temple in Sagaing, I was intercepted by a monk who asked me bluntly, "Do you have any books?" I had none to give him, but he hungrily seized on a German-made map of Southeast Asia I was carrying in my bag. We sat and talked for a while, and he told me how hard he tried to stay in touch with the scholarship of his Buddhist faith and with the learning of the secular world. He had been denied permission to go to Sri Lanka to study the sacred Pali language, which he wanted to master in order to read Buddhism's oldest texts. I said I would send him books. Admitting that he had accosted other foreigners with his singular request for reading material, he said they had tried to mail him books, but none ever arrived. He said he knew that packages for him were regularly intercepted by the government's religious authorities whose job it was to curb the potential political power of the monks. Aware he would not be permitted to receive books from abroad, he hoped only to cadge them from itinerant tourists who trekked to his remote monastery. A teacher in Maymyo told me a similar story. Books sent to him by a well-meaning foreigner had brought the police in their wake.

Decades of military rule had all but stripped Burma of the printed word by the time the country opened to tourism in a significant way—unless one counts the parody of a newspaper, the *New Light of Myanmar*, pub-

lished by the government, along with semiliterate tourism industry magazines intended to boost morale as much as business with their astounding
claims. The extremely modest Arakan beach resort of Ngapali was in their
pages "Asia's Miami"; a new gallery pushing slushily sentimental naturalist
paintings had already "influenced French, American and Japanese art
dealers"; and wonder of wonders, Myanma Air—the dreaded Burma Air-
ways of old—was declared "the world's first global airline." Under a couple of generations of blinkered soldiers not given to the broadening of
minds, the country had lost its points of reference. Every day the *New
Light of Myanmar* printed in the most prominent front-page position the
Four Political Objectives, the Four Economic Objectives, and the Four
Social Objectives. They read a bit like General Ne Win's Burmese Way to
Socialism in drag: a lot of nationalist bombast with the reins of the economy firmly in the hands of the ruling military. The introduction of that
creed in the 1960s had set Burma back at least a generation. The country
was so isolated that it could never bring itself to sign on to nonalignment.

CNN International and the BBC's world television news are now available in Burma, along with MTV and the Cartoon Network on half a
dozen channels in Maymyo. Students can find *Time* magazine in the
town market. A few of the young people I met (who liberated most of my
reading material) were angry about the state of education available to
them. One young man, waiting for admission to Rangoon University to
study science, said he didn't know why he bothered. It was too easy to get
a degree now. All you had to do is pay the right people 4,000 or 5,000
kyat and you could graduate without studying, he said. The others nodded
emphatically. For a number of years, many young people have been deciding to forgo higher education and look for a job in the burgeoning
tourism industry, even if only on the fringes. I remembered two students
in Rangoon who were driving a shared taxi when I encountered them at
the airport some years ago. I asked them to tell me about a religious holiday that was approaching. "I am so sorry," the more talkative one said.
"We don't know the festival days. We only know what days the foreign
flights come in."

A century ago, the spirited young Beth Ellis had her disappointments,
too, in the months she spent with her sister. Maymyo was so windy, she
said, that all manner of things blew through the house and had to be
plucked off the back wall of the compound. The piano lovingly shipped
and carted into the Burmese hills soon "produced such an extraordinary
conglomeration of sounds as would certainly have caused a German band

to die of envy" and then went entirely silent. Her hopes of cooking the latest in European dishes for her sister ran aground in the outdoor tin kitchen with an oven that looked more like a doghouse and turned most efforts into cinders. Anyway, chicken was the only meat available at the market. Mail ordering was hopeless "without an expenditure of all one's powers of sarcasm in letters of remonstrance."

Beth Ellis's small book has a larger importance, beyond its incisive and evocative description of this hill station in the making. There were many women in Burma, India, and other colonies who kept diaries or wrote books about a life in the outposts of empire that was far from the glamorous and pain-free existence that a dozen or more servants, a tropical garden, and hours of idleness on the veranda might otherwise suggest. The wise and witty accounts left by women—some anguished, some funny, some far more perceptive than anything written by the men in imperial service—are slowly and belatedly finding new audiences. Women in the colonies have taken hard knocks from historians, as the contemporary ethnologist Ann Laura Stoler pointed out in a 1989 article, "Rethinking Colonial Categories: European Communities and the Boundaries of Rule." Stoler, taking a new look at conventional views of colonial women, questioned one widely held assumption: that the introduction of European women in Asia created or intensified racism. A hundred years earlier, on the scene in Maymyo, Beth Ellis challenged another myth: that colonial life—and hill station life in particular—was one unending revel. "Their husbands away, or busy much of the day, deprived of their children's society, with few books, few amusements, and practically no duties, life is far from being an unqualified joy to these exiled women," Ellis wrote after watching her sister and their acquaintances desperately looking for something worthwhile to do day after day. "Let the British matron who would accuse her sister of idleness, frivolity and worse, consider these things, and forebear to judge."

6

A Malaysian Mix

Penang Hill and Maxwell's Hill

Cameron Highlands

Fraser's Hill

Modern Malaysia rising in the Cameron Highlands

Penang Hill and Maxwell's Hill

Malaya was Britain's only true Southeast Asian colony, and it was a small one, measured by the standards of India. All around Malaya were territories very different in culture and history: Siam, which was never colonized; French Indochina; the Dutch Indies; and the Philippines—first Spanish, then American. The Malay peninsula supported large Chinese trading communities and colorful Malay courts ruled by Islamic sultans who took their time about joining this thing called empire, preserving much of their traditional Muslim law and culture. The British were largely civil servants or members of a planter society that came to dominate colonial life here, as it could never have done in India, with its imperial-scale civil service and its greater geographic and economic diversity. Although it was not until the early twentieth century that London's hold on the Malay peninsula was secured, the British had been roaming the neighborhood for at least a couple of hundred years, establishing themselves incrementally in strategic outposts.

A "steady as you go" philosophy also characterized contemporary Malaysia as it first preserved—better than Indians have done—the public buildings, roads, and institutions the British left behind, and then began with rising prosperity to augment and improve on them, at least until recently, when the passion for skyscrapers rewrote much of the urban skyline. Their stewardship of the hill stations until very recently has been a good example of Malaysian deliberation, even if not all would applaud the changes that are now taking place.

The first proper colonial hill station in Asia began to take shape on Penang Island at the end of the eighteenth century, and the last imperial British hill towns were still works in progress as late as the 1960s. Malaya—and after 1957, independent Malaysia—was then recovering from setbacks in the 1940s and 1950s caused by a long Japanese occupation and an even longer Communist insurgency. Now the hill stations seem to be looking forward with uncommon confidence to the twenty-first century because, with characteristic Southeast Asian adaptability, Malaysians are remaking them with a new generation of travelers in mind.

In a tropical country with plenty of beaches, cool hill stations add a touch of diversity to the national image and enhance Malaysia's appeal to newly rich Asian tourists who outnumber and outspend Westerners all around the region. If that means massive hotels and condominiums on the hilltops and a golf club atmosphere, with fairways and greens on every piece of land that can be flattened by human effort, all the better, say the country's planners. Since Malaysians, like other Asians, have lately been caught up in a golfing frenzy, what better place to tee off than on rolling, grassy expanses chilled by a mountain night and watered naturally and gently by dew and mist. For those who like more thrills and noise, a postindependence hill station, the Genting Highlands, has been purposely built for gambling. Anyone who visits this monstrosity in the hope of seeing history reborn, however, leaves with a wish that this monument to cheap glitz will not be repeated elsewhere.

Penang Hill, the oldest British hill station, has so far escaped a total makeover to lure the new mandarins, and this hill station is nowadays more a local tourist attraction than an international resort. But who knows. Malaysian developers are famous in Asia for a proposal that would make Cambodia's magnificent temples at Angkor the backdrop for a tourist hotel and golf center. At least for the moment, the cluster of hills near the center of Penang Island, near the northern end of the Strait of Malacca, an area smaller in scale than the classic Asian hill stations and barely 2,000 feet above sea level, does not rank with Malaysia's Cameron Highlands, or even Fraser's Hill, also not a very large place. Both of these latter hill stations are in remote reaches of the mountainous spine of the Malay peninsula, closer to Malaysia's capital, Kuala Lumpur, and to Singapore.

Penang Hill, on its island, like Maxwell's Hill, on the peninsula near Taiping, were cheated by geography and history, and thus never quite established themselves among the great hill stations. On the international tourist circuit, Penang's beaches are better known than its hills, although the beaches also have their limitations, lapped as they are by the less-than-sparkling Malacca Strait. Yet Penang Island, or Pulau Pinang in Malay, is one of the country's most interesting states, with a pronounced character all its own. It also has one of Asia's great old hotels, the Eastern and Oriental, known by its friends as the E&O.

Scrappy Penang has left thorns all down the side of the mainland. Smuggling and drug running have kept Malaysian antinarcotics squads busy there over the years. Penang has also long been a center of multiple advocacy movements and protests, where social action groups and environmentalists flourish, to the annoyance of the central government, especially under Prime Minister Mahathir Mohamad, who in 1986 locked up a number of its activists as security threats. Malaysia's outspoken first prime minister, the late Tunku Abdul Rahman, who had a home in Penang, was outraged and said so to anyone who came to pay court. Penang always thought itself an intellectual cut above the rest. Not to mention a whole lot more economically energetic.

Chandra Muzaffar, perhaps the country's most tireless social activist, who did time in jail before he more or less reconciled himself with mainstream Malaysian politics, once explained to me what made Penang special. "I think it is partly because Penang has a more autonomous middle class than the rest of Malaysia, and these people do not depend on the government for jobs. It also has a strong educational tradition, with great fluency in English." The first English-language school in Southeast Asia opened here in 1816.

Penang has been a thriving commercial outpost for a long time, with a very large ethnic Chinese population that gave the island its unique character within the Malaysian union. The island's well-schooled, English-speaking workforce helped make Penang, once known as the Island of the Betel Nut Tree, the electronics center of Malaysia in the twentieth century. But then Penang has been a pioneering place for centuries.

The island, only 180 square miles in size, fell into British hands in 1786, when a persuasive trader and adventurer, Captain Francis Light, acquired from the sultan of Kedah the right to establish a base there for the East India Company. Light, a former merchant navy officer, renamed the island for the Prince of Wales, the future George IV, and began to build a settlement that he called George Town. Penang was administered as part of Bengal until 1805, after Light's death, when it became a full-fledged presidency of the East India Company, the fourth after Madras, Bombay, and Calcutta. But hopes that Penang would be an important naval base were never realized. In 1826, as British attention focused farther down the coast of peninsular Malaya, Penang was combined with Malacca and Singapore to form the Straits Settlement Presidency. Six years later, it lost the presidency government to Singapore. Its moment as a center of imperial authority was brief.

But during those early decades of the nineteenth century, before hill stations began to be built on the Indian subcontinent, the British in Penang quickly created the retreat on Penang Hill, where the air, an early visitor said, was especially bracing, open to breezes from the sea. The existence of a presidency headquarters in the island's lowland capital brought in enough civil servants and East India Company functionaries, troops, and merchants to warrant the building of at least a scattering of higher-altitude bungalows. A British governor's residence, Bel Retiro, was constructed on the hill, along with a small hospital and a kind of sanitarium called the

Convalescent Bungalow. An inn, the Crag Hotel, opened optimistically, but could not long survive the official eclipse of Penang. Although there were always civil servants or officials of the East India Company on the is-land—from time to time they were ordered to duty in Burma, in the same way Spain dispatched its functionaries from Mexico to the Philippines—the ranks inevitably thinned irreversibly with Penang's political decline. Besides, few of those official Britons remaining seemed to have had the wherewithal to spend much time or money in the hills.

To get to Penang Hill in its glory days, one began on horseback in George Town, then switched to a rented hill pony or sedan chair for the ascent. It was not until the 1920s that a funicular railway was built. The Penang Hill Railway, like many construction projects in the hills of Asia, was a phenomenal accomplishment. Ultimately, it allowed almost anyone with change for the fare to visit the small hill station, which soon became less a resort than the day-tripper's excursion it is now. People make the climb largely for the funicular experience, have cup of tea or a soft drink at the top, and come back down. A small hotel, the Bellevue, is there for those who want to stay and savor the scenery and breezes. From Penang Hill there is a broad view of the strait that separates the island from the mainland town of Butterfield. Frankly, I think a drive around the island, with its lovely Malay kampongs—clusters of houses with their exquisite painted-wood trimming—easily rivals the hill, the view notwithstanding. But then Penang is so small you can do both and be back at the E&O in time for dinner.

The best account of colonial life in Penang available to most foreign travelers is John Turnbull Thomson's *Glimpses into Life in Malayan Lands*, first published in 1864. Thomson was a surveyor sent to the region in 1838 at the incredible age of sixteen. This was apparently not so unusual; there are also accounts of planters still in their teens and twenties taking up resi-dence in the colonies. In India, Elihu Yale went to work for the East India Company in Madras in 1670 while in his early twenties. He was appointed governor of Fort St. George there in his mid-thirties and had time to come back later as a civilian to make a fortune. Some of that money went to en-dowing a school in New Haven, Connecticut, where his father had settled. The institution was the Collegiate School, which in due course became Yale University. In Ceylon, Thomas Skinner was still a teenager (with the rank of an army major) when he was put in charge of building a part of the road linking the port of Colombo with the former Sinhalese hill capital, Kandy. For many, putting long years into colonial service of one kind or another had less to do with good health and longevity, neither of which a career in the Indies promised, and more to do with the early age at which a young person, almost always male, sailed out to the East.

Although not entirely devoid of the prejudices of his time in his assessment of the "native races," Thomson, a civilian not in official service, was able to turn an honest, irreverent eye on the British colonial administration and the society it created. Allowing for the unforgiving absolutism of youth sitting in judgment on its elders, the arbitrariness and corruption among colonial officials that Thomson described were probably real, because he had as his witnesses and informants the local people he met while at work on whom the consequences of malfeasance fell so heavily. The Anglican clergy came in for especially sharp scorn; the young surveyor thought that the politically well connected bishops and vicars sent out to the colonies were spiritually useless and often more interested in making money on the side than serving either God or his struggling little congregations abroad. Thomson had a particularly keen understanding of daily life, upstairs and downstairs, because he had learned the Malay language early and developed total fluency. He rejoiced when the din of voices around him suddenly became conversation to his ears. "With the possession of the language of the country," he wrote, "the people no longer passed and repassed as groups of strange folk."

Thomson was fascinated by British social life in Penang and on Penang Hill in the 1830s and 1840s, and he described the lavish dinner parties and other amusements in evocative detail. A reader can feel the breezes on the verandas, hear the crunch of the gravel drive under horses' hooves, and see the gentlemen dismount from their carriages wearing "snow-white trousers" and black coats, accompanied by ladies in fine dresses. At dinner in the home of an obviously wealthy and generous planter, Thomson was regaled with wines, spirits, and ale and fed a choice of soups, fish, "joints of sweet Bengal mutton, Chinese capons, Keddah fowls, and Sangora ducks, Yorkshire hams, Java potatoes, and Malay ubis," followed by a rice-and-curry course, cheese, and fruit. There were card games and piano duets after the meal to fritter away another hour or two, and then the sated guests went home, their carriage lights twinkling down the road.

Because of his ability to communicate in Malay, a common language of Southeast Asia, then and to some extent now, Thomson was equally incisive and meticulously descriptive in his accounts of Malay and Chinese social rituals and relationships. He had friends among Chinese merchants, Malay rulers, and Indian and Ceylonese migrants. He shrewdly observed the importance of the *nonia* (or *nona* or *nyai*), a native mistress of a European in Southeast Asia. Given the youthful age and frequent isolation of colonial civil servants and planters, it was inevitable that sex and companionship would be sought and found in the neighborhood. The women chosen—who sometimes became legal wives before the arrival of European rivals—hoped for a good life and perhaps a niche in colonial society, or on the fringes of it. There was always the possibility of being cast out with indifference, if not cruelty, by a man who had tired of his plaything or needed a European wife for the sake of his career. Stories and novels about Southeast Asia are often populated by such women, Chinese, Malay, or Indian. A lot of them ended up in indignity on the veranda, their meager possessions thrown out in a small bundle at their feet—sometimes by a triumphant servant jealous of another native who had tried to rise above her station.

The most memorable and finely developed portrait of a *nonia* may be Pramoedya Ananta Toer's Nyai Ontosoroh, the Indonesian partner of a Dutchman and the mother of his children in a quartet of books about the life of Minke, a young Javanese man coming of age in colonial Dutch society. Minke falls tragically in love with the Nyai Ontosoroh's mixed-race daughter, Annelies, and in the process becomes very close to the older woman. Pramoedya endowed the Nyai Ontosoroh with a great measure of dignity and intelligence, making her rise above the small-minded, uncouth, and multiprejudiced Dutch, Javanese, and Chinese characters around her. In the first book, *This Earth of Mankind*, the attributes that struck Minke, the only Javanese student in a Dutch school, in his first encounter with Ontosoroh were her flawless command of Dutch and her table manners.

"Nyai ate calmly, like a genuine European woman who had graduated from an English boarding school," he thought as he watched her. "I earnestly examined the position of the spoons and forks, the use of the soup ladle and the knives, carving forks, and also the elaborate dinner service. It was all perfect. The white steel knife seemed to have been sharpened not on stone but on a steel grinding wheel, so there were no scratches. From everything I had read, even the position of the napkins and the finger bowls and the position of the glasses in their silver cases could not be faulted."

Pramoedya's story also demonstrates eventually the painful circumscription of a colonial mistress's rights, even over her own children, when Europeans intrude to take charge. In the end, Annelies is lost to both her mother and to Minke, her young Javanese lover, and Pramoedya makes us care. Many other *nonia* characters, lacking the depth of the Nyai On-tosoroh, were no more than vehicles for adding sex, a touch of oriental ex-oticism, or even witchcraft to a tale, since natives were known to cast spells.

For Thomson, who was nonjudgmental about the taking or not taking of an Asian wife or mistress, the great sorrow in the system flowed from the inevitable misunderstandings that ensued when a native woman tried, and failed, to turn a physical relationship into a permanent place for her-self in a lone European man's household. To her compatriots, if not always to the household servants, it was only natural that her role should be reg-ularized in some fashion. An intelligent and beautiful woman, often very young but frequently trained in her *nonia* role by an older practitioner, could not fathom rejection; nor could others in her society. "The children of passion know not, nor understand not, the energy that binds the son of the cold north to his destiny," Thomson wrote. "Each weighs the other by their own standards, so their actions are inexplicable. By our standard their actions are lewd, immoral and wicked. By their standard our actions are cold, prudish and unfeeling."

Almost a century passed between the founding of British Penang and the creation of the first hill station in peninsular Malaysia across the Malacca Strait. Maxwell's Hill, now known as Bukit Larut, is little more than an anachronistic extension of the Malaysian city of Taiping, some-thing of a resort city itself. The first colonial bungalows began to appear in this hilly part of Perak state in the 1880s, though there had been British administrators called assistant residents, stationed there for some time be-fore that. One of them was William Edward Maxwell, whose base came to be called Maxwell's Hill, and the name grew to encompass the whole settlement. In Maxwell's Hill, a small hill station where rest and convales-cence were the goals of visitors, official and otherwise, British colonial ad-ministrators built houses or were provided them by the government. Mis-sionaries were also usually in residence in cottages that bore their denominational names. Prominent among God's servants who sought rest in Maxwell's Hill were men and women from the American Methodist Mission in Malaya. As elsewhere in the Asian hills, missionary bungalows soon became permanent fixtures and local landmarks. "Turn right/left at the Lutheran bungalow," people seemed to say everywhere I went.

Though Maxwell's Hill was never a grand hill station on the scale of those in India or even Burma, because like Penang it was too far from the centers of power farther south in Singapore and Kuala Lumpur, people drawn to the Perak hills entertained the same hopes for development as those who later sought refuge in highlands farther south. Around Maxwell's Hill, there were early efforts to introduce fruit and vegetable farming and to import herds of cattle for grazing on high grasslands. As everywhere in Southeast Asia, overseas Chinese populations and new immigrants from China were quick to seize and profit from burgeoning business opportunities. People needed transportation into the hills, and small livery and porterage companies sprang up, first in Penang and later in other colonial centers.

Chinese and sometimes European merchants moved in to open provisions stores, offering to find and deliver all manner of consumer goods to hilltop bungalows. Chinese families seemed able to accumulate capital more rapidly and use it more effectively than either native Malays or immigrants from India and Ceylon. This economic pattern would later create serious tensions between Malaysian Chinese and Malays and lead to a comprehensive affirmative action policy favoring Malays in the economy and politics after Malaysian independence. No ethnic Chinese can become prime minister of Malaysia.

CAMERON HIGHLANDS

There are no other hill stations in Asia where the architecture, the atmosphere, and the tidiness imposed on nature by the colonial powers, most of all the British, are so carefully and consciously maintained as they are in the Cameron Highlands and Fraser's Hill. This link with history is not necessarily threatened by the rush into development. If you stand where the condos and giant hotels rising on the periphery are not visible, it is easier here than anywhere else to experience the calm, the freshness of air and the rustling, verdant tropical forests that beckoned and soothed the overheated and overwrought colonial. Contemporary planners usually have at least a dim notion of salable natural attractions and have done enough market research to know that newly rich Asians can also be sold nostalgia. Just hang around the flower gardens on a weekend at the Smokehouse, the ersatz English country inn, and watch the steady stream of young people taking pictures of each other in a vintage British telephone booth. In the Cameron Highlands, white plaster patterned with wood to look half-timbered covers a lot of concrete, and the effect, although not exactly authentic, is not bad.

Moreover, the highlands of the Malay peninsula are blessedly rich in rainfall, a natural restorative for even an abused landscape. Flower gardens explode with color. Patches of jungle are still vast, dense, noisy, and even frightening as they lurch eagerly toward narrow dirt roads and tracks in the hills that could easily disappear into the creepers. On hiking trails in Fraser's Hill, I felt the organic tropical forest breathing, whistling, shrieking, and shuddering all around in a way I had not experienced since plodding into a jungle in Borneo with Australian gold prospectors. Visitors to the Malaysian highlands are told to leave itineraries with hotels or friends when walking in the jungle and to take enough supplies to survive at least a twenty-four-hour disappearance if lost, during which it is helpful to light a small, smoky fire, since rescuers have no way of seeing a stranded hiker under the canopy of green.

In the Cameron Highlands, I followed a narrow dirt road into the wild undergrowth in search of the spot where Jim Thompson, the enigmatic American who created the modern Thai silk industry, disappeared inexplicably from Moonlight Cottage just before tea on Easter Sunday in 1967, apparently while on a walk in the woods. For the first time I understood exactly why his disappearance has remained a mystery despite the army of policemen, clairvoyants, swindlers, and adventurers who thought they would find him. No clue to his fate, not even a shred of his clothes, was ever found in jungle still so impenetrably tangled that walking only a few feet in any direction is hard work.

The Cameron Highlands is not a single place like Ootacamund or Maymyo or Dalat, but a region. Three towns and more than half a dozen hamlets are strung along a winding road that begins at Tapah, on the coastal plain, and rises to more than 5,000 feet (with higher peaks) before it drifts into the Blue Valley Tea Estate at more or less the end of the resort route sixty miles later. The gateway to the Cameron Highlands is Ringlet, a commercial town with a large Tamil population of South Indian and Sri Lankan origins. A Hindu temple marks one entrance to Ringlet, which is otherwise distinguished mostly by gas stations, service industries, and basic shops selling hardware, tools, and food. Although the natural setting of Ringlet is attractive, its altitude is below 3,000 feet, and the vegetation can be a little scrubby.

The two towns at the center of hill station life are Tanah Rata and Brinchang, with a village known as Kea Farm just beyond. Brinchang has taken the biggest hit from the bulldozers and cement mixers in recent years. A "Tudor-style" megahotel of more than 500 rooms built by the Equatorial chain has just joined the mix of smaller hotels and roadside wonders like a cactus park and butterfly farm, where, alas, most of the butterflies are pinned to cardboard to be sold as souvenirs. Brinchang's dusty back streets do lead, however, to the gilded extravaganza of the Sam Poh Temple, a Buddhist shrine that is testimony to the wealth of the local Chinese Malaysian farmers. Outside the temple gates, where there is a view of a sultan's retreat on a distant hill, you can have a Chinese seal, a chop, made from the phonetic rendering of a Western name. With inexhaustible Chinese ingenuity, the chop maker has somehow acquired a mammoth directory of foreign names, and he is pretty confident of finding most.

Like other Asian hill stations, the Cameron Highlands is a popular resort not too difficult to reach even without the proposed highway the Malaysian government seems to think is necessary to link it to other towns along the mountainous ridges of Pahang state. But the crowds that come are smaller, quieter, and more affluent than those assaulting the hill stations of India, for example, or thronging the streets of Baguio, now more a busy Filipino city than a resort. The Malaysians and Singaporeans who arrive in their sleek cars and buses are Southeast Asian statistics on wheels. Unlike in India and much of its neighborhood, population growth has been cut dramatically in Southeast Asia, income levels have risen rapidly, education is available to all, and a consumer culture creates an awareness of style and taste.

That gloss makes life in the Malaysian highlands both less harrowing and more boring for a traveler, of course. There are few spontaneous, cacophonous dramas here. No dire Gothic warnings to extortioners and molesters of women posted prominently at tourist sites. There are also no gaping class and culture differences on a South Asian scale. When a visitor strolls the sidewalks of Tanah Rata, the one-street tourist center of the upper Cameron Highlands, everyone—Malaysian and foreign—mingles and blends in an easy equality, eating at cheap sidewalk food stalls or in comfortable air-conditioned restaurants, buying or browsing in souvenir shops, hailing taxis, catching buses, or hiking up to the Smokehouse to enjoy a drink or tea in the garden among Home Counties flower beds. No heart-wrenching, sense-challenging roadside squalor. No betel spit.

The Malaysian highlands have always been sparsely populated. The first people in these mountains were aboriginals or migrants whose origins are lost in time who lived on shifting agriculture and hunting with blow guns and poison darts. Among other theories about what happened to Jim Thompson was that he had been done away with by forest people, though there was never any real evidence to support the idea. In Malay, aboriginals of differing linguistic and cultural communities who lay claim to being the first to live here are known collectively as *orang asli,* the original people. There are still *orang asli* villages of *atap*—leaves and thatch—scattered across the highlands, where a subsistence living is about all that can be expected. Ethnic Malay and Chinese Malaysians enjoy pointing out *orang asli* to foreigners: groups of men lounging at a bus stop, maybe, or a woman and child in the market place. To a Malaysian, it seems to be the tightly curled black hair and slight stature that is noticed first, not skin color in a country of many hues. An Indian Malaysian, taking me to an *orang asli* village in his taxi, added that universal all-purpose put-down: "They don't work hard like us." Unlike in India, the Philippines, or Vietnam, where the crafts of tribal people have attained a certain chic quality in many places and even carry substantial price tags, in Malaysia the *orang asli* have not made much artistic impact or have not been encouraged to revive or promote traditional work, except in Borneo, where most indigenous populations are not classified as *orang asli* but *bumiputra*—sons of the soil, a rank higher, equal to Malays in the political pecking order. On the peninsula, the *orang asli* seem as invisible now as they were when the first British civil servants hacked their way into the hills.

Although the Straits Settlements were established as a collection of territories governed by the British in the first quarter of the nineteenth century, British authority was not imposed on most of peninsular Malaya until much later. In the last quarter of the nineteenth century, Britain created a political union called the Federated Malay States—Pahang, Perak, Negri Sembilan, and Selangor—and had made Kuala Lumpur the capital by 1895. By 1914 there were British advisers in the rest of the Malay sultanates. Meanwhile, considerable British economic interests had developed, with plantations spreading across lowlands, particularly along the west coast, where tin mining and commercial agriculture shared the land. Rubber took off in the early twentieth century. By then Britain had cleared large areas of rain forest to create plantations and build roads. This was no mean environmental destruction; the character of western Malaya's climate must have been radically altered in a very short time. Dry barren hills sliced today by Malaysian highways were once tangles of undergrowth under canopies of trees. Jungles were too dense for travel except by boat or elephant, early adventurers wrote.

S. Robert Aiken, whose book, *Imperial Belvederes: The Hill Stations of Malaysia,* provides the most concise yet comprehensive history of the founding of the Malaysian hill stations, thought that William Cameron, the British surveyor who explored other areas of Malaya, probably never saw the highlands that later inherited his name. As early as 1885, when Cameron was at work in Perak state, there had been suggestions that areas of mountainous Pahang might be turned into health-giving hill stations, but no extensive exploration was undertaken for nearly forty years thereafter. And this despite the longings of many a European resident of the peninsula for a place of refuge larger and with more promise of self-sufficiency than either Penang or Maxwell's Hill.

Two expeditions in the 1920s rectified this oversight. According to Aiken, the first methodical exploration was led by H. C. Robinson, director of museums for the colonial government. That was followed by an intensive examination of the region by Sir George Maxwell, not the Maxwell of Maxwell's Hill, but a colonial official who had been instrumental earlier in the opening of Fraser's Hill. After studying the land and climate, Maxwell concluded that the highlands had great potential first of all for agriculture. He described the plateaus and pastures as not unlike those of Nuwara Eliya and Baguio—an interesting observation that tells us that by the early twentieth century hill station experts were very well traveled and equipped to make useful comparisons. The 1927 *Handbook to British Malaysia* suggested that, like Ootacamund, the highlands of Pahang might also become retirement communities for Europeans. Dozens of bungalows, two boarding schools, and the inevitable golf course had been built by 1940.

After 1926, when development began in earnest, the paved road from Tapah was constructed and tea plantations were established. Though the countryside is not completely blanketed by tea estates, as is the landscape of Nuwara Eliya, tea played a large part in the developing identity of the Cameron Highlands, with its planter society. Tea looms large in the local tourist industry. Plantations tours are popular, and the most common souvenirs for sale in the "handicraft" shops of Tanah Rata are packets of tea or, recently, tea bags and fancy tea blends that zing the old drink with newly fashionable flavors and spicy fragrances. Agricultural development was encouraged and supported from the earliest days of the Cameron Highlands.

A number of pioneering Chinese farms were soon established, especially in the higher valleys. Today, roaming the croplands around Kea Farm, a visitor sees the bright red household shrines dotting the fields of Chinese families who still work the land and produce modern Malaysia's finest vegetable crops. The Kea Farm vegetable markets are a tourist attraction in themselves. People drive all the way from Kuala Lumpur and Singapore to shop, insistent that nothing beats the taste of produce from the Cameron Highlands. Prices are fashionable too. A taxi driver told me that smart people went down to shop in Tanah Rata, where the same vegetables sold for a lot less.

The Chinese in the highlands suffered grievously during the Communist insurrection of 1948 to 1960, when they were caught between rebels and British-led antiguerrilla forces who destroyed many of their homes to prevent potential sympathizers from succoring the insurgents, most of whom were ethnic Chinese. The fate of the Chinese in Malaya during the period known as "the Emergency" was not unlike that of those Japanese-Americans who were rounded up to be relocated, detained, and denied the right to a livelihood by the United States government in World War II.

With all this fascinating history and engrossing terrain as backdrop, why was it that of all the great hill stations of Asia, the Cameron Highlands seemed the least warm and appealing? Looking back, I liked it least. This had nothing to do with its setting. Or the journey into the hills from Kuala Lumpur.

The roads of Malaysia are superb. India may never know their equal, at least not in this generation. The highway out of Kuala Lumpur's vast international airport at Subang—already slated for replacement by a new and bigger facility to the west near Klang—was six lane, then four lane, as the highway, which runs the length of western Malaysia, left the metropolitan area. The oil-palm groves and rubber plantations along the road were a little monotonous but beautiful nonetheless. Oil palms are squat, yet more shapely, cousins of their taller, more regal relatives, and on their trunks grow soft ferns and other gentle greenery. At Tapah, where we left the road to begin the trip into the hills, a good two-lane road took over. It was indistinguishable from an American country road, with guard rails and ample directional and distance signs. After the hair-raising, bone-rattling days on the road in India and Burma, why was this not a welcome change?

Perhaps it was because although the roads were the best I had encountered in Asia, the driver was the worst. He didn't want to go to the Cameron Highlands. He and the car company's representative at Subang tried to talk me into the Genting Highlands instead. I explained politely and without damning elaboration that I had been there and had no interest in returning. We set off late. I had just endured a night at Kuala Lumpur's astonishingly awful airport hotel. On the highway, the driver wandered all over the road without reason, sometimes straddling the dotted line that divided the two northbound lanes. He tilted his seat back to a near-reclining position. I took this to be cool. He delighted in passing cars with only inches to spare. He chatted on his cellular phone with friends. He smoked. He turned up the pop music until I turned it off. At seventy miles an hour, he opened the window wide to sneeze, frequently, spraying germs into the blast of hot air that roared through the otherwise air-conditioned car. "Excuse me," he said ritually after each explosion.

When we hit the sharply winding hill road, he wove wildly across curves—legend has it that there are 600 of them—swaying and braking suddenly, passing cars at construction sites where other drivers had wisely slowed down. I started out annoyed and got angry at not being able to concentrate on the exceptionally beautiful forests along the roadside, thick with broadleaf bamboo, tree ferns, and a mix of deciduous and evergreen trees. I arrived at the Smokehouse in Tanah Rata with a deeply entrenched headache and an unsettled stomach. Not a good beginning. "Nothing to do here," the driver observed, then departed sullenly when I declined his offer to return for me at the end of my stay.

Or maybe the problem was the 1930s Smokehouse, now called, unfortunately, Ye Olde Smokehouse Hotel. The longer I stayed, the more I thought of a tea shop in Hoddesdon, Hertfordshire, where two no-nonsense women presided when I live in England years ago. Their specialty was apple tart with custard and mild abuse. I found myself connecting them with the tendency of British men to seek masochistic sexual pleasure from women dressed up as headmistresses, school-dinner ladies, or nurse matrons, avatars of authority figures from a cozy British male childhood. I think I lived in England too long—eight years—to sustain a romantic image of the places that are too-too British, with their cold pretensions. At the Smokehouse, there was a whiff of an uncompromising superiority and enforced quaintness. To further prick the memory, Tanah Rata, the town nearest the Smokehouse, was awash with arrogant young Brits, tourists and expatriates alike. Smug was the word that came to mind.

It did not describe the warm, unaffected North Country British couple I met within minutes of arriving at the Smokehouse. They happened to be in the lobby asking to see a room as I was checking into mine, so I invited them up. When the staff left, they confided that they were staying somewhere else "up the hill" in the tangle of hotels in Brinchang, but had always wanted to see this place. They told me that friends of theirs had come to the Smokehouse to spend Christmas but were so put off by the atmosphere that they fled not only the hotel but also Malaysia.

It is more than a little unfair, however, to damn the Smokehouse for the alternately prissy and condescending atmosphere left behind by colonial Britain. In fact, the staff formed an unusually interesting group of young people. Two of them, the bartender and a duty manager, were Burmese exiles who heard that I had just been in Burma and were eager for news of their home country and for an outsider's opinion of where its military rulers were leading it. I learned a lot about the ease by which Burmese passed through Thailand, where everything is for sale, including false documents of all kinds to smooth the would-be immigrant's route. These young men had chosen Malaysia and liked it. Others pushed on to the West, armed with newly minted passports, visas, and other necessary—if fraudulent—papers.

There was a very cheerful part-time Malaysian waiter of nineteen, who announced at our first meeting over a cheese sandwich that she was not Malay but *orang asli*. "You know *orang asli*?" she asked incredulously after I nodded at her self-description, noticing for the first time her frizzy black hair and broad features. "And," she added for emphasis, "I am Christian." Her good command of English came from a Methodist school, she told me, resting her tray at her side to keep me company at lunch. While awaiting some exam results, she was planning to enroll in a Kuala Lumpur college to study innkeeping, she said. She had heard that New Zealanders were in charge, and that left open the possibility of foreign study some-where down the road. Given her goal of joining what she called "the hos-pitality industry," she seemed distinctly underwhelmed at having the rare opportunity to learn on the job at the Smokehouse for even a few months, a position she got through an auntie who once worked here. "I really wanted to work in a supermarket in Ipoh," she explained.

Why did no one I encountered in the tourist world of the Cameron Highlands seem either knowledgeable or particularly interested in its his-tory? There were maps and booklets full of facts about how much it costs to send a postcard to Brunei or how to dial the United States through AT&T's USA Direct, and lots of magazines for sale to investment buffs and computer nerds, but precious little information on the highlands. Did this apathy about origins among young people, this lack of curiosity about things around us, have something to do with growing up under a Malaysian political regime that is obsessed with the control of informa-tion and where an inquiring mind can lead one to grief? If newspapers were also hard to find, it seemed that was because no one thought them worth the effort of hauling them up to Tanah Rata. Malaysian newspapers and television reports don't so much cover news as inflate to ridiculous proportions every utterance or move of the prime minister, Mahathir Mohamad. Or, more recently, his deputy and heir apparent, Anwar Ibrahim.

In the absence of books and knowledgeable sources in the Cameron Highlands and Fraser's Hill, I had time to construct theories about why an Indian, Sri Lankan, Burmese, or Pakistani would be eager to talk about a town and to find in its byways a few people who are recognized and respected for their grasp of local history—and why this didn't happen in Malaysia. To paraphrase Santayana loosely, reading history saves a lot of trouble. In 1875, Frank Swettenham, who would later become governor of Singapore, visited this same state of Pahang, albeit at the invitation of the sultan, and was taken to a performance of pre-Islamic court dancing. His own account of the evening, included in J. M. Gullick's wonderful anthology, *Adventures and Encounters: Europeans in South-East Asia*, describes his growing curiosity, as the unusual dances progressed, as to what this was all about. The women who danced were revealingly dressed and lavishly adorned. The music was Javanese, not Malayan. Swettenham looked around for guidance. "But those of the audience whom I was near enough to question were, Malay like, unable to give me much information," he wrote.

At the Smokehouse, I went through parlors with shelves full of moldy books hoping for enlightenment, but to no avail. A few newspaper clippings saved by the management helped. From them I learned that the Smokehouse was not built until 1937, almost a decade after the tea plantations began to claim the hills. A picture taken soon after its opening shows the English country-style building sitting exposed in a clearing. The richness of its gardens came later, improving the environment considerably, in contrast to the negative impact made on the surroundings by many other Asian hill station hotels.

During World War II, when Japan overran Malaya, the Smokehouse became quarters for officers of the Imperial Japanese Army, who apparently took pretty good care of their attractive accommodations. After Japan's defeat in 1945, a British architect restored the hotel, enlarging it at the same time into the rambling assortment of corridors, stairways, nooks, and bedchambers it is today. The rooms, all different, are really all suites, carefully made to look as chintzy and floral as an English country inn demands. My suite was called Squire. My neighbors were Gwenlaura and

Hazelwell. Down the corridor were Glenlee and Fairhaven. I also found Ambleside, Wycombe, Glenmore, Warwick, and Elgin. Once all these quarters, with their wood floors and solid wood furniture, had wood-burning fireplaces, but they were all sealed after a guest lost control of his blaze and nearly gutted the whole building. We are treated these days to those electric heaters that tingle the chilblains of Britons everywhere, whereas open fires are restricted to the very pleasing pub, the Old Tap Room, and the adjoining saloon bar on the ground floor. Wood, leather, and rough terra-cotta floors make the pub especially appealing. Outside on the roof, there are also terra-cotta tiles, but frequent showers and day-long mists have turned them into small gardens of mosses and lichens and even a few patches of impatiens.

The last real innkeeper the Smokehouse had was Colonel Stanley Middleton Foster, a veteran of the brutal Burmese jungle campaigns of World War II who stayed on in Asia and bought the place in 1962. Some old books beside the hearth are still stamped "Foster's Smokehouse." Foster cribbed from antiques magazines to commission reproductions of old European furniture and haunted the antique markets of Kuala Lumpur and Singapore looking for bargains. In 1976, he told my colleague David Andelman of the *New York Times* how he bought what looked like a pile of old blackened candlesticks for $4 and found, after he had them cleaned and polished, that he owned a four-foot-high solid silver candelabra that had belonged to a British regiment when regiments traveled with candelabras. It had been lost in the confusion of war. Foster had it appraised: It was worth about $18,000.

Since 1977, the Smokehouse has been owned by a commercial company, Country Inns Sdn. Bhd., which manages another Smokehouse at Fraser's Hill and a new restaurant in Kuala Lumpur. The company has invested heavily in atmosphere. Except for a few tribal objects in one back sitting room, European antiques or pseudo-antiques dominate the decor. The whole place glows with copper and brass: pots, lamps, plates, sconces, horse brasses, bed warmers, vases, brass-framed mirrors. Yards of tapestry and chintz cover furniture grouped around oriental rugs in the main lounge. The nearby indoor-outdoor dining room is airy and attractive, softened by hanging plants.

Outside, the gardens that surround the Smokehouse sustain that wonderful mix of tropical and temperate horticulture that characterizes most hill stations. Here there are tree ferns and wild poinsettia hedges; morning glory vines envelop lampposts, fences, and any small structures they can find to embrace. In the formal flower beds, geraniums, impatiens, coleus, and salvia mix with anthurium, exotic ferns, and orchids. Across the road is the golf course, the oldest one in Malaysia. Its lush softness, fringed in tall wild grasses, never fades. Looking out of my neoleaded window over the gently rolling course and the darker, forested hills behind, I remembered the apt phrase "hysterical green" that the Indian writer Bill Aitken applied to his Himalayan valleys.

The Smokehouse is still the favorite of foreigners, especially British travelers, but Asian guests are rapidly becoming its mainstay year-round. Indeed, rich Asians can more easily afford this very expensive hotel than Westerners, some of whom balk at more than $100 a night for a bed and breakfast experience they can get at home. Although Malaysian food is very good, the menu is all Western at the Smokehouse, probably more for the chic appeal of "ye olde" image than for the tastes of its guests. Breakfast is oatmeal, bacon, and eggs. In the afternoon there are Devon cream teas with jam and scones. On an average evening, there will be hors d'oeuvres of asparagus with hollandaise, smoked salmon, grilled mushrooms in cream and wine sauce, and seafood or prawn cocktail. Soups might be French onion, Scotch broth, mulligatawny, basil-scented tomato consommé, cream of asparagus, or cream of mushroom. The roasts include beef Wellington, roast sirloin with Yorkshire pudding, lamb with red currant jelly, duck, turkey, or chicken with cranberry sauce. With a little notice, the chef was prepared to make steak, kidney and mushroom pie, oxtail stew with dumplings, or something ominously British called brown stew, also with dumplings. The steak category carries a footnote: "You may wish to season your steak with one of our sauces: pepper, mushroom, garlic, Bombay." Seafood encompasses oysters and lobster, and there are the predictable veggies: cauliflower with cheese sauce, bubble and squeak, sautéed onions, and roast potatoes. Then comes the sherry trifle, bread-and-butter pudding with custard, fresh fruit crumble with custard, and fresh strawberries and meringue with cream, as well as a number of crepe varieties. Not a single stick of satay. No nasi lemak. No gula malacca. What a shame. John Turnbull Thomson would feel right at home.

I decided to try Fraser's Hill.

FRASER'S HILL

It was in the hills of Malaysia that an insurgency added the fateful phrase "hearts and minds" to the vocabulary of antiguerrilla warfare. In 1952, Sir

Gerald Templer, a newly appointed British high commissioner in Malaya, announced that winning over the people's affection and trust, their "hearts and minds," with a comprehensive plan of protection and development would be his goal. Richard Stubbs, who has written a definitive study of that guerrilla war—a period known in Malaysian and British history as simply "the Emergency," said that Templer, later a field marshal, lived to regret the phrase. But by then it was part of the terminology of the postcolonial age.

The same idea in almost the same words had been floated by his predecessor as high commissioner, Sir Henry Gurney. But Gurney was gunned down in a bizarre ambush on the road to Fraser's Hill—a sign now marks the spot—and the articulation and implementation of the new policy was left to those who followed. Sir Henry and his wife were driving up to Fraser's Hill for a break in the cooling highlands when his car came under fire. The jungle is still dense along this road; then it easily hid the attackers. In Stubbs's retelling of the story in his book *Hearts and Minds in Guerrilla Warfare: The Malayan Emergency 1948–1960*, Sir Henry inexplicably got out of the car and walked toward the side of the road where he was hit with a shower of bullets and left to die in a drainage ditch. His wife and his personal secretary stayed in the automobile and survived.

The British took extravagant revenge. Whole Chinese villages were emptied, their people evicted for failing to turn over attackers. Other attacks had taken place in this area, and more were to come. In 1952 in Tanjung Malim, a guerrilla attack killed twelve people, including a high-ranking British colonial official with a war hero's reputation. Templer went to the town, rounded up community leaders for a sharp dressing down, put Tanjung Malim under an almost total curfew, and cut food rations. Never mind. Kuala Lumpur has named a park for him.

The first stage of the trip from the coastal plain to Fraser's Hill starts in Kuala Kubu Bahru and pauses at the Gap. Here a rest house that was once a resort in its own right marks the spot where a one-lane road to the hill—open for two hours to travel up and two to travel down throughout the day—meant an almost inevitable break unless one's timing was exceptionally accurate and the green light was on for the ascent. Normally, cars began to accumulate in a queue to await the Go signal, and passengers got out to stretch and find a snack. Malaysia was completing a new, second road to the hill when I passed the Gap last time, so that travel up or down could go on uninterrupted. By now the special function of the Gap tea shop—to entertain and feed those waiting for the next green light—will be slipping into history. At the Gap, the route that passes through scrubbier jungle than the road to the Cameron Highlands plunges into more luxuriant vegetation. At the end of the climb, Fraser's Hill is enveloped in a deep, dark rain forest, where wild boar still roam, and from which they emerge at night to forage in the town. Wild monkeys live among the thickly packed trees, vines, and giant ferns. There are more birds singing more melodiously in Fraser's Hill than in almost any other hill station. Perhaps the dearth of cars until now contributes to an environment that makes it worth the songbirds' while to perform. Easier access for automobiles, and the building of a second golf course, could spoil the sanctuary atmosphere, of course. But walking uphill and downhill with relative ease and safety will still be possible, thanks to miles of narrow sidewalks and designated jungle trails that lead away from roads into uncivilized wilds.

Fraser's Hill was named for Louis James Fraser, an entrepreneurial wanderer from Europe whose business in the Malay peninsula in the late nineteenth century has been variously described as mule-train operator, opium smuggler, and tin miner. S. Robert Aiken, using the writings of Fraser's contemporaries, said that Fraser lived for a time in Tras, at the edge of the mountains in central Malaysia, where he ran his mule-train transport service between Kuala Kubu, the gateway to Fraser's Hill from the west, and Raub, on the other, eastern, side of the mountain range not far from his home. He later turned to tin mining, and some time along the way built himself a fairly commodious bungalow, to judge from a photograph taken in 1918, more than a decade after his death early in the twentieth century. Fraser was described by those who met him as a frail, but surprisingly tough, old man. Tough also was the ascent to his lonely hill. Before the luxury of roads and cars, the Gap was the start of a long walk. In 1917, when the Gap rest house was still a resort of sorts and not the unlovely Chinese hash house it has become, the bishop of Singapore, J. C. Ferguson-Davie, stayed there. From the Gap he and a colleague hiked up to Fraser's Hill and thought the journey wonderful.

By 1920, the British government in Malaya had begun major development work on Fraser's Hill. Excavation began for a golf course, built by literally remaking the landscape to create a long valley stretching away from what would become the center of the town, still a very small collection of buildings: two hotels, some shops, a post office, and a few other government buildings. When I visited the town, the second golf course was taking shape a few miles above the first one. Bulldozers had mowed down even more jungle, causing erosion that muddied mountain streams and Fraser Hill's lovely Jeriau waterfall. Local people pointed this out to me, saying that the promise of a growth in tourism meant less to them than the salvation of this rich natural setting.

Dozens of bungalows and a large rest house were built in Fraser's Hill before World War II. They nestle gracefully among the misty mountains whose shrouded peaks seem very close and all enveloping. Fraser's Hill mercifully never developed as rapidly as the Cameron Highlands. The newest hotel, the monstrous Silverpark, sits atop its own small rise and does not intrude too much on the core of Fraser's Hill. Sleepy or stuffy—people call it both—this hill station is still more a hamlet with the feeling of an isolated summer camp than a recognizable town like Tanah Rata, Brinchang, or Ringlet, in the Cameron Highlands.

At the Smokehouse, a poor relative of its Cameron Highland's counterpart, a clerk-waiter showing me around kicked at the rough ground where the boars came out at night to graze in the gardens and the spots where unusual monkeys, "black with long tails," collect to hoot and chatter. I was right about the variety and melodiousness of the birds. A naturalist told me later that there are more than a hundred species of birds around Fraser's Hill, thriving on the insect life of the perennially wet forests and the seeds, blossoms, or fruit of many trees and flowers.

After long walks and a few drenchings in Fraser's Hill, it was time to read, and I really needed to find some books. I was reduced to reading old faux *Tatler* magazines and plaques on the walls of the bar and parlors at the Smokehouse, some of them actually quite interesting. From one I learned that the small inn had been erected in 1924 by the British Red Cross Society and the Order of St. John's of Jerusalem for the use of Britons, "especially of members of the imperial forces." The message concluded with thanks to Malaya for "unexampled cooperation . . . with the Motherland during the Great War." Another plaque was filled by a homily from Buckminster Fuller about the future prospects for humanity on Spaceship Earth. Nearby was a framed Hermès scarf featuring English post coaches in the snow. But no books.

There was only one solution. Early one morning, I left the hills for Kuala Lumpur, where there are good bookstores and shelves of volumes on Malaysia—though none on the Cameron Highlands or Fraser's Hill. I was lost in books for hours. Another task remained, however. That night, before leaving Malaysia, I ate the best nasi goreng I have probably ever enjoyed anywhere, and after it an exquisite air batu campur—fruits, nuts, glutinous rice, palm sugar, and shaved ice—as big as a banana split. They call it an ABC. All is forgiven.

7

DUTCH INDONESIA

Bogor, Bukittinggi, and Brastagi

Bukittinggi, in West Sumatra's Minang land; photo © Karen Petersen

$\mathcal{T}$HERE CAN BE SOMETHING darkly brooding, vaguely threatening, about Indonesia. It lurks there in the background, more consistent if less dramatic than the deadly moods that sweep over Sri Lanka now and then like black Indian Ocean thunderclouds, sending citizens in search of cover. The Indonesian brooding is not the momentary *amok* of the peninsular Malay or the spontaneous combustion of an Indian mob. A steady, if hidden, stream of potentially violent unease runs under Indonesia; it is a recurrent theme in the country's modern history. Fair or not, the lasting impression in Southeast Asia is that the Dutch colonialists who ruled the people of the Indonesian archipelago did nothing to drain away this subterranean flow. They were harsher than their fellow European imperialists in Asia and far meaner in bestowing benefits such as higher education, political participation, or widespread opportunities to amass independent wealth and prestige—all seeds of an independent middle class. Anticolonial uprisings, the first mass-based one in 1825 by Diponegoro, a mystical Javanese prince who became a national hero, were quickly suppressed.

Lewis Couperus, a Dutch correspondent for the *Haagsche Post* who traveled around the Netherlands Indies in the 1920s—he called the place India, generically, as did many of his fellow countrymen—observed the bitterness he encountered in the colonies about the lack of interest about them among the Dutch. In the colonies, he found a shortage of qualified Dutch citizens willing to work in the Indies, compared with the much larger corps of Britons of all vocations and professions who were prepared or even eager to go to India or Malaya. "Are there really so few young Dutchmen who are willing to seek a career round about the equator that, for instance, it was necessary to send out quite a number of young Danes as military dispensers?" he wrote in a letter. "Everyone tells me that the young Dutchman would rather seek a position in Holland than go so far away from home to the unknown colonies, where none of his people have ever been. It is a family matter—if one sheep crosses the bridge the others will follow." At least the Danes, who struggled with the Dutch language, were polite and engaging, Couperus noted. "I have often noticed that many Dutchmen despise to a certain extent everything that comes from India."

The Dutch period ended effectively with World War II, which sadly brought a cruel Japanese interregnum, during which many thousands of Indonesians were imprisoned, press-ganged, or executed, a familiar story in Southeast Asia that the contemporary Japanese are attempting to rewrite. With independence after the war came new horrors. Sukarno, the first Indonesian president, was a brilliant but impetuous leader not afraid to defy the world, in particular the United States. He withdrew Indonesia from the United Nations in 1965, despite the organization's role in helping to negotiate the country's independence and in assisting its efforts to acquire disputed territories. Sukarno flirted with China and encouraged an unsettling leftist populism at home. After a 1965 attempted coup—whether by Communists or others remains in dispute—there was a terrible pogrom against ethnic Chinese Indonesians in which perhaps three-quarters of a million of them died. General Suharto, who stepped into the chaos and gradually took power in a series of deftly calculated steps in the aftermath, perfected a quiet but fierce and personalized repression that dominated the rest of the century. He seemed to think that he could sweeten this and maybe fool the Indonesians by rapid economic growth (not least of all his family's own enrichment, as it turned out). After all this, Indonesia for decades did not feel like a place to go for frivolity or relaxation, unless one happened to be one of those legendarily disconnected tourists in Bali unaware of exactly where that happy island lies. Given this history, it is not unexpected that Indonesia was not known for its hill stations.

But hill stations there were. By the end of the colonial period, more than twenty towns could be at least loosely identified as such, most of them on the island of Java—though there were a few on the island of Sumatra and at least one, Kintamani, in Bali. The first and grandest of the Indonesian hill stations was Bogor, where Baron Gustaaf Willem van Imhoff, the Dutch colonial governor-general from 1743 to 1750, built himself a country residence he called Buitenzorg, a name meaning roughly "free of care"—*sans souci*. His use of this house as an semiofficial country residence predated the building of the first British hill stations by almost a century. Van Imhoff's successors eventually made Buitenzorg, as the town also became known to the Dutch, an official base in the hills, which it remained until the end of the colonial period. The house, completely rebuilt in the 1850s and enlarged over the years, is now the hill residence of the president of Indonesia.

Bogor is only thirty-eight miles from Jakarta, Indonesia's modern capital, and connected to it by a major highway that cuts traveling time to little more than an hour, making the small hill city almost a satellite town. Indeed, the cities of Jakarta, Bogor, Tangerang, and Bekasi are all now part of an urban sprawl that Indonesians—who love to create new words from acronyms or fragments of other words—call Jabotabek. The popular Lonely Planet guide to Java suggests that this might be a better base than

Jakarta for exploring the island. Even in the nineteenth century, a fast carriage and horses could make the trip from Batavia to Buitenzorg in four hours, a much easier journey than the long, punishing treks to most British hill stations.

Bogor, to use its original Javanese name, quickly grew out of its origins as a sleepy hamlet in the rainy, fertile hills and is now a busy commercial and industrial town of several hundred thousand people. It once was at least a semiclassic hill station, however, more so than Bukittinggi, in Sumatra, a popular highland retreat because of its climate and location in the heart of the Minangkabau country, or Brastagi, farther north in the Sumatran hills near Medan. Bogor was only semihigh at less than 1,000 feet, but that was enough to separate its climate from that of the steamy swamp of Jakarta, which the Dutch called Batavia. Mountains, some of them volcanoes at 4,000 feet, were nearby, creating the illusion that Bogor was both higher and more remote than in fact it was. Bogor was very much a government town, according to visitors during the colonial period. When the Briton Charles Walter Kinloch, who used the pen name "Bengal Civilian," spent some time in Bogor in the mid–nineteenth century, he found the entertainment very formal but the environment refreshing, if soggy from a daily afternoon shower. The mountain air seemed to improve his health, he noted, believing it to be better than the atmosphere of most British hill stations.

Buitenzorg was a long-established town in the 1850s, when British hill stations were still young. Moreover, a trip to Java would entail a bracing sea voyage as well as a chance to ramble in the less exhausting Javanese mountains. In the nineteenth century, it was an article of faith almost everywhere that an ocean trip could do wonders for one's health. Furthermore, as a Briton in colonial service in India, Kinloch, not unlike many other British travelers, was fascinated by the Dutch experience in the Indies. The British often judged the Dutch harshly, perhaps with good reason. But these critical comments preserved in books and used to salt lectures for audiences in Europe must have contributed substantially to the general perception that the Dutch Indies were a benighted backwater, not even on a par with the Spanish Philippines in social and economic development. What is lost in this perception, however, is the cultural refinement that was there when the Dutch arrived, a life many of them could little understand because it was often impenetrable to the outsider. Java, in particular, did not take kindly to interference. Almost any Indonesian trying to explain the Suharto phenomenon would sooner or later say to me, "Well, you have to understand that he is very Javanese."

The early history of Indonesia is a far more complex story than the ancient and medieval history of Europe; the languages of the archipelago are among the most arcane and in some cases the most difficult in the world to master. When the Europeans arrived, the islands that are now Indonesia were not a clean slate on which colonialism might easily draw the outlines of a new order. The colonial era stretched over centuries, but parallel to that story ran the unbroken histories of sultans and courts, a continuation of a royal past peopled by kings and emperors and ministers that reached far back into prehistory. Like the Vietnamese, the Indonesians fought a long and bitter war for independence, and the break with colonialism was clean and deep, more complete than anywhere else in colonized Asia. Reprimands from the Netherlands still sting and provoke angry responses in Jakarta. Right up to the eve of the twenty-first century, Indonesia has remained aloof and apart. Little known to the world, it has always been a source of surprises.

By the end of the sixteenth century, ports on the north coast of Java had become huge international bazaars that astonished the first Europeans to see them. At Bantam, travelers saw wholesale grain markets, warehouses of pepper and spices, hardware like cooking utensils and craftsmen's tools; medicines, cloth, and decorative objects from India; Persian and Arab jewelry; and satins, silks, gold-threaded brocades, porcelain, and lacquerware offered by Chinese merchants. An early Dutch visitor noticed that merchant communities seemed wealthy enough to support local aristocracies of sorts.

The Dutch became very active in Indies trade by 1600, sending numerous expeditions south and eastward via the Cape of Good Hope and westward through the Strait of Magellan. They were successful very quickly in intruding on the Portuguese monopoly in Southeast Asia, particularly in the Indonesian archipelago, which soon became known as the Netherlands East Indies. The free-for-all competition among Dutch traders became self-defeating, however. In 1602, the Netherlands, following the example of Britain's East India Company, chartered the Vereenigde Oostindische Compagnie, or United East India Company. Widely known by its initials in Dutch, the V.O.C. was granted a twenty-one-year monopoly, putting an end to rivalry. Like the British East India Company, the Dutch monopoly could recruit an army, build defenses, and conclude agreements with foreign rulers. All the major trading cities of the Netherlands had a say in the company's affairs and could send out their own vessels under the auspices of the V.O.C.

The Dutch company lasted until 1799, by which time a network of inter-island shipping routes had been established in the Indies, with smaller vessels bringing goods to be picked up by larger inter-oceanic ships in the main port of Batavia, now Jakarta. The Dutch appeared to be pretty much in control of this trade, even when their seas were forced opened to competition. J. M. Gullick, in his anthology *Adventures and Encounters: Europeans in South-East Asia*, includes a description of the Batavia network in 1832 written by George Earl, a British merchant seaman who later became a colonial official in Singapore. "Spices are brought from the Moluccas, coffee and pepper from Celebes and Sumatra, gold-dust and diamonds from Borneo. Tin from the government mines in Banka, and tortoise-shell, bees'-wax, dye-woods &c from Timor, Sumbawa and the other islands to the eastward." Earl discovered that many of the Dutch feeder ships, which he called "country boats," were often owned and commanded by Britons.

By the time the V.O.C. began functioning early in the seventeenth century, the Dutch were being harassed in the Indies by the British, who had earlier wasted a lot of time trying to find a northwest passage to the East across North America or around Russia and were in a hurry to catch up. The two great European mercantile companies skirmished around Java and the spice islands farther east in the first quarter of the seventeenth century, when a particularly ruthless Dutch governor-general, Jan Pieterszoon Coen, was in charge of the growing Dutch empire in what is now Indonesia. His treatment of native populations in some of the smaller islands was brutal, and he was a great fan of slavery. Furthermore, since his example seemed to condone rough behavior, lower-ranking Dutch administrators lost whatever inhibitions and restraints they may have had. The Dutch, in order to control the supply and thus the price of cinnamon, cloves, pepper, and other produce, decided which islanders could plant what spices. Village people abruptly cut off from the income of a traditional crop were left to fend for themselves, starve, or perhaps take up a new line like piracy. When there was defiance, often born of desperation, it became commonplace to punish whole island populations by deporting them to other regions of the archipelago, where they endured great hardships of adjustment. (Much later, Indonesia under General Suharto was still using banishment, especially to the prison island of Buru, as a form of punishment for people with unacceptable political notions.)

The colonial Dutch did not spare Europeans, either. In what has gone down in history as the 1623 Amboina Massacre, all the English officials along with their Asian employees at a trading post on that island were rounded up, tortured, and beheaded by the Dutch even though the two countries had a treaty of cooperation. Later in the century, the Dutch began to concentrate on expanding their Asian trading empire more at the expense of the Portuguese. Dutch explorers, foremost among them Antonie van Dieman, a mid-seventeenth-century governor, also ventured into the southern seas around Australia and New Zealand. Domination of the spice trade by the Dutch continued until late in the eighteenth century, when their defeat by the British in a war sparked by the Netherlands's recognition of American independence resulted in the 1784 Treaty of Paris, which gave Britain the right to free trade in the Indies.

Few Britons were more passionate in their convictions about what was wrong about the Dutch colonies than Sir Thomas Stamford Raffles, who lived in the governor-general's palace in Bogor from 1811 to 1815, when Britain briefly took control of the Netherlands Indies during the period of the Napoleonic wars in Europe. Raffles, with the title of lieutenant governor of Java and its dependencies, was only thirty years old when the British replaced the Dutch administration in order to prevent the French, who had conquered the Netherlands, from establishing themselves in Dutch possessions in Asia. Raffles, who would later become the founder of modern Singapore, worked for the East India Company, which still held the powers of government in the colonies. He joined the company at the age of fourteen and knew its workings well. He was convinced that the British could make a better job of governing the Indies than the Dutch, and he set about doing so in Java.

By all accounts Raffles had great energy and a comprehensive interest in everything around him. He established his authority over the sultans and courts of Java and its dependent states, including Bali and parts of Borneo. He tried to reform the administration of the colony and its cumbersome taxation system and cut back, though could never totally abolish, slavery and debt bondage. He left behind an antislavery movement modeled on Britain's, which was later supported by humanitarian-minded Dutch citizens. Raffles got into everything: the arts and sciences, languages, agriculture, archaeology, and more. His prodigious record stopped even the voluminous D.G.E. Hall, who said in his *History of South-East Asia*, a work of more than 1,000 pages, that his book wasn't big enough to encompass the range of Raffles's activities. And Raffles was in Java not quite five years. He later took this tremendous energy to Sumatra and Singapore. I am sorry that when I was a correspondent in Southeast Asia and had the opportunity to talk with Lee Kuan Yew, I never asked the creator of contemporary Singapore what he thought about Raffles, his spiritual predecessor, and whether he felt any kinship to him.

Dutch independence was restored after the defeat of Napoleon in Europe, and in 1814 Britain prepared to return Java to the control of the Netherlands, to Raffles's great disappointment. He was recalled to London in 1815 under a cloud of criticism for not having wrung more wealth out of the Dutch Indies. In truth, he did give Asia much more than he took, in the broadest interpretation of his work, and his detractors quite rightly could not prevent his receiving a knighthood. Apart from his administrative and judicial reforms, Raffles became known as a sympathetic promoter and conservator of Java's cultural heritage. From his base in Bogor, he nosed all around Java, touring at least once the ruins of the great eighth-century temple of Borobudur, which he ordered surveyed for the first time, with the aim of better preserving the monument. Two years after leaving Java, Raffles published a three-volume illustrated history of the island that remains a classic, a better work in the view of many scholars than anything the Dutch had produced.

In Bogor, Raffles decided to surround his official residence, the palace of the Dutch governors-general, with a botanical garden. With characteristic thoroughness, he did not leave the work to amateurs; he called in experts from London's Kew Gardens. The Bogor botanical garden, like many of Raffles's innovations, was nurtured and enlarged by the Dutch. Now called the Kebon Raya, it is still an oasis, albeit in a noisier, hotter city than Raffles knew.

I remember the Kebon Raya with special delight because it was a torrid morning in Jakarta when the taxi I had arranged the night before to take me to Bogor and Bandung arrived at the hotel in a nauseating state. The driver had slept in it all night—he told me proudly, so that he would arrive on time—and had apparently also had his evening and morning meals in the stifling vehicle. The cloud of stale food, sweat, and unwashed clothes could not be dislodged. With the windows open, the taxi didn't benefit much from the air outside, since Jakarta's streets were even more pungent. There are times in this port city, especially in its older quarters, when the sick-sweet odor of rotting sludge in drains and near-stagnant canals is close to unbearable. In the early eighteenth century, historians tell us, cholera was known to lurk in those noisome open sewers. It still does, though health officials are reluctant to admit the possibility when waves of diarrheal disease sweep the slums. Leaving the city for the fresh air of the hills, one can actually experience as well as understand what drove the Dutch governor-general to Buitenzorg in the first place. Being dropped at Bogor's botanical garden on such a day is bliss. Past the hawkers and layabouts outside the gates, the world looks much better.

There are about 250 acres of gardens, groves, greenhouses, and a maze of pathways at Bogor's Kebon Raya, with more than 15,000 species of plants, among them scores of varieties of palm—some say the most comprehensive collection in the world. The guides to Bogor inform us that philodendron was introduced to Southeast Asia from South America by way of these gardens. As in the Caribbean, philodendron grows into a magnificent outdoor vine in this rainy climate, with huge glossy leaves of deep or mottled green. The Kebon Raya otherwise contains many of the same plants and trees found in the botanical gardens of other hill stations established at about the same time and also with the help of botanists and naturalists from Kew.

Bogor's gardens, completed in 1817 after Raffles was gone, are adjacent to the Presidential Palace, where several statues of nude women, from the notoriously extensive collection of President Sukarno, are grouped in a grove, I was told; I did not make the effort to see them. In one corner of the garden proper, there stands a monument to the memory of Olivia Raffles, Sir Thomas Stamford Raffles's first wife, who died at Bogor in 1814. She was forty-three, more than a decade older than her husband, when he buried her in Batavia. He was also in his midforties when he died, twelve years later. The colonies did not promise life everlasting.

Raffles would find more work to do in the East before his death, however. In 1818 he was named lieutenant governor of Bencoolen, now Bengkulu, a British trading port and settlement on the west coast of Sumatra, an island otherwise occupied by the Dutch. Again he lobbied against turning over Bencoolen and other Sumatran towns to a restored Dutch empire; again he lost. That may have been providential. In 1819, he landed on the island of Singapore, which he dexterously acquired for the East India Company and Britain by playing politics in a squabble among competing Malay sultans. But that is another story, one without hill stations.

In Sumatra, Raffles had enough time to explore the hill country around Bukittinggi, an old Dutch fortress town in the heart of Minangkabau country. The Minangkabau are an unusual Muslim people on an island that has seen a lot of Islamic militancy, some of it more nationalistic than religious. Much about Minangkabau history is murky, or fanciful. Raffles was eager to look at the region's archaeological artifacts, just as he had been to wander through the historical sites of Java. By the time Raffles took office in Bencoolen, he had remarried in England and brought his new wife, Sophia Hull, to the Indies. Although they were able to travel together on a number of adventures, their life was full of personal tragedy. They had several babies who died in Sumatra, where malaria and other diseases were endemic. In 1923, a ship taking them to England caught fire at sea, and although they survived, most of Raffles's papers and collection of antiquities and specimens was lost. He died three years later. After his death, Sophia gathered what letters and other documents she could find in a documented biography, *Memoir of the Life and Public Services of Sir Thomas Stamford Raffles.*

Among the letters she collected was one he had written to a patron in England about the expedition he and Sophia made through the Minangkabau region. Much of the trip was done on foot, trekking over rocks and through deep mud at the rate of sixteen to twenty miles a day. All along the route, Raffles studied every statue or inscribed stone he could find, as he imagined the life that was once lived in courts since reduced to ruins. "A few peasants now cultivated those spots which had formerly been the pleasure-grounds of the rich," he noted in Paggaruyung, where he thought the scenery was splendid. "I may safely say that this view equalled any thing I ever saw in Java; the scenery is more majestic and grand, population equally dense, cultivation equally rich."

Nearly two centuries later, it is still possible to share his delight. Setting off from Bukittinggi one morning to traverse by car, more or less, the same terrain Raffles covered on foot or on horseback, I found that my taxi had arrived with not just a driver but also a guide, Budi Agnesya, who had arranged my highland trip back in Padang a few days earlier. This turned out to be an unexpected blessing, since Budi's family had strong intellectual and cultural ties to the region; his uncle, A. A. Navis, is one of Sumatra's leading writers, and I was introduced to him through his nephew. Setting out from Bukittinggi for the Minang heartland, we stopped first for the usual breakfast break not far from town.

For the price of a cup of coffee—home-grown Sumatran *kopi,* served in a big glass with rough brown sugar for a sweetener—what an eyeful of glory we got! The precarious back porch of the roadside café clung to the rim of a deep, long valley. In the distance, there were the ubiquitous green, green rice fields of Indonesia. But here there was more. Rose-red leaves atop the cinnamon trees and huge yellow daisies bobbing in the morning sun splashed unexpected color over dense tropical undergrowth. Off to one side, the soaring, stylized curved horns on the rooftops of Minangkabau villages could be glimpsed through a tangle of trees. The attraction of the Sumatran highlands—both here in Minangkabau country and farther north in Batak land—is not only the scenery but also the extraordinary artifacts and architecture of daily life, and the character of the people who create them. More than in almost any other hill station I could recall, the highland towns of Sumatra still belong to the mountain men and women, not to lowlanders or foreigners.

The Minangkabau have created an unusual culture in the hills of West Sumatra. Though matrilineal, they are also devoutly Muslim, but they have no problems living with a relatively egalitarian social system and an economy in which women inherit all the property. The Minang have produced poets, thinkers, novelists, educators, politicians, and even revolutionaries of national stature in Indonesia. Daily life in Minangkabau country is governed by intensely complicated rules of etiquette known as *baso-basi*, which an outsider cannot help but offend in some way or another. The Minang are forgiving, however, because they are also cosmopolitan in their own way. Villages get together to invest in satellite dishes and tap into television from as far away in distance and culture as Australia. Part of growing up here, especially for young men, includes a stint abroad in the *rantau*, a word that means roughly "anywhere but here." Anthropologists love the Minang, who tolerate them in return. The Minangkabau themselves seem to be fostering a revival of their traditional arts, to judge by the number of those breathtaking Minang spires on new public buildings rising over the white-walled, red-roofed cityscape of Padang, the West Sumatran provincial capital and an Indian Ocean port.

There are two routes to Bukittinggi from Padang by road, the more popular one inland through Padang Panjang, where a magnificent center for the study of Minang culture and architecture has been created around a rebuilt *rumah gadang*, the Minang version of a Southeast Asian longhouse. The *rumah gadang*, or "big house," is the center of communal life for the extended Minang family. At Padang Panjang, the large rectangular wooden structure built a story above the ground on stilts has six saddle-shaped sections of overlapping thatched roofs, three to the left and three to the right of the central entrance. The six soaring pinnacles, rising like three gigantic pairs of wild buffalo horns, are tipped in silver. Below the tiered roofs, the exterior walls of the great house are intricately carved and colorfully painted in designs drawn from nature and the imagination of folk artists. The house and four small but similarly ornamented rice barns in front of it are set in gardens and shrubbery native to the area. Indoors, this *rumah gadang* is a museum, gallery, bookshop, and the offices of the Center for Information and Documentation on Minangkabau Culture, a private foundation.

There is not a lot of foreign tourism in West Sumatra, and the small museums made of these big houses, this one and another in Bukittinggi, on the edge of the town's pathetic little zoo, are often empty. When I would show up at the door, I was often greeted in Dutch, as I was in the restaurant at the hotel where I stayed, as if only something in my history would have brought me here. In these small museums, dusty tableaux with ungainly mannequins are set up to demonstrate how life was lived. But mostly, an empty *rumah gadang* is a dark interior space with a vaulted ceiling and galleries of rooms around the walls, sometimes on two or more floors, where the visitor can give free range to the imagination, picturing the family councils, the wedding feasts, the unremarkable moments shared by children, grandparents, cousins, and friends. Longhouse cultures are found elsewhere in Southeast Asia—among the best known are in the Malaysian state of Sarawak, on Borneo, where I once spent time with an extended family that had made its traditional home into a kind of motel, with private individual quarters opening on a long, cool veranda shared by all. The whole operation of life went on over at least a generation or two of family garbage, conveniently tossed off the split-bamboo deck walks outside, to accumulate on the ground below. Nothing, however, beats the Minangkabau longhouse for decorative detail, from its spired rooftop to the musical instruments, cooking utensils, and the gold and silver ornaments of the women within.

Bukittinggi, less than fifteen miles north of Padang Panjang, is not a particularly pretty town; its architecture is more all-purpose modern than that of the surrounding historical villages. Bukittinggi was neither a Minang town nor a hill station at its inception, but a Dutch fortress, Fort de Kock, built in 1825 to withstand attacks from nineteenth-century Islamic zealots. But Bukittinggi, with its horse-drawn taxis called *bendis*, its labyrinthine street market, fast food restaurants, and every kind of shop, including a good bookstore or two, also has the region's best (albeit new) hotels—including a Novotel and a much nicer Indonesian luxury hotel, the Pusako—and that makes it a good center for exploring the legendary Minangkabau homeland. The town, with its remnants of the old Dutch fort and a fine Dutch clock tower, is cool but not cold: Its altitude is less than 4,000 feet, and it is barely fifty miles from the Equator. But the days are refreshingly clear and the nights cool. It is not a bad town for walking, especially in the section of parkland called the Jalan Panorama, which overlooks Sianok Canyon, part of a rift valley running the length of Sumatra, a volcanic island about the size of California.

Much of Minang history and lore springs from the hilly farmland east of Bukittinggi, notably around the town of Batusangkar. There in a pasture the event occurred, according to legend, that gave the Minangkabau people their name, which translates variously as "victorious buffalo" or "sharp-horned buffalo." Versions of the story differ, but the bare framework is essentially this: A king from the neighboring island of Java, vowing to subdue the folks thereabouts, was persuaded by a Batusangkar ruler to allow the battle to be fought by proxy—in this case buffalo—to save human life. The Javanese king agreed and sent for his biggest bull. Meanwhile, the people of Batusangkar had been starving a nursing buffalo calf, while fitting its small head with sharp metal horns. When the calf was set loose to face its opponent, it raced for the belly of the big beast in search of milk, fatally goring the much larger animal and saving the people from subjugation.

To go back into the mists a little further, the Minangkabau creation myth revolves around Mount Marapi, one of two volcanoes—the other is Mount Singgalang—visible from Bukittinggi and many other places in the highlands. Legend says that the Minang came down from Marapi to build their first earthly settlement at Pariangan, a few miles from Batusangkar. Pariangan is still there, reached by a narrow road climbing into the hills. Families struggle to keep their ancestral homes in repair along Pariangan's single unpaved street; not a few dwellings are in progressive stages of collapse. But the place remains important to the Minang. There are many other sacred spots in these hills and valleys. On the grassy fields of Batusangkar, there are banyan trees with resident spirits and the tomb of a sultan that is reputed to change in size each time it is measured. Megaliths are scattered here and there; one with a large hole in it was supposed to have been used by restless warriors whose peaceful king told them to attack it whenever they felt like stabbing something. That's the story the groundskeeper told, anyway. There are no doubt other explanations. Many facts in Minang history are no more incontrovertible now than they were in Raffles's time.

Pagarruyung, the town that captured Raffles's imagination, has a fine collection of buildings in traditional style that together illustrate Minangkabau thinking. One is a reconstructed royal palace, a *rumah gadang* of grand proportions erected to replace and replicate a nearby royal residence destroyed by fire in the 1970s. Nearby, an imposing white mosque has been constructed, and behind it a local government headquarters built in traditional style. For the Minangkabau, the three are symbolic of a philosophy rarely found in Muslim societies: a belief that there can be a separation of religion, culture, and civil authority. Officially, Indonesia encourages this kind of thinking. At independence, its leaders invented a national philosophy called Pancasila, or five principles, to avoid making religion the definition of nationhood and prevent a drift toward an Islamic state. Indonesia, with about 200 million people, the majority of them Muslims, contains the world's largest Islamic population.

Among Indonesia's minorities are Christians from various ethnic groups. Many Chinese Indonesians, like other "overseas Chinese" in Southeast Asia, have joined Christian—often Roman Catholic—churches. But among ethnic Malays and other indigenous or near-indigenous groups, the most boisterous, energetic, and successful people converted in substantial numbers by missionaries are the Bataks of highland North Sumatra. It is hard to imagine so different a culture sharing an island, however large, with the Minangkabau. Whereas the Minang have choreographed exquisite, stylized dances for special occasions, Bataks are given to robust singing. The Batak, unlike the Minang, are patrilineal in inheritance. If the mosque is the center of Minang belief, the chapel brings Batak communities together. Not all Bataks are Christians, of course, but missionaries did make significant inroads among two major communities: the Karo and the Toba Bataks. Mary Margaret Steedly, a Harvard anthropologist who has lived in Karoland, says that the term *Batak* was apparently invented to distinguish six culturally related "infidel" peoples of the highlands—Karo, Toba, Mandailing, Angkola, Simelungun, and Pakpak—from the Muslim Malays of the coastal lowlands. Bataks, before and after Christianity, had their own spiritual systems, compellingly described by Steedly in *Hanging Without a Rope*. Half a century earlier, the European ethnologist Edwin M. Loeb made an interesting observation about Batak philosophy, which may go some distance in explaining their ability to incorporate Protestant Christianity, at least in its message of seizing control of one's destiny. "The entire life of the Batak is one of self-seeking," Loeb wrote, "not with the idea of improving one's life in the next world, but of improving one's lot here and now."

The Toba Bataks live around Samosir, an island the size of Singapore thrown up into a bottomless inland crater lake—both crater and island formed by horrifically huge volcanic eruptions perhaps 75,000 years ago. Samosir is about a hundred miles southwest of Medan, the provincial capital of North Sumatra, a physical, colorful, and vital region. There can't be many places in Indonesia where the hapless stranger is dragged into a frenzied folk dance by an entertainer who later asks for his partner's shirt as a souvenir. Or where a waitress, like a greasy whirlwind, flies out of the kitchen to heave water over children amusing themselves by watching a foreigner eat. Or where a lad takes visitors home to meet his granny and is rewarded by a public scolding because he has come when the floors of the house are not polished to their highest standard.

My husband and I once spent a week being worn down by Bataks in Prapat, a resort town on Lake Toba that is sometimes classified as a minor hill station itself, though it is not very high in altitude or distinguished by its history. From Prapat, small boats ply the lake, connecting scattered Batak villages, marked by individual saddle-roofed houses built on a more modest scale and without the ornamentation of the Minang big house. At Tomok, the first town most people encounter, there is (beyond the souvenir stalls) a genuinely fabulous old royal tomb with a puzzling assortment of carvings. The ethnologist Loeb was convinced that the Bataks were much influenced by Hinduism and Buddhism, though some Batak statuary looks almost Mayan. At Ambarita, farther north, a pleasant village boasts a collection of stone thrones, or platforms, that come equipped with a variety of stories. But none of these relics are apparently very old. A Toba Batak's idea of a small excursion to any of these settlements on Samosir seems to involve flying over the water at reckless speed (given the state of the craft), hiking in the hot sun, eating heartily, and being pursued aggressively by craftspeople selling their wares before hurtling back to Prapat ahead of a sudden, ugly squall.

Farther north and closer to Medan is Sumatra's only true hill station, Brastagi, in the Karo Batak region. Brastagi—also spelled Berastagi, with a virtually silent *e*—was founded in 1908 by and for foreigners, primarily the Dutch colonials based around Medan, in an administrative region that had been the Deli Sultanate, a petty Islamic kingdom. The Dutch did not conquer these highlands until 1904. But Brastagi, on a plateau about 5,000 feet high, soon had all the classic hallmarks of a hill station: "This is the Switzerland of Deli, because of the vast hills, the mountain air, and even the soil upon which palms and bamboo do not flourish, but where strawberries are grown," wrote the Dutch journalist Couperus in the 1920s. "Every Deli man who can manage it has his weekend cottage at Brastagi, and even the English come over from Singapore to get a breath of fresh air." Couperus enjoyed the views from Brastagi, especially of the triple-peaked Sibayak volcano, and he was happy at the cheerful Hotel Brastagi, where on Saturday nights "an amateur quartet from Medan plays untiringly." A photograph from that period shows the Brastagi Hotel as a rather plain, two-story building not much larger than a comfortable suburban European home, with a row of French doors on the ground floor opening on a terrace and garden. Since Couperus visited, Brastagi's accommodation has expanded with a few luxury hotels, but the town is still quite small and surrounded by farmland.

Just as the British, Americans, and French promoted the growing of fruit and vegetables around their hill stations, the Dutch quickly made Brastagi a marketing center for fresh produce. The town also attracted missionaries, and Christianity became another growth industry. There were Karo Batak living in the area; their settlement, Rumah Brastagi, gave the modern town its name. But it was a Dutchman building his hill station villa who first noticed all the good land that seemed to belong to no one in particular and who subsequently persuaded the Karo to try large-scale agriculture. The Dutchman was Joost von Vollenhoven, the chief administrator of the Deli region and the founder of "Brastagi the hill station." Local Batak people from whom he leased his land were open to discussions about agricultural experimentation. In 1911 an agricultural expert, H. M. Botje, arrived from the Netherlands, more or less in the same way that botanists were dispatched from Kew to British colonies. Agriculture was not new to North Sumatra, however. This corner of the Dutch Indies, especially the flatter areas near the coast, became extensive plantations in the late nineteenth century. The Dutch came late to northern Sumatra, and with resources slimmer than in earlier centuries, they shared the land with other Europeans, while retaining colonial power.

In Karoland, potatoes were the first new crop promoted by Botje. But, in Steedly's telling of the story, the very success of the venture—potatoes growing in all directions—prompted manipulation of the price by Chinese middlemen in Medan. An agricultural cooperative system introduced consequently by Botje collapsed, and Karo farmers, already skilled at their work, thereafter went their separate ways and prospered. Commercial farming boomed, and the local Batak clan, the Rumah Brastagi Purbas, further benefited from the rising value of their land, farmed or fallow. Dutch colonial policy supported their land rights and the independent free enterprise of Karoland, which proved to be a lucrative source of tax revenues for colonial administrators. Steedly called it "colonialism on the *very* cheap."

The North Sumatra highlands are still known for their fine produce, especially fruits, which the traveler encounters on the breakfast table at dawn. Along the road to Brastagi, there are orchards growing pungent durians, spiky rambutans, and the sweet markisa, or passion fruit. In the 1920s, Couperus was enthralled by the fecundity of the Brastagi highlands and the "noble majestic Nature" that caused the wild things to bloom and grow in profusion, as if to heal wounds gashed into the landscape by human development. He marveled at native trees—palms, breadfruit, and giant ferns among them—"always harmoniously outlined in clumps, as if the godheads of these trees were courtiers who knew how to group together the things which enhance each other's beauty."

But Couperus, like so many others, was also struck by a latent dark sorrow in the air, even in upbeat Batak country. "Just in front of the Governor's pasangrahan, lost in the solitude of the mountains, hangs the strange atmosphere of Indian evenings, a brooding sadness, an inexpressible melancholy," he wrote of an evening in Brastagi. Until the singing began, that is, and a old man with a lute began to tell his musical stories. Couperus fell under the spell of the Batak singer's joy in performance, "and his happiness made me also smile contentedly in this hour of dusk and melancholy."

8

REBIRTH
IN VIETNAM

Dalat

The Palace Hotel in Dalat

THE FRENCH HAD BIG DREAMS for Dalat. Designed, like Baguio, by a great urban planner—in this case, Ernest Hebrard—Dalat would be more than a French hill station in Annam, Vietnam's middle kingdom. It would be the focal point of a greater Indochinese federation comprising Vietnam, Cambodia, and Laos. It would be a spacious, health-giving city for the enjoyment of polite pleasures, with broad avenues, large parks and gardens, a grand hotel or two, and a lake meandering through its heart. On the periphery, there were pine forests and several sparkling waterfalls dropping into dark, damp glens. On the horizon were the twin Lang Bian peaks, which the sentimental, mammary-obsessed Vietnamese describe as the breasts of a beautiful woman "whose exquisite figure with its bewitchingly graceful lines gave shape to this lovely mountain city," according to a local guidebook. In more than a few ways, the Vietnamese and the French were made for each other.

Dalat is a pleasure still. Moreover, it is perhaps the only major hill station in Asia remaking itself, after years of war and the privations of a collapsed economy, faithfully and deliberately in its historical, colonial image. The famous French villas along the avenue Tran Hung Dao are being restored. At the height of its glory days, Dalat had as many as 2,300 substantial country homes, a few owned by rich Vietnamese and the rest by expatriate French, who often designed them in the styles of their home regions. In the Lam Dong provincial library I found reproductions of architectural plans for homes that recalled Normandy, the Basque country, Savoy, and Brittany. Others were modeled on Alpine chalets. In the 1980s, when Vietnam was still miserably poor, Dalat's city government had dreams of researching and restoring these houses, then in a state of serious decay. But there was no money. Now there is foreign investment, and outsiders are making everything possible. French companies are back managing the city's two premier hotels, the Palace, now the Sofitel Dalat Palace, and the former Hotel du Parc, renamed the Novotel Dalat. Both hotels have been lavishly refurbished and staffed with cheerful young Vietnamese who cannot speak a word of French, a state of affairs that produces the predictable grumbles from French tourists, who register their sadness and displeasure in the Palace guest book.

Putting aside for the moment the inevitable specter of overdevelopment, symbolized by an epidemic of karaoke cafes in the town center advertising digital sound, Dalat seems for the present to be in bloom. But then so much of Vietnam has opened like a flower after a long winter. In particular, women of all ages, down to schoolgirls on their bicycles, are emerging as colorful butterflies from the cocoons of those long dark years that followed Hanoi's overthrow of South Vietnam in 1975. The ugly uniforms of cheap slacks and military-style overblouses in dull, dark colors that reflected the cheerless orthodoxy of life in the decade after unification are gone. So are most restrictions on private initiative. When I first came to Dalat in the mid-1980s, I heard stories of ruined lives, as producers of the famous fruits and vegetables of the highlands were no longer able to sell their harvests in Saigon, or Ho Chi Minh City as it was then officially renamed. First their trucks were commandeered by triumphant northern Communists; then their rights to free trade were eliminated. Dalat's large central market hollowed into an empty shell, with unpurchasable government-made goods on display in unimaginative, dust-covered arrangements. Even the rats moved out.

In the years after Hanoi's troops took the South, Vietnam had something called the Economic Police, which I learned about later from a redoubtable woman, Nguyen Thi Thi, who had been rounded up by them for the sin of creativity. Thi was a Socialist Hero of the first order, so when the North Vietnamese reorganized the South, she was put in charge of rice distribution in the Saigon region. It occurred to her that many of the people running neighborhood outlets in her network had skills they were not using. So she began to encourage them to turn the food-distribution centers into small manufacturing operations making noodles, cakes, cookies, and cereals from a variety of grains. The goods could be sold when rice was picked up. The plan was a huge success. By 1981, more than 1,000 distribution centers had become tiny bakeries and noodle factories. That's when the Economic Police moved in. Sixty armed officers surrounded her headquarters. Thi, then about sixty years old, locked herself in and held out, telling the besieging policemen that she had plenty of food in stock, so they should be prepared to wait a long time. She was saved from a jail term by a rift in the city's Communist leadership that gave people sympathetic to her the chance to get the siege lifted.

Dalat, about 150 miles northeast of Saigon and less than fifty miles inland from the South China Sea, was always a suspect town in Hanoi's eyes. It had been the favorite haunt of Vietnam's last monarch, the Emperor Bao Dai. After the defeat of the French in 1954 at Dien Bien Phu and the collapse of France's Indochinese empire, thousands of anti-Communist Roman Catholics poured south and many settled in Dalat. South Vietnam established a university here and built a nuclear research reactor with

American help. It was the site of the Saigon regime's national military academy. Furthermore, Dalat escaped much of the damage of the war between North and South Vietnam. American troops were not permitted to go there for rest and relaxation, thereby providing tempting targets for Communist guerrillas, so there was little fighting or physical destruction, except in the 1968 Tet offensive. At the end of the war, the town and the region collapsed quickly under a North Vietnamese advance. Dalat's middle class was hit hard by the fall of South Vietnam. Families retreated into a grim subsistence, trying to hold on to a bit of land or some small property to make a home for themselves and their children.

It was in Dalat in the 1980s that I first learned about Vietnam's own POW-MIA tragedy. This was a time when families of Americans still officially unaccounted for after the war were lobbying hard to make Hanoi tell more about what it knew about the missing, or even the dead, if death was the fate that had befallen many who disappeared into enemy hands. In Dalat, I heard the story of Duong Quang Trong, who had vanished at the age of twenty-nine somewhere in the Central Highlands in the closing days of the North-South war. The face of his mother, Nguyen Thi Tu, is still clear in my memory; it was drenched with tears as she told me the story thirteen years later. Tu had no support groups, no leagues of families of the missing, no counseling to help her live with her anguish. Official vilification was all she got because her handsome officer-son had fought for South Vietnam, and pity was in short supply in the North. When peace came, the family was stripped of its property and was lucky to find a home in an old grain storehouse. At sixty-three, Tu spent her days picking strawberries on the plot of land near Dalat's Valley of Love that was all that remained of their once-prosperous produce business. Tu and her husband, Marcel Marniconi, a Corsican-Vietnamese, who adopted the name Duong Van Trung, had become prosperous selling fruit and vegetables to American bases. At the end of the war, most of the family went to prison camp.

This missing soldier's mother may have had all the wrong credentials, but she was not alone. Later in the Red River Valley near Hanoi, I met an old farmer who had never been anything but loyal to the Communists and their cause. He took me into his small parlor off a new threshing floor I had come to see when the Vietnamese wanted to show us how they were returning farms to private ownership. There he had three photographs of boys from three generations in his family who had vanished in Hanoi's wars—with the French, Americans, and Cambodians—and whose fate the family never learned. In Hanoi, army officers told me later that the country was always too poor to afford the luxury of tracing the missing or returning the remains of the dead, many thousands of them in battles stretching over several decades. Not only southerners had to bear the pain of final but unresolved separation.

Dalat's revival began after 1986, when its central market was reopened to private stallholders. Landowners were again allowed to grow fruit and vegetables for sale wherever they could find customers. It was still a shabby town, however. The old Palace Hotel was a barren shell with dirty windows, though its grand old rooms still had considerable character. Young people were fleeing Dalat, which seemed to have no future for them. At Sunday masses in the Cathedral, the congregation seemed to be largely old people and some younger women and their children. The rebirth was slow, but it did become steady. When local private enterprise got harnessed to foreign investment in the early 1990s, the town really took off.

By the mid-1990s, Dalat was exploding with activity. In 1997 everywhere I went there was construction. Drainage systems, sidewalks, and roads were being repaired. Small shops were becoming more and more numerous and glossier in decor. Beauty salons proliferated. Tourism was generating jobs. This time at the Cathedral's early Sunday mass, young men formed a significant part of a generally more youthful congregation. "Not so good for the government," a church official chuckled. The heavy hand of the Communist bureaucracy seemed to have been lifted. At the city post office—with its jazzy, illuminated Eiffel Tower–style telecommunications transmitter outside and the Palace's Café de la Poste across the street—clerks smiled and were helpful. Citizens seemed to ignore the police, who were much less noticeable. When I wandered into a maze of narrow walks in search of an old French cemetery and emerged in the front yard of an army officer who seemed to be at home baby-sitting, he came out—in uniform, with a small child on each arm—to give me directions.

The only apparatchik encountered on this visit was a boxy woman at the Cartographic Printing House 2, which was once the imposing headquarters of the Indochinese Geographic Service, a branch of the French Geographic Institute. The building is still an attractive architectural landmark, and my guidebook told me that it housed "valuable documents of Vietnam from the times of King Tu Duc" and a wonderful collection of historical and contemporary maps. As I started up the driveway, Ms. Apparatchik, wearing a very serious suit and an unfriendly look, blocked my way. She wanted to know why I was there. I said I wanted to look at the maps. "You get a tourist map," she said. "That's all you need. Foreigners are not allowed to look at the maps in here." She wanted to know where I was staying and what I was doing in Dalat. She lectured me on the folly of paying so much money at the Palace Hotel when there were so many cheaper places. I tried being conciliatory by acknowledging that the Palace's food prices were truly outrageous and the fare not very good. She softened for a second, but quickly recovered. Noticing my camera, she announced that taking pictures of the building was also forbidden. I photographed it from across the street, where there was a miniature restaurant called the American Café, which served Pepsi Cola.

It took the French decades to create in Dalat one of the finest of the Asian hill stations. The first Frenchmen did not explore the Central Highlands and the Lang Bian Plateau, where Dalat was eventually built, until late in the nineteenth century. Like so many highland areas in colonial Asia, the Central Highlands were populated by indigenous tribal mountain people. They were subsistence farmers, fishers, and hunters, not related to the mainstream ethnic Vietnamese who lived along the coast. At one point, a Vietnamese king tried to build a barrier to keep tribal groups out of lowland areas, where people knew little about the truculent highlanders except that they were aloof and invincible. A century later, American forces would recruit highlanders to join the fight against Hanoi. A good number of them were still holding out long after the Yanks departed.

The French consolidated their hold on Indochina—Cambodia, Laos, and the three parts of Vietnam: Tonkin, Annam, and Cochin—in 1862. By 1876, they had begun to send expeditions into the highlands to assess their economic and strategic worth. Some small garrisons were established. With the incidence of tropical diseases high in Vietnam, and the example of the British and Dutch before them, the French soon began to think about their need for *stations d'altitude* as health resorts. Alexandre Yersin, a Swiss-born physician who signed up with a French shipping company and sailed to Indochina as a ship's doctor before settling in Vietnam to become the colony's leading authority on tropical diseases and their cures, was the first foreigner on record to explore the Lang Bian Plateau and recommend the establishment of a sanitarium there. Yersin's account of the region, which he visited in 1893, impressed the French governor-general, Paul Doumer, who not only sent larger expeditions into the area and ordered the construction of a road but also went to have a look at the plateau himself.

Doumer was sold on Lang Bian. All that was left was to decide where to build a town. On that he got conflicting advice. Yersin had recommended a site at what is now Dankia, near Dalat. But Etienne Tardif, a young French military doctor who was part of the 1898–1899 road-building expedition led by Capt. Paul Guynet, strongly urged that the site that is now Dalat, at barely 5,000 feet, be chosen instead. Until his death in Europe more than half a century later, Tardif inexplicably felt the need to defend his choice in books and articles. Perhaps this was because the enthusiasm for completing a town at Dalat seemed to fall off precipitously after Governor-General Doumer left Indochina and was replaced by Paul Beau, who did not share his predecessor's passion for a hill station. Although some building occurred in Dalat before World War I, it was not until about 1915, and most notably in the 1920s, that the French colonial administration began to focus on this hill station and a few others that never amounted to much by comparison.

Again, the whims and inclinations of the governor-general made a difference. Albert Sarraut, who arrived in 1912, began to invest public funds in the development of the town and in the building of a road connecting the Central Highlands with Saigon. After World War I, Governor-General Maurice Long went a step further and commissioned Hebrard, a Prix de Rome laureate, to draw up a plan for Dalat. In Vietnam, Hebrard gave vital support to an architectural movement that tried to create a classic style with Vietnamese touches—"une architecture indochinoise," he called it—and it can still be seen in some museums and public buildings in Vietnamese cities. But Hebrard's plan for Dalat held few surprises for those who knew hill stations. There would be a health complex, a golf course and playing fields, parks, schools, and offices and homes, but no industry. Environmental protection was built into his 1923 proposals and into later modifications made in the 1930s by the architect Louis-George Pineau.

The population of Dalat grew accordingly. Lam Dong Province's official figures for the city show that it had only 1,500 people in 1923. That grew to 10,000 by 1937. "By 1940," wrote the geographer Robert R. Reed, "Dalat was a provincial center of education and political administration, an important religious retreat and nexus of Christian missionary activities, a primary hub of transportation and communications, and a strategic market town, where forest products, handicrafts, and exotic mid-latitudinal vegetables and fruits produced by highland peoples and Vietnamese migrants were assembled for shipment to Saigon and other lowland cities." After the fluctuations of the World War II years and the Vietminh insurgency, the influx from the North following the division of Vietnam in 1954 pushed the population up to 90,000 by the 1970s. By 1990 it was around 120,000.

As a hill station, albeit a latecomer, Dalat had few peers anywhere in Indochina, although Cambodians who remember the 1960s or earlier recall that Bokor, above Kampot town in the mountains the French called the Chaine d'Elephant, was once a glittering little Cambodian jewel of a sanitarium-resort, with a luxury hotel and casino. Residents of the area told reporters from the *Phnom Penh Post* who rediscovered the ruined town after a kind of peace returned to Cambodia in the 1990s that they remembered rolling out a carpet of pure white for every visit by King Sihanouk in the 1960s. Sihanouk was then prince who had renounced his crown to become the country's political leader. He liked the town, where he had a villa, and chose it as the setting of one of his quirky, self-indulgent films, *The Rose of Bokor.*

The hill town, now in ruins, has been a barometer of Cambodian national life. It was first built in the 1920s. By the end of that decade, the Bokor Palace Hotel was in operation and a parish church had been constructed to serve visitors who came to convalesce, hunt, or just relax in the cooler air. Fresh fruit and vegetables were abundant. But the moment of joy was short-lived. In the mid-1940s, Communist Vietminh guerrillas fighting to force the French out of all of Indochina—Vietnam, Cambodia, and Laos—sacked the town and the hotel. The jungle did the rest. After Cambodia won independence in 1954, Sihanouk rebuilt Bokor, adding his own retreat and some government offices to the residential mix. The Palace Hotel was restored. But then along came the Lon Nol coup that overthrew the Sihanouk government, which in turn was followed by the Khmer Rouge insurgency. Bokor took a few more hits and has yet to recover. Renegade remnants of the Khmer Rouge were still in the region as late as 1997, along with gunners' nests and sandbagged fortifications. But given the tourist potential of Cambodia—politics permitting—Bokor is bound to get someone's attention. Lately its only residents have been police in hammocks and a few rural people who harvest rattan.

For Dalat as for Bokor, the 1920s were boom years for construction. In 1922, Governor-General Long officially opened the Langbian Palace Hotel, which was owned by the French Indochinese government. Although the Palace has since been through several renovations, its spacious, graceful essential form has not changed. Rooms are large and high-ceilinged, with casement windows and French-style shutters to block out the daytime sun. Bathrooms are tiled artistically and fitted with brass fixtures that still survive. Dining rooms and lounges were and remain grand. No building in Dalat has a finer setting, on a hill with lawns rolling down to the lake created in 1930. The hotel grounds are a botanical garden in their own right, and much more pleasant to stroll in than the town's official gardens.

The hotel's history, however, has not been a particularly happy one, all the more wonder that its extravagant fittings have weathered the years. The thirty-room Palace was first managed by a company called Frasetto and Sice. The staff totaled sixty-eight, three Europeans and sixty-five Vietnamese. The arrangement did not last. By 1925, management was taken over by the Société des Grands Hotels Indochinois, which had been affiliated with Frasetto and Sice. The Grand Hotels Indochinois went bankrupt during the Depression, and the French government lost big money in trying to keep the hotel afloat. At one point, the Palace's furniture was confiscated for debt repayment. Yet the Palace was still considered one of Indochina's best hotels, a peer of Hanoi's Metropole.

The Palace was rescued by an Italian, Eduoard Auguste Feraudy, who later apparently became a French citizen, or at least posed as one. Feraudy was the manager of the Continental Hotel in Saigon in 1931 when he heard about the Dalat Palace's dire problems. It took two years to negotiate a three-year contract to run both the Langbian Palace and Hotel du Parc across the street, built about the same time. An early photograph in the Palace Hotel's archives shows the two hotels standing virtually alone in a forest clearing in the 1920s. By the time Feraudy and his wife, Léontine Buysson, took over, the two had serious competition: the Hotel d'Annam, Hotel de Bellevue, Hotel Mostini, and Grand Hotel de Dalat. Feraudy thought a casino might give him an edge, but the French government vetoed that project, so Feraudy settled down to run the Palace and the Parc expertly until his retirement in 1942. The hotel retained its preeminence. Feraudy and his wife never left Dalat. They are buried there.

During World War II, by which time Dalat had a magnificent train station and a cog railway connecting it to Phan Rang, on the South China Sea coast, south of Cam Ranh Bay, business flourished because many French families were unable or unwilling to return home with France under German occupation. By 1945, a quarter of Dalat's population was European. The number of French villas had climbed to nearly 1,000. Near the war's end, in March 1945, the Japanese occupied Dalat and took over the Palace Hotel to house officers, as they had done with leading hotels in Burma and Malaya. The French army came back at beginning of 1946. By then, pictures show that the Palace had been stripped of much of its external ornamentation, but the hotel's archives give no clue when or why this happened.

The French did not stay very long. In 1954, they were driven from Vietnam by a Communist guerrilla army. The country split in two, with a

Communist North and an anti-Communist—if not quite democratic—
South, and the face of Dalat was changed in several ways. The French departure left their villas and public buildings to uncertain futures. The
thousands of Catholics who fled Hanoi and settled in Dalat and in other
towns and cities of the South augmented the Christian population of the
highlands and saved its churches. Vietnam's last emperor, Bao Dai, who
loved Dalat and had spent a great deal of his time there, went into exile in
France.

Bao Dai's palaces are hugely popular tourist attractions for Vietnamese
from all parts of the country. What is known as Palace Number Three,
built between 1933 and 1938 by French and Vietnamese architects, is not a
particularly graceful mansion but is most closely associated with Bao Dai
and other Vietnamese leaders. Its 1930s "modern" style—flat roofs, some
rounded corners, and unadorned windows—left it without much ornamentation outside, though the twenty-six rooms indoors were finished in
attractive hardwoods, and there was a certain spaciousness without
grandiosity. The Art Deco furniture and accessories came largely from
France. Outdoors, an almost-formal European-style garden was created
behind the house.

The Emperor Bao Dai was born Nguyen Vinh Thuy, the son of King
Kai Dinh, in the royal city of Hue, on the Perfume River, which was also
an intellectual capital and famous culinary center. Successively a puppet of
the French (Vichy and otherwise), the occupying Japanese, and, for a year,
even Ho Chi Minh, Bao Dai then served as head of state in the new
South Vietnam until the monarchy was abolished by referendum. Historians say he had little talent for governance and considerable skills at socializing and the chase. He hunted a great deal around Dalat and grew
very attached to the place, or so the story goes. Local people say that he
tried to turn large areas of the highlands into a private hunting reserve,
barring all but the invited. In his Palace Number Three, he worked in a
ground-floor study and set aside a corner bedroom for himself upstairs
with a small "moon-watching balcony" on the garden side. The balcony,
and the house in general, were apparently great sources of relaxation. His
family—a wife, who had been a beauty queen, the Crown Prince, and
three princesses—spent time with him there in rather modest rooms of
their own. But the years were short. Queen Nam Phoung decamped to
Paris in 1949 and died there of cancer. In 1954, after the Geneva treaty that
extricated France and split Vietnam into North and South, Bao Dai, rejected in Saigon, eventually settled in a chalet on the Côte d'Azur and
later married a Frenchwoman. He never returned to Vietnam.

Vietnamese tourists love to wander Bao Dai's favorite palace, as they do the extraordinary tombs of his ancestors in Hue, touching what they are allowed to touch and being photographed amid the paraphernalia of royalty. Other doomed leaders also spent time enjoying the quiet hills of Dalat from Palace Number Three. Among them were Ngo Dinh Diem, who engineered Bao Dai's final fall, and Nguyen Van Thieu, two South Vietnamese presidents who shared little except the fate of being first courted and then abandoned by Washington as successive American administrations searched frantically for a viable government in Saigon.

While a lot of these things were happening, a boy named Tuyet Nguyen was growing up in Dalat under the care of French priests and schoolmasters. Now a journalist in the United States, he remembers the town as an oasis of calm in a turbulent country in the late 1940s and 1950s. Nguyen was born in Saigon in a Catholic family. "My father had disappeared in the war, and my mother sent me to Dalat, to a boarding house run by priests who took care of me and put me in school," he told me. "Most of the kids there had lost one or both of their parents or were the children of French soldiers, sometimes Eurasians, or of French business people." The school in which he was enrolled was the distinguished Lycée Yersin.

I think the distance from Saigon to Dalat was no more than 300 kilometers, but in those times it took a whole day to go there from Saigon. When I was a kid, we traveled up by convoy because of the war. The convoy was led by a tank or military truck or jeeps with soldiers. The condition of the road was very bad. But Dalat was untouched by war—all the wars, really. There was never any fighting, even from Dalat down to Nha Trang on the coast or north of us in the highlands. For us kids, it was a marvelous time. All of us were very poor, but I don't think that happiness has anything to do with that.

The Lycée Yersin cost nothing to enter, as long as you had good grades. Most of the kids who went there—boys and girls—were not from rich families. In the morning a van would come and take us from the boarding house to the school. Breakfast was French-made porridge. For people like us, boarding houses were not rich. I don't remember having lunch. But at three o'clock every day there was a piece of French bread and a banana for everybody at school. We called it *gouter*—the snack. The Lycée Yersin was a secular school. All the teachers—we called them professors—came from France. A good thing about the French was that they really cared for education. All my teachers came from the Sorbonne or had Ph.D.'s from the Sorbonne. The curriculum, all the school programs, were based on the French education system. Even later, when I was at the University of Saigon, all the professors in the school of letters were from the Sorbonne, all of them.

The impact of the French on Vietnam was very strong. It's something the Americans never had. The French really changed society upside down, through the food, the language, the culture, even the construction of houses.

Nguyen discovered later that his deep immersion in French culture had two notable effects: When he fled to Paris during the final days of Saigon, he found himself entirely at home in France. But earlier in Saigon as a university student, he had also learned how much his French education and his idyllic life in Dalat were resented by others who had been living very different lives. "When I went back to Saigon after the lycée and went into another boarding house for the university, I saw that they hated people who had a French education. Those people came from the Delta, where all the fighting was, and they hated me because I had been able to get a good education. We never fought as students, or anything like that, but the resentment was always there between the Vietnamese-educated and the French-educated Vietnamese."

Nguyen remembers very vividly the life he and his friends enjoyed in the forests of Dalat after school hours.

We really lived in the forest. We ate the food we found there. At those times there was no TV or movies. The only thing we could spend time on was hunting and fishing. And in the summer, when the pine needles dry up, they fall on the ground and form a kind of carpet. We used to get a piece of wood that we polished. And then you use it to slide downhill on the needles. The forest was in a wild state then. We were always there, finding something to do.

In 1954, after the battle of Dien Bien Phu, the children at the Lycée Yersin were asked to help care for convalescing French soldiers. "They took my school and turned it into a hospital and we were all asked to help," Nguyen said. But the French were soon gone, and the South Vietnamese elite moved in. "When the government in Saigon took over, they created the military academy, the University of Dalat, the seminaries. They started building a heavy-water reactor. But even then Dalat was always considered a resort city. The President had a house. The generals all had their houses because of the military academy. Dalat became mainly agricultural. It supplied the flowers for Saigon."

Nguyen recalls that most tourists who visited Dalat in the years he lived there were family groups who came to stay a while. For a number of years, the road to Dalat was thought to be too dangerous for casual travel, though in the 1960s tour buses were again able to make the trip without a military escort. Now the road from Saigon, though not much improved physically, is a busy route, and people flock to Dalat in cars and buses. Tourists and business people can also fly to Dalat several times a week, to an old airfield at Lien Khuong, about twenty miles away, which reopened in 1992. There are hopes of reviving a railway line to the coast at Phan Rang, and of rebuilding the Saigon road, which passes through struggling tea plantations as it climbs to the hills.

Traveling the tourist circuit with Vietnamese is great fun, since they are warm, inquisitive, generous people who want to draw an outsider into whatever activity is at hand. Having seen Dalat's palaces, the flower garden where tribal people's handicrafts are sold inside while they beg outside the gate, the newly refurbished golf club that may or may not prove to have created an ecological disaster in the lake below, any number of interesting churches and an old French cemetery gone to seed, I thought it would be novel to take the narrow-gauge excursion train ride to Trai Mat, with its locally famous Linh Phuoc Pagoda. The recently restored (by the Swedes, says the guidebook) small red-and-white train to Trai Mat is all there is at the moment to lure visitors to Dalat's rather grand railway station, although enterprising Vietnamese women have set up stalls there to sell their homemade shawls, snacks, and other handiwork.

A crowd of Vietnamese tourists was accumulating when the ticket office opened. The fare table posted on the wall was a little obscure, but I was sold a round-trip excursion for about $5. Since I had no idea how long or short the trip would be, it was hard to tell if that was a bargain or not. When the diesel engine was ready to go, we were all herded toward two small coaches. Then a smiling conductor stepped in to look at my ticket, take me out of the line, and show me to a car farther forward that I had earlier assumed was where the crew sat, since it was attached to the driver's compartment. The engine driver came out to say "hello" and "excuse me," the extent of his English vocabulary. He bowed lightly and returned to the cab. I looked around. This was obviously the club car. There was a upholstered sofa and two armchairs sharing a table on which a potted philodendron had been placed. The wall had posters. There were wide windows. The whole scene suddenly became hilarious. I realized that for $5, I had bought a business class ticket to Trai Mat.

So, apparently, had a well-dressed family from Saigon and a couple who never identified themselves or spoke except to ask the others what I was. "American," the Saigon patriarch said. That much I understood. "No!" said

the others. "Yes, American," he insisted. By now we were two to a chair and
passing around the bananas, candy, and bottled drinks. All I had with me
was water, but I threw that into the mix and had it promptly returned. I was
the guest. The ride could not have taken more than half an hour, but it
passed through exquisite farmland, a patchwork of greens and reds and yel-
lows. Flowering vines covered the narrow gulch through which we passed.
And then we were in Trai Mat, a crossroads town of no great architectural
interest but much eating and drinking in countless little cafés.

The routine, I was told by my fellow club car passengers, was to get out,
walk to the Linh Phuoc Pagoda, spend an hour or so, and come back to
the train, which left promptly. Before the hopeful eyes of shopkeepers and
food vendors, dozens of us dutifully disembarked and walked up the
town's narrow main street, a tide advancing on the pagoda, off to one side,
up an alleyway. Linh Phuoc is a work in progress, and part of the purpose—perhaps the greater part—is to contribute to its construction. The
pagoda, set at the edge of more farmland that is very pleasing to the eye, is
distinguished by its large standing statue of the Boddhisattva Avalokitesvara in the temple forecourt. Avalokitesvara is a familiar figure in Mahayana Buddhism, which is prevalent in Vietnam and different from the
Hinayana or Theravada Buddhism of Thailand, Laos, and Cambodia.
Some of my fellow passengers took turns being photographed with the
statue. Others made a quick move to the noodle stalls. (How do these
people eat so much and stay so thin?) But most entered the temple to pray
before the seated Buddha inside, and then to give generously to the completion of his house.

The sign at the entrance says, in Vietnamese and English: "Ladies and
Gentlemen, The construction work of Linh Phuoc Pagoda has not been
completed because the cost of this project is higher than the local Buddhists' budget. Therefore we call on the Buddhists and benefactors from
everywhere to help us complete Buddhist cultural work soon. We look
forward to your golden generosity. We genuinely pray Buddha to bless
you." A row of women with ledgers and cash boxes sit just inside the door.
What's an American to do: give too much and appear to be showing off or
give too little and incur disdain? Fortunately, there was a chart on the wall
listing all recent donors and their donations. The average gift was 10,000
dong, or about $1 at the time. That seemed safe, so I presented my requi-
site dong notes and received a certificate of blessing. Then a fellow club
car passenger stepped up to the table and with a flourish and a look of immense pride, laid down 100,000 dong.

9

PHILIPPINE AMERICANA

Baguio

Abraham Lincoln still watches over Baguio

$\mathscr{I}$S THIS PLACE AMERICAN OR WHAT? Checking into the Club John Hay in Baguio was like registering at summer camp all over again. I expected to be issued a towel and a hockey stick. Breakfast was cafeteria style; we got to push our damp trays past a battery of icky juice dispensers and make our own instant coffee. A short hike away, en route to the zany camp bakery called Solana's Manna, a statue of Abraham Lincoln peered over the hollyhocks.

Freeze the frame there. Unfortunately, those of us who tramped the piney hills in 1997 and stayed in those spartan rooms and cottages with cultural roots in the Poconos or upstate New York were the last to enjoy the only American colonial fuddy-duddy still left intact in Southeast Asia. By the turn of the twenty-first century, Club John Hay, a former American military camp ceded to the Philippines in 1991, will become another pan-Asian golf resort, rebuilt, jazzed up, and "developed."

Like how? I asked. "Oh, a championship golf course, a luxury hotel, and maybe a shopping mall," a public relations person said brightly.

"Then this is the end of Club John Hay," I said.

"Oh, no," she replied cheerfully. "It's just the beginning."

Club John Hay and the city of Baguio just beyond its gates, the only true hill station in the Philippines, were planned and built from ground up in the first decade of the twentieth century by eager new American imperialists who acquired the islands in 1898 during the Spanish-American War. Baguio remained a very American town into the 1930s, said Lewis Gleeck, who probably knows more and has written more about the U.S. colonial experience in the Philippines than anyone else. The only American hill station in Asia, Baguio had its country club for the well-to-do who came for the season. But the guys who lived there year-round, self-propelled entrepreneurs of more limited means, were more apt to get together for morning coffee at John Nill's Pioneer Shoe Shop and for evening drinks and sometimes a meal at Mike Ryan's Shamrock Hotel. There were men like J. J. Murphy, who had worked on the first road to be built to Baguio and then stayed to open a movie house, and Joe Rice, who tended bar, ran a taxi service, became a truck gardener (with seeds from Denver), and finally struck it rich in property and gold mining. Both are among the *Americans on the Philippine Frontiers*, a book Gleeck wrote in the early 1970s. Gleeck himself settled in the Philippines and is curator of an extraordinary collection of Americana from the colonial period, now housed in the library of the Ateneo de Manila. "Keeper of the flame" is how one American scholar described Gleeck.

Although Baguio is now a Filipino city of more than 150,000 people, the largest urban area in northern Luzon, the original American plan for the town—with its broad avenues, imposing public buildings, and spacious parks—is still discernible under the sprawl that has transformed its vistas. Washington never intended to let Baguio take shape by happenstance. From the moment it was decided to create a hill station that would also serve as an American colonial summer capital, the search for a top town planner was on, led by no less than Secretary of War William Howard Taft and W. Cameron Forbes, then a member of the governing Philippine Commission and later American governor-general of the Philippines. After approaching Frederick Law Olmsted, Jr., a landscape designer and the son of the creator of New York's Central Park, and Charles F. McKim, one of the leading architects in the United States, Washington settled in 1904 on the famous city planner Daniel H. Burnham.

Burnham, who was also asked to redesign Manila in a burst of American thoroughness, spent only about nine days in the Baguio region, most of it on horseback, according to the most comprehensive early history of this American Simla, Robert R. Reed's *City of Pines*. Burnham wisely foresaw a town with many functions: a resort for health and recreation, a marketing center for the mountain region, an administrative capital, and a city where people of all income groups would live and work. At the center, on a meadow, he sketched in a park that now bears his name. With its lake and playing fields, Burnham Park is the most popular place in town, especially on weekends. He planned a municipal center and a site for colonial government offices as well as a commercial district. Set apart was a mansion for the governor-general.

Gently curving roads led into the hills, but Burnham insisted—contrary to British practice in India—that the ridges and hilltops remain natural. "The placing of formal architectural silhouettes upon the summits of the surrounding hills would make a hard skyline and go far toward destroying the charm of this beautiful landscape," he wrote. He warned against allowing timber companies a free hand and proposed a system of forest protection so that indigenous species would not be lost. As Burnham's 1905 plan evolved and was adapted over the following decade, Baguio added distinctive features: a large teachers' camp for training and relaxation, more parks, schools, hospitals, and a hotel, the Pines, which had earlier been a convalescent center.

"The Pines Hotel was a grand place, with a lot of history and character," Consuelo Almonte-Shaffer remembers. She went to Baguio first as a child and later with college friends from the University of the Philippines; the town was the Fort Lauderdale of Filipino campus life at vacation time in the 1950s.

A special place was the Kalinga Room at the Pines. But all the hotel was a showcase. Almost every visiting dignitary would be taken to this hotel. The ceilings, statues, and walls were carved of heavy, dark *narra* wood; most of the decorations were made by natives of Baguio, who had their own distinctive arts and handicrafts. I believe the Pines had more character and beauty than today's Manila Hotel. I was told that the Pines had burned to the ground in the 1980s and was never rebuilt. The Hyatt Hotel, which tried to replace the grandeur of the Pines, was leveled by an earthquake in the early '90s.

Almonte-Shaffer, who now lives in New York, said she was half-afraid to return to Baguio, the scene of so much youthful pleasure, because she has heard that its elegance and romance are gone, along with its landmarks.

She is probably too close to being right about that now that Club John Hay is being bulldozed into modernity. The rest of Baguio town is already a hot, almost treeless conglomeration of fast-food restaurants, stores, and offices, with sidewalks as crowded as those of Times Square on a summer evening. There are exceptions. The civic center with its graceful town hall remains, and so does Burnham Park, an oasis named for the planner who wisely and presciently made it a centerpiece of the town. Almonte-Shaffer's family gravitated there when she was a child.

"In the mornings outside our summer house the air was crisp and misty," she recalled.

By noon, the sun would be strong but the wind kept the air cool. I remember wearing a sweater while sitting in Burnham Park, with the heat of the sun on my face. Burnham Park was at the center of town, like Central Park, and everyone congregated there among the beautiful flowers. In those days, an experience like that was rarely seen in cities in the Philippines. Baguio was also the only place in the country where we could see pine trees.

The city was not born fashionable. Although Baguio was not formally chartered until 1909, and then great efforts had to be made by Cameron Forbes, the governor-general, to get Americans and wealthy Filipinos to buy land and build houses there, the military had made the area a rest and recreation center by 1903. In 1906, the first simple permanent buildings were erected on the 1,760 acres of what was then known as Camp John Hay. Most of the camp was completed by 1920, including a hospital and an open-air amphitheater and garden designed by Major General J. Franklin Bell, the American commanding officer in the Philippines. His house and amphitheater will be spared the wrecker's ball in the reconstruction of the camp, I was told. The Lone Star Steak House won't be so lucky. For some Filipinos, this funky bistro with plastic cactuses provided a first glimpse of the American carnivore in action, and a first taste of steak. Consuelo Almonte-Shaffer was introduced to a T-bone at Camp John Hay, which she remembers as an "exclusive American military resort," to which Filipinos had to be invited.

The inspiration for this singular American hill station sprang from the same sources that nourished colonial dreams of escape from tropical torpor everywhere in Asia. By the time Americans got around to Baguio, European colonialists had made it an article of faith among the pale races that Westerners' bodies (and sometimes their minds) fell to pieces in the tropics. Few heeded the warnings of many a medical expert who told these Caucasian flowers that they were wilting in part because they insisted on overeating, overdressing, drinking too much alcohol, and sleeping in closed rooms to avoid "miasmas." The British and Dutch in particular clothed themselves as they would at home, where it is almost never truly hot. They taught their cooks to prepare heavy, starchy meals fit to fuel a body through a dismal, chilly North Sea winter. A small school of academics, mostly American, has sprung up to explain this insanity as some kind of calculated policy of separation that called for distinctive (and, the imperialists thought, superior) living habits that must never be tinged or compromised by proximity to natives. However, this inability to adapt may have been only that: a reflection of a stodgy, unimaginative people afraid to jettison convention. Errant behavior was sometimes known as "going tropo."

Americans, with greater experience in warm climates and frontier living, were more casual in the Philippines, diarists of the time noted. But even if they knew how to dress more appropriately, there was always a fear of illness or exhaustion. All the other colonialists had hill stations. Americans wanted one, too. When they set about very methodically to create their model town in the Cordillera Central, a rugged mountain range in northern Luzon about 120 miles north of Manila, Baguio was a village inhabited by Igorot people, tough mountaineers who had held off the Spanish for centuries and whose skills in hydraulic engineering had made them, like the early Sri Lankans, one of the most successful irrigators in Asia. The Igorots created the phenomenal rice terraces at Banue, north of Baguio, in the Mountain Province. They would later lend their expertise to American engineers building the road into Benguet Province and Baguio, which would become its capital.

The Spanish had come close to building a hill station of their own in Baguio. They established a small sanitarium at La Trinidad, a few miles away. But first Igorot resistance and then a nascent anticolonial revolution in the lowlands preoccupied them in the last years of empire. The first American promoters of a hill station in these pine-covered mountains knew about La Trinidad and the potential of Baguio, a highland ringed by cliffs, wooded hills, and rocky peaks. Dean C. Worcester, an American zoologist who had done research in the Philippines under the Spanish and later was named to the Philippine Commission, which acted as an American governing body in the islands, knew about the region but had never managed to visit it because of illness. He was transfixed when he finally saw the place in 1900.

"We were literally dumfounded when within the space of a hundred yards, we suddenly left the tropics behind us and came out into a wonderful region of pine parks," he wrote after his first inspection of Baguio. "At the same moment, a delightful cold breeze swept down from the heights above us. It took us but a short time to decide that here was an ideal site for a future city." Worcester's words are mounted on the wall of a small and apparently doomed museum on the grounds of Club John Hay.

Nearly a century later, Consuelo Almonte-Shaffer remembers similar impressions of Baguio. "I remember Mines View Park, where we enjoyed the view of distant hills and the Benguet gold mines below. In those days it seemed to be the whole wide world below us, with flowers scattered down the sides of the hills." The soft faraway hills are still there on the horizon at Club John Hay, and still—miraculously—green. Indeed, taking off from Baguio's small airport—whose runway is used as a short-cut between two local roads by taxis and ambling schoolchildren until a Klaxon warns of an incoming aircraft—the rolling hills and velvet peaks below seem never to end.

Worcester, like Burnham after him, always envisioned Baguio as more than a health-giving resort. It would be a Philippine Simla or Ooty, a well-equipped summer capital for the hot season. This was not a popular idea among Filipinos and a good number of Americans in Manila, who thought that the new imperialists should be spending more money on the Philippines and less on keeping themselves cool and happy. Ironically, it is now Filipinos in Baguio who are clinging to the American vision of the town, fearful that Filipino redevelopment, with the usual Asian dose of money politics involved, will destroy its unique character, making it indistinguishable from any other highland resort in Southeast Asia.

Dean Worcester, confronted with skepticism on all sides, took his case for a hill station in Baguio directly to Secretary of War Elihu Root in Washington, into whose department the newly acquired islands fell. A committee was dispatched to the area and concluded that not only would Baguio be good for the health of "white women and children," but it would also be an ideal place to station reserve troops on call for service anywhere in the Philippines. And, of course, it would be that perfect sanitarium. But now the practical troubles set in. The committee, one of whose leaders was Worcester, recommended building a road to Baguio from the nearest railhead at Dagupan, near the coast of the South China Sea to the southwest. This recommendation nearly proved fatal to the unborn Baguio project. Construction of the road turned out to be a far more costly and difficult project than anyone had imagined.

Americans had reached Baguio on horseback with relative ease and did not seem to be aware of how hard it would be to turn mere trails into all-weather roads passing through deep gorges and over relentless folds of rocky, if forested, mountains. The roads would have to serve not only a summer capital but also the year-round agriculture industry the colonial government hoped to encourage. But if the British could build impossible roads to the tops of mountains, surely the Americans, the greatest road builders since the Romans, could do so also. The plan adopted by Worcester's commission envisioned a road that would cut inland from Dagupan and snake into the Cordillera along the Bued River. An army engineer, Captain Charles W. Mead, was put in charge of the project, since he had earlier surveyed the route for a possible railroad line. Work began in January 1901. Mead thought the road would cost about $75,000 to build and would be completed relatively quickly. Four years later, when the road was finally finished, the bill was $2 million. By then, Mead had been replaced first by his chief engineer and then by Major L.W.V. Kennon, who finished the job in 1905 amid a storm of protest in the Filipino press. The highway is still commonly known as the Kennon Road.

"My family would go to Baguio during the off-season summer recess—that was after Easter week, when Baguio was packed with affluent families trying to escape the heat of the cities," Consuelo Almonte-Shaffer wrote in notes about her childhood she collected for me. "We would take the bus up along the winding roads to the top of the Baguio plateau. The way to Baguio was both scenic and exciting. My sister and I would cover our eyes, since we were both very scared to see the steep cliffs along the zigzagging road that had no guard rails. Farther up, we could watch the Igorots climbing up the mountains barefoot with bundles on their heads. We also saw small native huts made of bamboo and nipa leaves." Then and now, the Kennon Road is blocked from time to time by rock slides in the rainy season or after an earthquake.

Kennon was a skillful manager with a knack for recognizing and accepting innovation, said Robert R. Reed in *City of Pines*. His workforce of 3,000 construction laborers comprised forty-six nationalities, with nearly as many languages, beliefs, and appetites.

> Major Kennon fed them well, provided essential medical care, guaranteed adequate wages, allowed married men to keep their families in camps, offered for sale ample quantities of cigarettes and cigars, and even permitted the establishment of gambling houses and bars in certain restricted areas. Unlike his predecessors, moreover, Kennon was not completely tied to the notion of Western superiority in all matters of engineering and human organization. In fact he proved willing to accept any technological suggestions of merit that could facilitate construction activities. Consequently when the hooves of draft animals wore thin on the sharp river gravels used to macadamize the road, Kennon adopted the Japanese innovation of shoeing them with small mats made of straw and hemp. When the mats proved inadequate, black hostlers from the American South fashioned special iron shoes to protect the hooves of both oxen and carabao. Even more significant was Kennon's willingness to employ Igorot hydraulic techniques to make major cuts into mountain spurs and wash earth into places where it served as roadfill.

Frank Jenista, an American diplomat and scholar who wrote about American governors in the high Cordilleras north of Baguio, noted in his fascinating book *The White Apos* how important the personality and character of an administrator were to colonial relations with the mountain people who had so successfully rebuffed the Spanish. Americans had some of their most challenging and rewarding experiences with the Ifugao—a distinct group among the mountain people collectively called Igorots—who lived, farmed, and took the heads of their enemies in the region around the Banue rice terraces that bears their name.

"For the Americans," wrote Jenista, who as the son of missionaries went
to school in Baguio and later taught there,

> just the sheer visual spectacle of Ifugao was enough to overwhelm those see-
> ing it for the first time: the magnificent rice terraces which turned the
> mountain slopes into giant staircases and range after range of steep, forbid-
> ding mountains, some stark and bare, others covered with luxuriant tropical
> forests. The people and culture were equally striking: superb physiques,
> uniquely Ifugao "bowl" haircuts, spear-carrying warriors, gongs pounding
> out wild rhythms and bare-breasted women dancing at canaos honoring the
> ancestral spirits, human heads decorating the homes of the brave—all these
> struck the imagination of the turn-of-the-century American.

The Ifugao stood their ground. Told that head-hunting was henceforth
illegal, they refused to adopt this innovation and challenged the Americans to fight it out. Americans made mistakes. Arrested for taking heads,
Ifugao died in the confinement of jails. Nevertheless, Jenista said, the independent spirit of the Ifugao "struck chords of admiration and respect
among the Americans who perhaps remembered a similar proud spirit
among the American Indians before the conquest broke them." In the
end, some good working relationships and close personal liaisons were
built between the Americans and the mountain people, Ifugao and others.
Jenista made the interesting observation that this pattern was not uncommon in Southeast Asia, where people of the lowlands "stereotyped the
mountain people as primitive, hostile and naïve" and made little effort to
learn their languages or understand their cultures. "Western colonial authority intruded into the Southeast Asian world and virtually without exception (and, indeed, virtually without regard for geographical, cultural or
temporal limits) developed relations with highland people that were
largely congenial, in contrast to the inimical colonial relationships with
lowland cultures." All around Southeast Asia certain Western authority
figures—the "white apos"—have been incorporated into local folklore.

When the United States acquired the Philippines as a by-product of
the Spanish-American War—a very controversial conflict over Cuba,
halfway around the world—it was a bad moment to debut as an imperial
power in Southeast Asia. Anticolonialism was building, and two years
earlier Filipinos had begun an armed fight for independence from Spain.
The Spanish made matters worse by executing a great Filipino nationalist,
José Rizal, in 1896, despite his sincere and public disapproval of armed rebellion. Fortunately for Spain, the rebellion fell into factionalism and dis-

array. Andres Bonifacio, a firebrand who pressed for war against the Spanish, was condemned, pardoned, then executed anyway on the orders of a rival Filipino revolutionary, Emilio Aguinaldo. Under Aguinaldo, the rebels concluded a kind of peace treaty with the Spanish in 1897—or at least took money to call off the fighting, and went into exile. When an American fleet arrived in 1898 to sink Spanish ships during the war, Aguinaldo was brought back, armed by Commodore Dewey, and encouraged to resume his revolution in alliance with the Americans.

Hopes were high among Filipino nationalists, who became willing partners of the United States in the expectation that their freedom would now come from Washington. They formally declared independence from Spain in June 1898. But they were soon disappointed. At about the same time that Filipinos were writing a constitution and preparing to set up a government, Washington was deciding to send troops to claim the Philippines for the United States. In the Treaty of Paris, signed in December that year, Spain relinquished the Philippines for $20 million, a deal Filipinos refused to accept. President McKinley later told a group of Methodist pastors that he had prayed over the problem of what to do about the Philippines and had concluded that the Filipinos could not be left to their own devices, vulnerable to European powers in mercantile competition with the United States. Spain might, in fact, try to reestablish itself in the islands, the president thought.

Filipinos promptly turned their guns on Uncle Sam. The campaign was, of course, bound to fail against superior American arms and experience. Filipino guerrillas, who were strong enough to consider attacking the Spanish in Manila in 1898, were pushed back and scattered by the Americans in 1899 and 1900. Aguinaldo, still the rebels' political leader and strategist, was finally captured in 1901 and publicly accepted the sovereignty of the United States in an eloquent statement acknowledging that the Filipino people wanted peace. Under the American flag he said that Filipinos "repose their trust" in Washington's promises that liberties would be granted by a generous nation.

The Filipinos were not, ultimately, entirely disappointed by Washington, where Congress took an active part in making policy on the new acquisitions. Almost immediately, American administrators were taking steps to give the Philippines the national political institutions the Spanish had never created. By 1902, there was an elected national assembly, which later became a bicameral legislature modeled on the U.S. Congress. Autonomy grew steadily, though not at the pace many Filipinos sought. In

1934, the American Congress passed the Tydings-McDuffie Act, promising complete independence and a new constitution in 1946. In the interim, the Philippines would be an American commonwealth. In 1935, Manuel Luis Quezon became its first president. Though Filipino historians and politicians have argued that the promise of independence was an act of economic self-interest in Washington, this was a period when a strong current of anticolonialism was being felt in informed American public opinion. Followers of Mahatma Gandhi said that they sensed this when they toured the United States to drum up support for Indian independence. Despite the devastating interruption of World War II, Washington honored its pledge to the Filipinos, and the Republic of the Philippines was finally free on July 4, 1946.

Almost from the moment the United States acquired the Philippines in 1898, or at least from the time that the reality of imperialism set in, Washington began sending to Manila a corps of very able administrators and specialists in critical fields, who set to work with zeal, the positive side of manifest destiny. Rudyard Kipling egged them on with a famous poem, "The White Man's Burden," which may be unacceptably prejudiced and patronizing now but then certainly reflected the thinking of do-gooders of the age. The Americans looked for gaps left by nearly four centuries of Spanish rule. Schools were built and teachers trained, with the aim of providing universal education. A national health bureau, often working through the schools, tackled endemic problems. "Gradually, the epidemic diseases that had been taking their toll of Filipino lives for centuries were brought under control," the Filipino historian Horacio de la Costa noted. Encouraged by the Americans, the ethnic Chinese built more schools, hospitals, cemeteries, and businesses for their communities.

In both the accounts of the Chinese role in Philippine life and the record of American imperialism, there are often pro-Spanish biases among some Filipino writers drawn from the solidly Roman Catholic Spanish-speaking elite, who had their counterparts in the Spanish American colonies. Indeed, the ruling elite of the Spanish Philippines was much more closely linked to Spain's New World colonies, particularly Mexico, than to Spain. Acapulco was the port to which ships from the Philippines headed, crossing the Pacific laden with goods from the East to be sold or used in the colonies or transshipped to Europe. Spanish-Americans were sent to Manila to run the Philippines. As in its colonies in the Western Hemisphere, Spanish officials in the Philippine Islands did not encourage local industry or even, until late in the day, plantation agriculture. Like Spain itself, as well as its American colonies, the Philippines became a valuable but limited point of commerce—goods in, goods out—without developing much of an economy of its own to sustain long-term growth. Education in the Philippines was very limited. Filipino and foreign critics remarked on the near-absence of practical vocational training compared with the large numbers of priests graduating from religious schools.

As for the Chinese, the tiny Spanish-speaking elite kept them at arm's length and literally in ghettos in Manila, though in rural areas some Chinese-Filipinos were able to become substantial landowners. The Chinese were the unacknowledged backbone of the national economy and ultimately of political life in the Philippines, where the term *mestizo* implied Chinese-Filipino parentage more than Spanish-Filipino blood. Nearly every major political figure, from the nineteenth-century nationalist hero José Rizal to former president Corazon Aquino, a leader of the People Power revolution that overthrew the dictatorship of Ferdinand Marcos in 1986, had a mixed Chinese and Malay-Filipino ancestry. Furthermore, the Chinese provided all the practical trades and services.

While I was in Baguio, a small but wonderfully stocked museum at Camp John Hay that specialized in exhibits of mountain tribal life mounted a special exhibition called "Heritage: A Pictorial History of the Chinese in the Philippines." It traced the rapid progress of the Sangleys, as Filipino Chinese became known, because they announced on first arrival—perhaps as early as the thirteenth century—that they had come *seng-li,* to trade. The old photographs showed the Sangleys in every corner of economic life. The accompanying texts credited them with the introduction of the cast-iron plow and sugar making in the countryside and the development of a range of trades and industries in the towns: printing, carpentry, masonry, blacksmithing, weaving, dyeing, and food processing. Chinese cooking filled bowls and dictionaries. The Tagalog language includes numerous Chinese loan words.

As in other Southeast Asian colonies, many Chinese became Christians, often without losing completely their inherited traditional spiritual practices. On a road in northern Luzon, a Chinese farming family had built an ornate red-and-gold shrine with a miniature pagoda roof, then placed inside it, not incense or objects of Buddhist worship, but a small statue of El Niño, the Christ Child. A certain eclecticism, even ecumenicism, seems easier to achieve in the Philippines than in the Muslim-majority nations of Malaysia and Indonesia, where Islam can accommodate architectural differences—the shape of the mosque or minaret—but not much intermingling of beliefs, symbols, or practices. As I traveled across Asia, I looked forward to the "anything goes" Philippines.

But after two months almost literally on the road, through snow and ice and searing heat, uphill and down, with no serious mishaps or great inconveniences, everything started to fall apart where I least expected problems: in the Philippines. The hurdles were small at first, but nonetheless the kind of inconveniences that most other Southeast Asians would no longer tolerate. Inexplicably, nobody in the bank kiosks at the airport seemed to want to cash traveler's checks, but were happy to take hard currency. Later in Baguio I discovered that only one bank, the Philippine National Bank on Sessions Road, was authorized to cash traveler's checks at all, and these indifferent bankers had made the process as complicated and time-consuming as possible. After visiting two departments on two floors, I was sent to stand in an all-purpose queue leading to six teller windows, of which only two were open for business. The tellers seemed to be conducting major financial transactions, to judge by the deliberation they demonstrated. Most people were only trying to withdraw or deposit small sums to their personal accounts, however. Sixty-three people were ahead of me in the line, which snaked three times back and forth across the lobby. It took more than forty minutes to reach the front, where a teller asked for more signatures and documentation.

In Manila, the old Manila Hotel had also let me down, failing to deliver the promised room on the side overlooking the Manila Bay, where I had spent many days and nights as a reporter. After all the bubbling expressions of "welcome back," the receptionist said they were not expecting me until later, and would I mind a view of the city. But more serious bad news soon followed. Philippine Airlines had canceled my confirmed, paid-for and ticketed flights to and from Baguio. Sorry, the flights were now full. Clearly, in my absence, my ticket had been sold at a good price, perhaps with a little commission, to a persuasive traveler. A concierge scrambled to find a taxi to drive me to Baguio early the next morning, at about six times the cost of the airfare. I probably paid about $50 too much, Baguio drivers told me. But it was still cheaper than a hotel car and just as safe and comfortable. When I called the Club John Hay in Baguio before leaving Manila to say that my travel plans had changed, I discovered that I had no room; it had been booked for February instead of March. We still disagree over whose fault that was, but fortunately, the John Hay came through with accommodations in the main club building, a former American officers' mess and quarters. From then on things went fine.

The drive from Manila to Baguio honors no schedule. It can take four-and-a-half hours. It can take six or more if a sudden landslide occurs and the rocks can be cleared enough to open a lane for cars. The first part of the journey is by highway and then a two-lane road, with cars passing recklessly along the shoulders without warning. The highway cuts straight across the flat rice fields and sugar plantation landscape of Luzon. Somewhere around halfway through the trip, my driver—Consorcio D. Agena, Jr., on his business card, or, more familiarly, "Onnie," following the Filipino custom of going by a nickname—took a "shortcut" in defiance of road signs pointing another way to Baguio, and we soon plunged into a vast wasteland of ash and lava left over from the 1989 volcanic eruption of Mount Pinatubo, about twenty-five miles away. The scene was remarkable in its profound devastation, eight years after the event. On every side the view was an unbroken field of gray, with clouds of ash stirred up by traffic. Dust was still settling on people who had come bundled like mummies to beg at the side of the road. Trucks methodically carted away ash and rocks, but there seemed no end to the supply, which in places appeared to cover what were once fields with layers of volcanic matter many feet deep.

The Philippines, and certainly the Filipinos, do not deserve the terrible pounding they take periodically from natural catastrophes. Manila and Baguio are among the places destroyed or badly damaged over the years by earthquakes. Typhoons rip houses from the land and flip ships over in the seas. Years ago, I went to report on a ferry that had overturned in a storm, and I stood with a crowd of stoic but shattered people waiting on a pier to learn who had survived or what bodies might be found and brought to shore in the driving rain and wind. The ferry had been overcrowded; people on the dock said that it was common for boatmen to make some money on the side by selling "extra" tickets.

After the ash of Mount Pinatubo and before the climb into the Cordillera begins, there is little else of interest to see on the road from Manila to Baguio beyond rice and sugarcane, unless one derives some entertainment from counting gas stations, fast-food restaurants, and Protestant churches. The phenomenal growth in recent decades of Protestantism, in particular evangelical Protestantism, gives new meaning to the Philippines' distinction of being the only Christian country in Asia. There is not a town along the route to Baguio that does not have a Protestant church of one kind or another. And this is a country so saturated by Roman Catholicism under the Spanish that the running joke is that the Philippines' colonial history can be summed up neatly as "four centuries in a convent and forty years in Hollywood." The late Filipino historian (and Jesuit) Horacio de la Costa noted in his fascinating 1965 collection, *Read-*

ings in Philippine History, that a passion for religion seemed to be a hall-mark of the Filipino. Today, mainline bookstores are packed with religious publications of every kind, from tales of the miraculous to mundane advice on family life. There are also quite heavy theological works available to the general reader, though these do not attract as many browsers, from what I observed. The ability to run amok for the faith is manifest not only in the zeal with which a number of Filipinos volunteer each year to reenact the Crucifixion but also in the fervor with which the antiabortion crusade is waged. In Tarlac and Baguio, and no doubt in numerous other places, the church has erected huge statues of unborn fetuses to assault the senses and the consciences of passersby. Family planning in the Philippines engenders perennial emotional debate between a social welfare lobby arguing that the country cannot sustain its present rate of population growth and a rock-hard anticontraception Roman Catholic hierarchy that has never relinquished its proclivity for interference in affairs of state, a privilege it acquired under the Spanish.

Religion apart, there is a nice wacky quality about life in the Philippines, surely the friendliest, most open society in Southeast Asia. Lunch in any popular restaurant can be an experience in good-natured pandemonium. Conversation never stops; no deadly northern European silences here. Waiters may be lightning fast or a little slower, but there is always a natural ebullience. No need for a forced, "Hi, my name is Bong-Bong." Life is very hard for many Filipinos, but shrieks of delight and contagious laughter enliven even small excursions, like a walk through the flower gardens at Club John Hay, where giggly couples, friends, and families take turns on weekends posing for pictures among the strange flowers from foreign temperate zones: tall hollyhocks, intensely colored dahlias, mountains of snowy daisies, and a virtual ground cover of petunias and snapdragons. A gardener who came to check on his charges at sunup on a quiet weekday morning told me this Filipino-American friendship garden had been an American idea. He added, moreover, that he wished that the Americans had never left because nothing was what it used to be anymore. Like many others, he feared he would lose his job in the three years of "redevelopment"—a scary word—ahead.

"I cherish the sweet memories of the good old days," Consuelo Almonte-Shaffer said. "In Baguio the markets where my mother would take us to see mountain people with colorful beads on their heads and necks selling their fresh fruits and vegetables and their handicrafts are now heavily congested. Western fast food is crowding out our *carinderias.* The cool nipa huts are replaced by shantytowns and so many pine trees have been cut down." Before leaving Baguio, I took a taxi to all the tourist sites beyond the gates of Camp John Hay and its still-cool forested hillsides. I began in town, with what was left of Burnham's city, and saw crowds lounging on the grass by the lake in Burnham Park while children played soccer in one of its fields. We climbed the hill to Lourdes Grotto, but not the 252 steps pious pilgrims ascend in Holy Week; there is a road. From there, large parts of the city are spread out below, a density of white and pastels under the sun. A few clusters of mountain people had come out in costume to have pictures taken for money. We paused at the Mansion House, the presidential retreat whose gates are modeled on those of Buckingham Palace. Families were taking turns being photographed there, a picture souvenir of a summer capital trying to cling to its raison d'être. We went to the Philippine Military Academy, where only graffiti on a nearby wall saying "I love Gringo" is left as a reminder that not so long ago this place was a seething well of rebellion. "Gringo" Honasan, who tried more times than I can remember to overthrow the government, was now a senator, and his alma mater, the military academy, is just another tourist attraction with flower beds and murals for busloads of city folk. I toured the tonier neighborhoods around Outlook Drive and saw the abandoned and decaying former hideaways of the Marcos family dictatorship, appropriately as empty as the legacy Ferdinand Marcos left his country. I remembered those heady days in 1986 when Filipinos by the thousands flooded Manila's Rizal Park and Rojas Boulevard to celebrate his overthrow. Vendors did a brisk business selling T-shirts that proclaimed: "Proud to be a Filipino." Heads have been higher ever since.

And then I went back to John Hay to walk around, sit on benches, read all the historical plaques, visit the silly little Cemetery of Negativism, where earnest Americans "buried" bad things like sloth and mendacity, and photograph the old, white-and-green-painted buildings that are about to disappear—or may already be gone as I write. These summer camp cottages and lodges scattered around the piney woods were never really distinguished architecturally; no Savoys or Hill Clubs or Candacraigs here. But they were truly American in inspiration, style, and spirit—and, rightly or wrongly, an American military presence in the Philippines for nearly half a century after independence kept them that way. Now, later than anywhere else in colonized Southeast Asia, the people whose land on which this sole American hill station rose have come to claim it.

BIBLIOGRAPHY

Addleton, Jonathan. *Some Far and Distant Place*. Athens: University of Georgia Press, 1977.

Aiken, S. Robert. *Imperial Belvederes: The Hill Stations of Malaysia*. Kuala Lumpur: Oxford University Press, 1994.

Aitken, Bill. *Seven Sacred Rivers*. New Delhi: Penguin Books India, 1992.

Allen, Charles, editor. *Tales from the South China Seas*. London: British Broadcasting Corporation and Andre Deutsch Ltd., 1983.

Baker, Sir Samuel White. *Eight Years in Ceylon*. London: Longmans, Green, 1891. Reprint.

Barr, Pat, and Ray Desmond. *Simla: A Hill Station in British India*. London: Scholar Press, 1978.

Bhatt, Vikram. *Resorts of the Raj: Hill Stations of India*. Ahmedabad, India: Mapin Publishers, 1997.

Blavatsky, H. P. *The People of the Blue Mountains*. Wheaton, Illinois: Theosophical Press, 1930.

Bond, Ruskin. *Rain in the Mountains: Notes from the Himalayas*. New Delhi: Penguin Books India, 1996.

_____. *Ruskin Bond's Green Book*. New Delhi: Roli Books, The Lotus Collection, 1995.

Bond, Ruskin, and Ganesh Saili. *Mussoorie and Landour: Days of Wine and Roses*. New Delhi: Lustre Press Pvt. Ltd., 1992.

Buck, Edward J. *Simla Past and Present*. Delhi: Summit Publications, 1979. Reprint.

Burgess, Anthony. *The Long Day Wanes: The Malayan Trilogy*. Harmondsworth: Penguin Books, 1982.

Cabaton, Antoine. *Java, Sumatra and the Other Islands of the Dutch East Indies*. London: T. Fisher Unwin, 1911.

Caddy, Florence. *To Siam and Malaya in the Duke of Sutherland's Yacht Sans Peur*. Singapore: Oxford University Press, 1992. Reprint.

Caine, W. S. *Picturesque India: A Handbook for European Travellers*. London: Geo. Routledge and Sons, 1898.

Christie, Agatha. *The Mysterious Affair at Styles*. New York: Berkley Books, 1991. Reprint.

Cohen, Stephen P. *The Indian Army: Its Contribution to the Development of a Nation*. Berkeley: University of California Press, 1971.

Cohn, Bernard S. *Colonialism and Its Forms of Knowledge: The British in India*. Princeton: Princeton University Press, 1996.

Collis, Maurice. *Into Hidden Burma: An Autobiography*. London: Faber and Faber, 1953.

Cooke, Hope. *Time Change: An Autobiography*. New York: Simon and Schuster, 1980.

Cordiner, James. *A Description of Ceylon*. Dehiwala: Tisara Prakasakyo Ltd., 1983. Reprint.

Couperus, Lewis. *Eastward*. London: Hunt and Blackett, 1924.

de la Costa, Horacio. *Readings in Philippine History*. Manila: Bookmark, Inc., 1965.

Dozey, E. C. *A Concise History of the Darjeeling District Since 1835, with a Complete Itinerary of Tours in Sikkim and the District*. Calcutta: Jetsun Publishing House, 1989. Reprint.

Eden, Emily. *Up the Country: Letters Written to Her Sister from the Upper Provinces of India*. London: Oxford University Press, 1930. Reprint.

Ellis, Beth. *An English Girl's First Impressions of Burmah*. Wigan: R. Platt, 1899.

Elsmie, George. *Thirty-Five Years in the Punjab*. Edinburgh: D. Douglas, 1908.

E.M.M.L. *Guide to Kodaikanal and Its History*. Kodaikanal: Lillingstone, 1909.

Ferguson, John. *Ceylon in the Jubilee Year, with an Account of the Progress Made Since 1803, and of the Present Condition of Its Agricultural and Commercial Enterprises*. New Delhi: Asian Educational Services, 1994. Reprint.

Galbraith, John Kenneth. *Ambassador's Journal*. New York: Paragon House Publishers, 1988.

Gleeck, Lewis E. *Americans on the Philippine Frontiers*. Manila: Carmelo and Bauerman, 1974.

Goonetileke, H.A.I., editor. *Images of Sri Lanka Through American Eyes: Travellers in Ceylon in the Nineteenth and Twentieth Centuries*. Colombo: United States Information Service, 1975.

Guide to the Tourist Places of India with Hotels and Trains at a Glance. New Delhi: Ram Publications, 1996.

Gullick, J. M. *Adventures and Encounters: Europeans in South-East Asia*. Kuala Lumpur: Oxford University Press, 1995.

Hall, D.G.E. *A History of South-East Asia*. London: Macmillan Press Ltd., 1981 (fourth edition).

Hankin, Nigel B. *Hanklyn-Janklin, or a Stranger's Rumble-Tumble Guide to Some Words, Customs and Quiddities Indian and Indo-British*. New Delhi: Banyan Books, 1992.

Hart, Mrs. Ernest. *Picturesque Burma, Past and Present*. Philadelphia: J. B. Lippincott Co., 1897.

Hayes, Michael, and Ker Munthit. "The Wilted Rose of Bokor Mountain." *Phnom Penh Post,* April 4–17, 1997.

Hockings, Paul. *Blue Mountains: The Ethnography and Biogeography of a South Indian Region.* New York: Oxford University Press, 1989.

Hooker, Sir Joseph Dalton. *Himalayan Journals: Notes of a Naturalist in Bengal, the Sikkim and Nepal Himalayas, the Khasia Mountains &c.* (2 vols.). New Delhi: Today and Tomorrow's Printers and Publishers, 1969. Reprint.

Imperial Gazetteer of India, Vol. 18. New Delhi: Today and Tomorrow's Printers and Publishers. No date given. Reprint.

Jacquemont, Victor. *Letters from India, 1829–1832.* Translated by Catherine Alison Phillips. London: Macmillan, 1936.

Jenista, Frank Lawrence. *The White Apos: American Governors on the Cordillera Central.* Quezon City: New Publishers, 1987.

Jennings, Sir William Ivor. *The Kandy Road.* Peradeniya: University of Peradeniya Library, 1993.

Kanwar, Pamela. *Imperial Simla: The Political Culture of the Raj.* Delhi: Oxford University Press, 1990.

Kennedy, Dane. *The Magic Mountains: Hill Stations and the British Raj.* Berkeley: University of California Press, 1996.

Kipling, Rudyard. *Plain Tales from the Hills.* Harmondsworth: Penguin Books, Ltd. 1987. Reprint.

Kipling, Rudyard, and Wolcott Balestier. *The Naulahka: A Story of East and West.* London: Macmillan and Co., 1928.

"A Lady Pioneer" [Elizabeth Sarah "Nina" Mazuchelli]. *The Indian Alps and How We Crossed Them.* London: Longmans, Green and Co., 1876.

Lewis, Norman. *A Goddess in the Stones: Travels in India.* New York: Henry Holt and Co., 1991.

———. *Golden Earth: Travels in Burma.* London: Jonathan Cape, 1952.

Loeb, Edwin M. *Sumatra: Its History and People.* Kuala Lumpur: Oxford University Press, 1972. Reprint.

Macdonald, David. *The Land of the Lama: A Description of a Country of Contrasts and Its Happy-Go-Lucky People of Hardy Nature and Curious Customs; Their Religion, Ways of Living, Trade and Social Life.* London: Seeley, Service and Co., 1929.

MacMillan, Margaret. *Women of the Raj.* New York: Thames and Hudson, 1988.

Marshall, Henry. *Ceylon: A General Description of the Island and Its Inhabitants.* Dehiwala: Tisara Prakasakyo, 1982. Reprint.

Mathew, K. V. *The Faith and Practice of the Mar Thoma Church.* Kottayam: Mar Thoma Theological Seminary, 1985.

Mitchell, Nora. *The Indian Hill-Station: Kodaikanal.* Chicago: University of Chicago Department of Geography, 1972.

Muggeridge, Malcolm. *The Green Stick: Chronicles of Wasted Time,* Vol. 1. London: William Collins Sons & Co., 1972.

_____. *The Infernal Grove: Chronicles of Wasted Time*, Vol. 2. New York: William Morrow & Co., 1974.

Ohn Pe. *Maymyo or Pyin Oo Lwin*. Rangoon: International Press, 1980.

Orwell, George. *Burmese Days*. Harmondsworth: Penguin Books, Ltd., 1984.

_____. *Homage to Catalonia*. New York: Harcourt Brace & Co., 1980.

Panter-Downes, Molly. *Ooty Preserved: A Victorian Hill Station*. London: Hamish Hamilton, 1967.

Peebles, Patrick. *Social Change in Nineteenth Century Ceylon*. Delhi: Navrang, 1995.

Pinn, Fred, editor. *Americans at Darjeeling*. Darjeeling: Heritage Publications, n.d.

Pramoedya Ananta Toer. *This Earth of Mankind*. New York: William Morrow and Co., Inc., 1991. Translated by Max Lane.

Price, Sir Frederick. *Ootacamund: A History*. Madras: Government Press, 1908.

Raffles, Sophia. *Memoir of the Life and Public Services of Sir Thomas Stamford Raffles*. Singapore: Oxford University Press, 1991. Reprint.

Rambo, A. Terry, et al. *The Challenges of Highland Development in Vietnam*. Honolulu: East-West Center, 1995.

Raslan, Karim. *Ceritalah: Malaysia in Transition*. Singapore: Times Books International, 1996.

Reed, Robert R. *City of Pines: The Origins of Baguio as a Colonial Hill Station and Regional Capital*. Berkeley: University of California Center for South And Southeast Asian Studies, 1976.

_____. "The Colonial Genesis of Hill Stations: The Genting Exception." *Geographical Review* 69, no. 4 (1969), pp. 463–468.

_____. "Remarks on the Colonial Genesis of the Hill Stations in Southeast Asia, with Particular Reference to the Cities of Buitenzorg (Bogor) and Baguio." *Asian Profile* 4, no. 6 (1976), pp. 545–591.

Rose, Sunny. *Dalat Lanbiang*. Dalat: Tre Publishing House, 1996.

Russell, William Howard. *My Diary in India, in the Year 1858–9*. 2 vols. London: Routledge, Warne and Routledge, 1860.

Saili, Ganesh, editor. *Glorious Garhwal*. New Delhi: Roli Books, The Lotus Collection, 1995.

Solverson, Howard. *The Jesuit and the Dragon*. Montreal: Robert Davies Publishing, 1995.

Spear, Percival. *The Oxford History of Modern India, 1740–1975*. 2nd edition. New Delhi: Oxford University Press, 1978.

Spencer, J. E., and W. L. Thomas. "The Hill Stations and Summer Resorts of the Orient." *Geographical Review* 38, no. 4 (October 1948), pp. 637–651.

Steedly, Mary Margaret. *Hanging Without a Rope: Narrative Experiences in Colonial and Post-Colonial Karoland*. Princeton: Princeton University Press, 1993.

Stephens, Ian. *Pakistan*. London: Ernest Benn, 1963.

Stoler, Ann Laura. "Rethinking Colonial Categories: European Communities and the Boundaries of Rule." *Comparative Studies in Society and History* 31 (January 1989), pp. 134–161.

Stubbs, Richard. *Hearts and Minds in Guerrilla Warfare: The Malayan Emergency 1948–1960.* Singapore: Oxford University Press, 1989.

Sud, O. C. *The Simla Story: The Glow and Afterglow of the Raj.* Simla: Maria Brothers, 1992.

Swettenham, Frank. *A Nocturne and Other Malayan Stories and Sketches.* Kuala Lumpur: Oxford University Press, 1993.

Tardif, Etienne. *La Naissance de Dalat, 1899–1900.* Vienne: Ternet-Martin, ca. 1948. (No date of publication given.)

Taring, Rinchen Dolma. *Daughter of Tibet.* London: John Murray, 1970.

Thomson, John Turnbull. *Glimpses into Life in Malayan Lands.* Singapore: Oxford University Press, 1984. Reprint.

Thukral, Gurmeet, et al. *Woodstock School.* Minneapolis: Roth Publishing Co., 1993.

Truong Tro and Vuong Lan, editors. *Da Lat: Thanh Pho Cao Nguyen.* Dalat: Uy Ban Nhan Dan Thanh Pho, 1993.

Twain, Mark. *Following the Equator: A Journey Around the World.* New York: Dover Publications, Inc., 1989.

Unrau, Ruth. *Hill Station Teacher: A Life with India in It.* North Newton, Kansas: Kidron Creek Publications, 1997.

Warren, William. *Jim Thompson: The Legendary American of Thailand.* Bangkok: Jim Thompson Thai Silk Co., 1986.

Westlake, Graeme D. *An Introduction to the Hill Stations of India.* New Delhi: Indus/HarperCollins, 1993.

Whitaker, Zai. *Hills in the Clouds: A Guide to Kodaikanal.* Madras: B. I. Publications Pvt. Ltd., 1993.

Withington, William A. "Upland Resorts and Tourism in Indonesia: Some Recent Trends." *Geographical Review* 51 (1961), pp. 418–423.

Wright, Gillian. *Introduction to Hill Stations of India.* Hong Kong: Odyssey, 1991.

Wyckoff, Charlotte Chandler. *Kodaikanal: 1845–1945.* Nagercoil, India: London Mission Press, 1951.

ACKNOWLEDGMENTS

$\mathcal{M}$ANY OF THE PEOPLE who helped me in many ways in the writing of this book are quoted or mentioned in its pages and bibliography. But there are also those who are not named whose assistance and encouragement were immeasurable. A book on the hill stations of colonial Asia in all its varieties might not have existed at all had it not been for Laura Parsons of Westview Press, whose knowledge of the region and the genre made her receptive to an idea few others understood. I was introduced to her by Sumit Ganguly of Hunter College at the City University of New York, who also arranged for me to meet his parents in Calcutta; and Nandini and Romen Ganguly, veterans of many hill station "seasons," who generously shared their reminiscences.

Jane Cummings, executive director of the Kodai Woodstock International association, offered me access to the Internet websites of Kodaikanal and Woodstock schools, which put me in touch with alumni on several continents. At the University of Virginia, Philip McEldowney, the librarian and a Woodstock graduate, took the time to compile a bibliography of books on hill stations all over India. I was directed to him by another Woodstock alumnus, Rodney Jones.

Patricia Herbert of the British Library in London was equally generous with her expert advice on Burma and her willingness to find and supply me with accounts from old official gazetteers. Sarah Timewell at Geographic Expeditions in San Francisco brought me up to date on contemporary Burma and recommended places to stay and see in Maymyo and other hill towns. In New York, Kyaw Tha Hla translated articles from Burmese-language publications given to me in Maymyo by their authors. At the University of Pennsylvania, David Nelson, the librarian for South Asia, opened his magnificent collection to me and helped me locate out-of-print books that would otherwise have been very difficult to trace.

In New Delhi, P. J. Anthony, a friend and colleague, took time to plan an itinerary that efficiently packed an unbelievable amount of travel into barely a month of revisiting the distant hills of North and South India, and then sent me on to Sri Lanka without a hitch, in a part of the world where almost anything that can go wrong usually does. In New York, Nancy Newhouse, editor of the *New York Times* Sunday travel section, was always open to suggestions for articles about Asian places, however remote or unfamiliar, that I visited as a foreign correspondent. Some material in this book, therefore, first appeared in different forms in the *Times* travel pages.

Joseph Lelyveld, executive editor of *The Times,* not only allowed me to take three months leave to travel in the Asian hills but also shared his own recollections of Maymyo, and told me that George Orwell's memorable description of the town was to be found not in *Burmese Days* but, of all places, in *Homage to Catalonia.*

As always, my husband, David Wigg, was my first and most trustworthy critic.

Finally, there are those no longer alive: the reporters, memoir writers, and diarists who over two centuries jotted down their joys and tribulations in colonial service, bringing to life the West's encounters with some of the world's most fascinating cultures. Their history is now part of Asia's as well as ours.

INDEX